T0330825

Climate Change and Anthropos

Anthropos, in the sense of species as well as cultures and ethics, locates humans as part of much larger orders of existence – fundamental when thinking about climate change. This book offers a new way of exploring the significance of locality and lives in the epoch of the Anthropocene, a time when humans confront the limits of our control over nature. Many scholars now write about the ethics, policies and politics of climate change, focusing on global processes and effects. The book's innovative approach to cross-cultural comparison and a regionally based study explores people's experiences of environmental change and the meaning of climate change for diverse human worlds in a changing biosphere.

The main study site is the Hunter Valley in southeast Australia: an ecological region defined by the Hunter River catchment; a dwelling place for many generations of people; and a key location for transnational corporations focused on the mining, burning and export of black coal. Abundant fossil fuel reserves tie Hunter people and places to the Asia Pacific – the engine room of global economic growth in the twenty-first century and the largest user of the planet's natural resources. The book analyses the nexus of place and perceptions, political economy and social organisation in situations where environmental changes are radically transforming collective worlds.

Based on an anthropological approach informed by other ways of thinking about environment–people relationships, this book explores the social and cultural dimensions of climate change holistically. Each chapter links the large scales of species and planet with small places, commodity chains, local actions, myths and values, as well as the mingled strands of dystopian imaginings and strivings for recuperative renewal in an era of transition.

Linda H. Connor is Professor of Anthropology at the University of Sydney, Australia.

Routledge Advances in Climate Change Research

Climate Change and Anthropos
Planet, people and places

Linda H. Connor

Routledge
Taylor & Francis Group
LONDON AND NEW YORK

earthscan
from Routledge

First published 2016
by Routledge
2 Park Square, Milton Park, Abingdon, Oxon OX14 4RN

and by Routledge
711 Third Avenue, New York, NY 10017

Routledge is an imprint of the Taylor & Francis Group, an informa business

British Library Cataloguing-in-Publication Data
A catalogue record for this book is available from the British Library

Library of Congress Cataloging-in-Publication Data
Names: Connor, Linda, 1950– author.
Title: Climate change and anthropos : planet, people, and places /
Linda Connor.
Description: Abingdon, Oxon ; New York, NY : Routledge is an imprint
of the Taylor & Francis Group, an Informa Business, [2016] |
Includes bibliographical references and index.
Identifiers: LCCN 2015035496 | ISBN 9780415718530 (hardback) |
ISBN 9781315869728 (ebook)
Subjects: LCSH: Climatic changes. | Climatic changes—Social aspects.
| Global warming—Social aspects.
Classification: LCC QC903 .C527 2016 | DDC 304.2/5—dc23LC
record available at http://lccn.loc.gov/2015035496

ISBN: 978-0-415-71853-0 (hbk)
ISBN: 978-1-315-86972-8 (ebk)

Typeset in Goudy
by FiSH Books Ltd, Enfield

This book is dedicated to the people of the Hunter Valley, especially those who struggle against the unfettered expansion of the coal industry.

Qui justa pro causa certant denique vincent

Contents

Figures and tables

Figures

Tables

Acknowledgements

The research on which this book is based was carried out in the Hunter Valley between 2008 and 2012. It was part of a collaborative project with Glenn Albrecht and Nick Higginbotham, with whom I have been researching environmental change in Hunter Valley communities for more than a decade. Apart from our many adventures on field trips, much of the excitement of this research has come from our mutual engagement with ideas and methods from our different disciplinary perspectives (anthropology, environmental ethics and social psychology). As a research team, we set out to develop a strong interdisciplinary framework for a regional and community-based study of environmental change. We were motivated by our interest and concern for the Hunter Valley: as an ecological region defined by the Hunter River catchment; a dwelling place for many generations of people; and a key site for resource extractive capital accumulation focused on the mining, burning and export of black coal.

Results of our research have appeared in publications and presentations over the years and some are cited in this work. In completing this book, I am fulfilling an undertaking written into the original grant application, to produce a monograph focusing on contributions of the ethnographic research to understandings of climate change. I am indebted to Glenn and Nick for their insights throughout the life of the project and for travelling with me on this journey.

The research assistants who worked on this project were an invaluable part of the team. Sonia Freeman, who was the senior project manager from 2008 to 2011, was an accomplished operational coordinator who also took responsibility for much of the media and document analysis. Her dynamic intellectual engagement with our research is reflected in co-authorship of a number of publications. Gillian Harris provided valued assistance for several years, especially on the topic of spirituality and climate change. The contribution of others is also much appreciated: Nick Maclean, Vanessa Bowden and Justine Chambers. The Hunter Valley Research Foundation (now the Hunter Research Foundation) proved an efficient and effective organisation in conducting the two phases of telephone survey interviews.

A book on this subject crosses into many areas of scholarship, and over the years of researching and writing I have relied on ideas and advice from colleagues in disciplines that include archaeology, geography, history, sociology, statistics and political economy, as well as fellow anthropologists. I thank all these people for their interest and timely contributions when called upon. I want to mention by name Fran Baker, Belinda Burbidge, Stephen Hancock, Jonathan Marshall, Phil McManus, Rebecca Pearse, Stuart Rosewarne and Peter White. Thank you to Paul Roche and Nick Riemer for the Latin. My persistence with the writing has also been sustained by the interest and encouragement of family, friends and colleagues.

Hunter regional newspapers have been an important resource for this study. The *Newcastle Herald* provides detailed and rigorous reporting on regional issues and has cast a particularly strong investigative gaze upon the often-opaque dealings between the mining industry and New South Wales state government. Several *Newcastle Herald* journalists require special mention for their high-quality, consistent reporting on issues of particular relevance to the subject of this book. Thanks to Matthew Kelly, Damon Cronshaw, Greg Ray, Michelle Harris and Joanne McCarthy, and also to Peter Lewis, whose daily cartoons are an inspiration and a delight.

The research project was supported by a grant from the Australian Research Council (DP0878089). Lake Macquarie and Upper Hunter councils made contributions to the funding of the survey research. I am also grateful for grants to assist with the preparation of the manuscript from the Faculty of Arts and Social Sciences, and the Department of Anthropology at the University of Sydney.

There are two people who deserve special thanks for their contributions to the writing of this book. I have benefitted from daily conversations on Hunter Valley affairs with Nick Higginbotham over many years, especially insights from his astute reading of local politics and his empathy for residents caught in the sacrifice zones of the resource extractive economy. I am grateful to him for reading the draft manuscript at short notice; the book has benefited from his constructive criticisms. Gina Krone, my research assistant for several years, has kept me on track through the thick and thin of writing. She has project managed the book and all the databases with efficiency and aplomb. Her editing skills, intellectual acumen, patience and good cheer have kept me going and improved the book at every level. I cannot thank her enough and wish her every success in her own PhD project that is now underway.

I am indebted to the people of the Hunter Valley who generously participated in the study in so many ways. They are too numerous to name, and pseudonyms have been used for those whose words are quoted in private interviews. I feel privileged to have had the opportunity to learn from their lives in the many places and situations encompassed by the study. This book is dedicated to them.

Acronyms and abbreviations

AAC	Australian Agricultural Company
ABS	Australian Bureau of Statistics
AGL	Australian Gas Light Company
BHP	Broken Hill Proprietary Company
CAG	Climate Action Group
CAN	Climate Action Newcastle
CANA	Climate Action Network Australia
CRDC	Climate Ready Dora Creek
CSG	coal seam gas
CTAG	Coal Terminal Action Group
DCCG	Dora Creek Catchment Group
EDO	Environmental Defender's Office
EIS	environmental impact statement
ENGO	environmental non-government organisation
ENSO	El Niño-Southern Oscillation
GFC	global financial crisis
GHG	greenhouse gas
HCEC	Hunter Community Environment Centre
HEL	Hunter Environment Lobby
HTBA	Hunter Thoroughbred Breeders Association
HVPA	Hunter Valley Protection Alliance
ICAC	Independent Commission Against Corruption
IK	Indigenous knowledge
IPCC	Intergovernmental Panel on Climate Change
IQ	*Inuit Qaujimatuqangit*
LGA	local government area
LK	local knowledge
LMCA	Lake Macquarie Climate Action
LMCC	Lake Macquarie City Council
LMS	London Missionary Society
LtG	Lock the Gate Alliance
MTpa	mega tonnes per annum
NSW	New South Wales

NSWMC	New South Wales Minerals Council
NVDA	non-violent direct action
OPEC	Organization of the Petroleum Exporting Countries
PAC	Planning Assessment Commission
PACC	Pacific Adaptation to Climate Change
PEL	petroleum exploration license
PWCS	Port Waratah Coal Services
REDD	Reducing Emissions from Deforestation and Forest Degradation
RT	Rising Tide Newcastle
SIDS	Small Island Developing States
SLR	sea level rise
SOE	state-owned enterprise
TEK	traditional ecological knowledge
TK	traditional knowledge
TN	Transition Newcastle
TT	Transition Towns
TTCP	Transition Town Coal Point
UNFCCC	United Nations Framework Convention on Climate Change

Introduction

Culture and combustion go together. The use of controlled fire by *homo erectus* at least 750,000 years ago may have enabled new hominin adaptations, such as the exploitation of new food sources and the diaspora to the colder climates of Eurasia (Klein 2009: 261–2, 412–4). There is evidence that ancient humans burned coal at Neanderthal sites in Europe more than 50,000 years ago (Pettit 2013: 152). But it was *homo sapiens* that 'releas[ed] the genie of coal' (Freese 2003: 13) only a few thousand years ago. Mastery of the dangerous pyrotechnics of coal combustion (and later, oil and other fossil fuels) set modern humans on a finite trajectory of global warming. 'Fire unwinds, unbinds and reverses the work of photosynthesis. The mass combustion of fossil fuels does this irreversibly, unmaking worlds made through the deep history of photosynthetic life' (Walker 2016: 272).

From the perspective of planet-wide thinking, anthropogenic global warming readily evokes apocalyptic scenarios. James Lovelock grapples with the spectre of future humanity as 'survivors of a failed civilization' (Lovelock 2007: 202). The peak international climate science organisation, the United Nations-sponsored Intergovernmental Panel on Climate Change (IPCC), which collates and analyses thousands of data sets and climate models from around the world, increasingly echoes these concerns in the registers of scientific discourse. The Fifth Assessment Report from the IPCC is emphatic, with lead statements like: 'Warming of the climate system is unequivocal, and since the 1950s, many of the observed changes are unprecedented over decades to millennia' (IPCC 2013: 4). From the standpoint of those scientists who work in the deep time of the planet's past, climate changes of varying scales, between cold and heat, wet and dry, glacial and interglacial periods, are a reality to which all forms of life have had to adapt over eons.

Modern humans evolved towards the end of the Pleistocene epoch, the last 'ice age', over 2.5 million years in duration, in which glaciers advanced and retreated over continents positioned much as they are today. For thousands of years the human species has adapted to climate change of a non-anthropogenic kind. The most striking example is the Neolithic revolution – the invention of agriculture at the end of the Pleistocene, when the earth warmed by a few degrees,[1] creating conditions favourable for the growth of wild grasses and other species amenable to domestication. The Holocene, the geological epoch of the past 12,000 years, has been a period of relatively warm Earth climate in which modern humans have expanded and thrived in every continent except Antarctica. But large-scale climatic changes throughout the Holocene have also claimed many victims. One oft-cited example is the Medieval Warm Period, 500 years of higher average temperatures from AD 800 to AD 1300. This period is associated with a flourishing of populations in Europe and the Circumpolar North, while cycles of megadroughts contributed to civilizational collapse, famine, warfare and depopulation in places as far apart as East Asia, New Mexico and the Mayan lowlands of Central America (Fagan 2008).

So what is different about climate change now? Humans have always encountered negative environmental change such as extreme weather events, volcanic eruptions, earthquakes, depopulation from epidemic disease, loss of food sources, pestilence,and pollution. Many of these cataclysms have been anthropogenic. Now humans are changing geophysical processes on a planetary scale, prompting atmospheric chemist Paul Crutzen and ecologist Eugene Stoermer to envision a new epoch fusing geophysical and human agency. They coined the term 'Anthropocene' to refer to the epoch starting in the late eighteenth century when humankind began to remodel the planet's ecosystems with the invention of the coal-fired steam engine (Crutzen and Stoermer 2000). These anthropogenic impacts are accelerating, long term and difficult to reverse. The co-occurrence of the beginning of the Anthropocene with the growth of industrialised economies and massive increases in the exploitation of fossil fuels has led some scientists to propose that capitalism rather than late Holocene human life is the progenitor of this ill-fated era. Indeed it must be noted that the industrial revolution was preceded by the great expropriation of church and peasant property in the sixteenth century, creating landless labourers and fluid capital. The Capitalocene concept has been followed by a procession of neologisms identifying various prime movers in the planet's warming (Haraway 2015).

For the purposes of this book, I avoid indulging in terminological proliferation beyond Anthropocene. The significance of resource extractive capitalism in present times will become clear enough. Anthropocene provides an etymological and conceptual link with my focus on Anthropos, which speaks to the broad scope of anthropology as a discipline. It encompasses the species being of *homo sapiens* and the ontological foundation of 'the human condition' in diverse morally grounded experiences of the lifecycle, attachment, suffering and freedom. In the Anthropocene, humans confront the limiting conditions of our existence as geological agents and as a species among other species on the planet.

The crisis of climate change is a crisis of human civilisation and an immense challenge for human reason, ethics and imagination. The historian Dipesh Chakrabarty has suggested that to understand our current plight, and deal with the consequences of global warming, we need human reason more than ever, but its purpose should be to 'think like a species', and understand ourselves as part of the history of planetary life. He argues that we need to '... bring together intellectual formations that are somewhat in tension with each other: the planetary and the global; deep and recorded histories; species thinking and critiques of capital' (2009: 213).

It is worth exploring this idea of 'species thinking' further. It implies that critiques of capitalist globalisation and proposed solutions to its excesses and inequalities are not sufficient to solve the problems of climate change. Nor do science and technology provide an ethical framework for action. We have to enlarge our perspective on human history to the deep time of geological change – the shift from the last ice age, when humans evolved, through to the Holocene epoch and then to the rapidly warming atmosphere and acidifying oceans that will define the Anthropocene. And we have to confront the plight of humanity as a whole, something international conventions and agreements have been unable to achieve. Unchecked climate change will outlive capitalism, and the lifeboats for the rich and powerful will eventually run out (Chakrabarty 2009: 212).

People inhabit the planet but they also dwell in local places. Anthropology's insights into the dual nature of Anthropos – our condition as an animal interdependent with other life forms on the planet as well as the role of cultural diversity in our adaptation and survival – are useful equipment for the challenge of species thinking. Anthropologists have always brought different intellectual traditions into conversation with one another. We know how to explore the practical materiality of human survival across the planet's ecosystems as well as the varied worlds of language and imagination in which humans dwell. Our research engages with activity in life worlds that connect with processes of transformation, inequality and exploitation in societal contexts.

The anthropological study of climate change now encompasses a diverse field of research problems and situations. Anthropologists are engaged in professional and interdisciplinary teams that investigate climate change from perspectives that include science and technology studies, policy and political economy, social movement analysis, and media and communication. In their overview of approaches to climate change research in cultural anthropology, Carla Roncoli and colleagues (2009: 104) comment:

> This shift is not new to anthropology: for the last twenty years, the practice of 'ethnography' has been expanding from physical localities, in which people have long-lasting social ties built on kinship and proximity, to multi-sited networks composed of people whose lives are connected and who share meanings and practices through media, institutions, and technology.

The 'multi-sited' rubric has been written into the design of almost every anthropological research project for the last two decades, and characterised many more, less explicitly, in the years before that. Whether claiming to be multi-sited or not, the challenge for ethnographic projects is to attain the deeply contextualised understanding of the research problem at hand through the practice of participant observation. This practice is best summarised as the researcher's direct, multiple and often contingent interactions in different contexts with people/agents/actants who are connected by virtue of common interests, problems or predicaments that they or the researcher have defined. The 'sites' in multi-sited research designs have never been tightly specified, even by the originator of this term (Marcus 1995), and have been creatively defined in many ways – such as networks, institutions, social media, geographic places, markets, interest groups, historical periods, organisations, events or any combination of these.

The phenomena of anthropogenic climate change and other forms of adverse environmental change that are the focus of this book appear in the domain of applied science as urgent problems on a planetary scale, demanding solutions that require new knowledge contributed by many disciplines. The research questions about climate change that anthropologists formulate must engage with this wider problem domain, often requiring interdisciplinary collaboration and participation in conflict-prone domains of policy, governance and advocacy. Regional studies of climate change necessarily involve a multi-sited approach, and are not immune from the pitfalls of multi-sited research, where single or small numbers of researchers spread themselves too thinly over sites or suffer intellectual entropy from the sheer effort of mobility and 'keeping track' of what is going on. As the anthropologist responsible for the ethnographic component of the project that informs this book, exploring 'climate change, place and community' in the Hunter Valley of New South Wales (NSW), I was fortunate to have co-investigators from other disciplines – social psychology and environmental ethics – as well as research assistants and occasional collaborators who together contributed intellectual depth and methodological expertise to the project that none of us could have achieved alone.

The research project set out to discover residents' experiences in a particular region where the reality of anthropogenic climate change is variously accepted, denied, suppressed or contested but where certain forms of environmental change are starkly manifest in consequential ways. It draws on a range of methods, including participant observation with selected groups, place-based communities, and the issues that activate conflicts and debates around environmental change; a longitudinal population survey of climate change perceptions, values and actions; semi-structured interviews with community members and key informants; and media and document analysis. Each of these methods yields different information and insights that do not necessarily converge. Working through these conundrums was an interesting and challenging part of writing this book.

The chapters in Part I take the long view of climate change in place and time, as a process in the ecocosmic sphere. Chapter 1 discusses the impacts and adaptations of environmental change among societies in highly climate exposed regions of the planet – the Circumpolar North and the islands of the South Pacific Ocean – that share a subordinate position in the geopolitical spheres of climate governance and capital accumulation. Chapter 2 turns to the transformations of landscapes, life forms and modes of being that characterise the Hunter Valley as a *topos* – a place that has been densely encountered, created, experienced and imagined – over scores of generations. Part II draws on ethnographic research in quotidian worlds of Hunter Valley residents – the mythological and ontological significance of weather and climate in Chapter 3, and the dialectic of perception and place in the experience of environmental change in Chapter 4. Part III explores the political and cultural intelligibility of climate change phenomena. Chapter 5 develops the idea of activation as a way of conceptualising how action (or inaction) on environmental change is expressed in different social contexts. Chapter 6 foregrounds the strands of dystopian imaginings and ideas of immortality that are embedded in envisioned futures conjured up by the prospect of the Anthropocene.

This book offers a new way of thinking about the significance of locality and lives in relation to the prospect of anthropogenic climate change. The social processes and effects of climate change are now well documented in the fields of ethics, policy and politics. My focus on cross-cultural comparison and a regionally based ethnographic study highlights other important perspectives on the capacity of human communities to respond to the predicament of global warming. Anthropological analysis reveals the limitations of the immortality strivings of Anthropos in the risky present world but also the practical imagination that can activate future recuperation and renewal of the ecocosmic sphere.

Note

1   See IPCC 2007 www.ipcc.ch/publications_and_data/ar4/wg1/en/faq-6-2.html on average temperature changes between ice ages and interglacials (4–7°C).

References

Chakrabarty, D. 2009. 'The Climate of History: Four theses'. *Critical Inquiry* 35 (2): 197–222.

Crutzen, P. J., and Stoermer, E. F. 2000. 'The "Anthropocene"'. *Global Change Newsletter* 41: 17–18.

Fagan, B. 2008. *The Great Warming: Climate change and the rise and fall of civilizations*. New York: Bloomsbury Press.

Freese, B. 2003. *Coal: A human history*. New York: Penguin Books.

Haraway, D. 2015. 'Anthropocene, Capitalocene, Plantationocene, Chthulucene: Making Kin'. *Environmental Humanities* 6: 159–165.

IPCC (Intergovernmental Panel on Climate Change) 2013. *Fifth Assessment Report: Climate Change 2013*. Available at www.ipcc.ch/report/ar5/wg1/#.Unmx4igRbzI (accessed 20 July 2014).

Klein, R. G. 2009. *The Human Career: Human biological and cultural origins*. Chicago: University of Chicago Press, 3rd Edition.

Lovelock, J. 2007. *The Revenge of Gaia: Why the earth is fighting back and how we can still save humanity*. UK: Penguin Books Limited.

Marcus, G. 1995. 'Ethnography in/of the world system'. *Annual Review of Anthropology* 24: 95–117.

Pettit, P. 2013. 'The Rise of Modern Humans'. In: *The Human Past*. Scarre, C. (ed.), pp. 127–173. London: Thames and Hudson, 3rd edition.

Roncoli, C., Crane, T. and Orlove, B. 2009. 'Fielding Climate Change in Cultural Anthropology'. In: *Anthropology and Climate Change: From encounters to actions*. Crate, S. and Nuttall, M (eds), pp. 87–115. Walnut Creek, California: Left Coast Press, Inc.

Walker, J. 2016. 'The Creation to Come: Pre-empting the evolution of the bioeconomy'. In: *Environmental Change and the World's Futures: Ecologies, ontologies, mythologies*. Marshall, J. P. and Connor, L. H (eds), pp. 264–281. London: Routledge.

Part I
The ecocosmic sphere

1 Precarious places in a warming world

All humans live on Earth as emplaced beings, part of the same interconnected ecosystem at a planetary scale; this is the species condition of Anthropos. Humans also live in different worlds, both at varying socio-spatial scales and with qualitatively different realities: the cosmological worlds that encompass imagination and myth, experience and the practice of living. All human worlds have striking asymmetries – of power, resources, life chances – that are manifest in dynamic and conflicting ways. Social science discourse expresses these asymmetries with a number of commonly used relational terms – such as global South and global North, developing and developed, first world and third world – that broadly refer to the interdependence of countries, regions and peoples that are respectively richer and poorer, more and less industrialised, more and less politically influential in the global arena, more and less bound by colonial pasts and post-colonial presents. The process of anthropogenic climate change has added a new unifying dimension to the species condition of humans and other life forms: the future for all has become precarious as greenhouse gases (GHGs) accumulate in the atmosphere, the world warms and oceans acidify. Climate change may be the ultimate experience of entropy for Anthropos and other living beings, as planetary systems become increasingly disordered because of life-destroying heat. The process also deepens inequalities. Economic growth based on accelerating carbon emissions is not only toxic for the whole planet, but also this form of capital accumulation is characterised by exploitation and inequalities of power and resources that intensify climate change hazards for certain populations, social groups and locations.

This chapter takes up these large themes in a necessarily synoptic style, beginning with an overview of climate change policy and governance as it pertains to the global South, leading into a discussion of anthropological research that has grown from a longstanding disciplinary concern with human ecology and environment. I then consider anthropological studies of people in places that are precariously exposed to climate change but who have little power in international climate change arenas.

Intimations of entropy

In affluent industrialised societies of the global North publics are highly exposed to science-derived understandings of anthropogenic climate change through mass media, internet and other sites of civic discourse. Government policies are shaped to varying degrees by the scientific projections of global warming. Sceptical and denialist information, mostly sponsored by interests vested in carbon-intensive economies, is a disordering force that has popular currency and government influence in some countries, including Australia. In the poorer societies of the global South, emission reduction policies and programmes of multilateral organisations have an impact on government policy and on perceptions of educated urban publics (Wolf and Moser 2011). The United Nation's collaborative initiative on Reducing Emissions from Deforestation and Forest Degradation (REDD) now has active programmes in 48 countries, including Nepal, Indonesia, Solomon Islands and Papua New Guinea in the Asia Pacific region. The United Nations Development Programme's Pacific Adaptation to Climate Change (PACC) project aims to implement 'best-practice adaptation' by hosting pilot projects in 14 Pacific Island countries, under the rubrics of coastal zone management, water resource management, and food security and production. The World Bank's decision to limit funding for coal-fired power generators in developing countries and increase support for alternative energy sources (World Bank 2013) came soon after the International Energy Association *World Energy Outlook 2012* report declared that no more than one-third of remaining proven fossil fuel reserves can be consumed by 2050 if the world is to stay within a 2°C temperature increase (International Energy Association 2012).

Fishers, rural food producers and the urban poor, still dominant population segments in developing countries, are less likely to be exposed to climate change discourse even while local development projects increasingly incorporate adaptation components, with varying effectiveness (see Barnett and Campbell 2010; Ford 2009; Fuller 2016; Pokrant and Stocker 2011; Rudiak-Gould 2013). Indigenous people living on ancestral lands, typically in the remoter parts of developed nations considered highly exposed to climate change impacts, have been involved with various projects for many years. A plethora of organisations and funding bodies is involved in climate change initiatives around the world. In addition to the annual climate change conferences held under the auspices of the main international governance instrument, the United Nations Framework Convention on Climate Change (UNFCCC), there are many involved agencies, committees and programmes of the United Nations and other multilateral organisations like the World Bank; national aid donors such as AusAid and USAID; regional associations like the Arctic Council and the Pacific Islands Forum; and national, provincial and local governments. In the realm of civil society, there are transnational non-government organisations including the Red Cross, Greenpeace and World Wildlife Fund as well as countless community-based groups sponsored by churches, schools, foundations, charitable organisations and local residents. Countering these civil society initiatives are peak fossil fuel bodies like the Canadian Association of Petroleum Producers and the Australian Coal Association, as well as corporate-funded foundations such as Koch, Heartland and ExxonMobil, which promulgate denial and scepticism of anthropogenic climate change using sympathetic scientists, opinion leaders and media outlets, in what sociologist and environmental scientist Robert Brulle (2013) has termed a 'climate change countermovement'.

The global governance of climate change to address its anthropogenic causes can only be described as disorganised and ineffectual, and few national governments have mustered the political will to do better (Leahy *et al.* 2010). Dryzek *et al.* (2013) have summarised the impediments to good governance that result in inaction on emissions reduction in the world's 'climate-challenged society'. They identify two main factors: one, that sovereign state governments often call on others to 'bear the burden', while reaping the benefits of a more stable climate; and two, that powerful developed states are the product of several hundred years of history where environmental conservation has never been a core priority because it has never needed to be (Dryzek *et al.* 2013: 96–7). Failures of agreements at a global level are hampered by numerous competing interests, such as individual nations' reliance on carbon intensive economies, and the perceived threat of 'global government' stripping away freedom from nation-states (Dryzek *et al.* 2013). Developed and developing nations dispute who should be held accountable – those with the largest historical or per capita emissions (such as the USA and Europe), or those with rapidly growing annual emissions rates and large populations (such as China and India).

The political inertia that defines global governance on climate change, as evidenced by the Kyoto protocol and the 2009 Copenhagen conference, are examples of what Leahy *et al.* (2010) define as 'two-track thinking', where the acknowledgement of dangerous human-induced climate change is maintained within the status quo of 'business as usual'. In Australia for instance, the former Labor government of Kevin Rudd simultaneously committed to a 40 per cent increase in coal exports over the next decade, while maintaining that climate change is the great moral challenge of our time (Curran 2009). Carbon pricing or marketisation (emissions trading schemes or carbon taxes) fall into this 'two-track' category, where addressing the threat of a warming climate sits firmly within a neoliberal capitalist world-order (see Paterson and Newell 2010). Dryzek *et al.* remark that within these carbon marketisation strategies, manipulation is easy; richer countries can offload production of goods onto poorer countries, thereby giving the appearance of reducing emissions, and they can 'buy carbon credits from poorer countries ... [and] purchase offsets from poorer countries that promise to grow trees – but in practice do no such thing' (2013: 104).

Environmental directions in anthropology

Anthropology's practitioners assert that their fecund discipline can make unique contributions to understanding anthropogenic climate change: in ethnographies of 'first line' communities that are experiencing ruptured lives and livelihoods; in anthropologies of industrial societies where science and politics construct nature as society's other, as expressed in Bruno Latour's 'bicameral collective' of the Moderns (2004); and by participating in interdisciplinary and applied research. Kay Milton abjures anthropologists to 'watch the discourse as it unfolds, questioning everything – the science, the politics, the economics, the morality – exposing implicit assumptions and hidden agendas, forcing debate, in the words of Mary Douglas, onto "a franker plane"' (2008: 58).

Ecological thinking goes back a long way in anthropology, with antecedents in the 'basic needs' functionalism of Bronislaw Malinowski (1944), the technological determinism of Leslie White's 'cultural evolution' (1949), the cultural ecology of Julian Steward (1973) and the cultural materialism of Marvin Harris (1979). While much of the earlier research was carried out in small-scale societies of the global South, the OPEC (Organization of the Petroleum Exporting Countries) oil boycott of the early 1970s catapulted a lot of scholars into 'anthropology at home', particularly in the USA (Wilk 2009) where new research funding opportunities opened up. Household energy use practices, 'folk' models of thermostats and energy costs, and popular environmental values were among the range of topics subjected to ethnographic study (Wilk 2009: 271–2). These researchers drew on earlier ecological currents in their field, and combined them with economic anthropology and then the study of consumer culture that burgeoned in the 1990s (Wilk 2009).

The subject of climate change was a latecomer in the subfields that became known as environmental and ecological anthropology (Pokrant and Stocker 2011). In the 1990s global warming had emerged as an area of study, often combined with other disciplines as in the compendious *Human Choice and Climate Change* in four edited volumes (Rayner and Malone 1998). Anthropologists undertook studies of climate change in localities of the South, emphasising the necessity of understanding cultural specificity in relation to geophysical models and large-scale processes of environmental change. A notable example is the special issue of *Climate Research*, which published a set of papers from the Society for Applied Anthropology meeting in 1999, focusing on the methodological contribution of ethnography to climate change studies, and in particular the impacts on African societies of the 1997–1998 El Niño Southern Oscillation (ENSO) climate conditions (Magistro and Roncoli 2001). Magistro and Roncoli (2001: 93) argued that understandings of climate change action should be informed by anthropological analyses of 'cultural meanings, collective myths, and social memory' as well as by the large-scale, quantitative data that characterise climate change forecasts generated by bodies such as the IPCC.

Monographs, compilations and reviews of climate change research in anthropology and related fields that have appeared in the last decade have echoed the importance of the domain of 'culture', but have also highlighted other strengths that the discipline brings to the field of climate change. Archaeologists have documented the ways diverse human groups have shaped and responded to environmental change over many millennia. Brian Fagan, a prolific writer in the archaeology of climate change in human history and prehistory, has commented on some of the socio-political outcomes:

> Climate has helped shape civilization, but not by being benign. The unpredictable whims of the Holocene stressed human societies and forced them to either adapt or perish... such as the switchover to farming during the Younger Dryas in southwestern Asia in about 10,000 B.C. and the demise of states like Tiwanaku, both in times of drought. The collapses often came as a complete surprise to rulers and elites who believed in royal infallibility and espoused rigid ideologies of power.
>
> (2005: 252)

Curious about diversity across the planet's population, socio-cultural anthropology has examined the full spectrum of modes of human being, particularly attending to the life of peoples and ideas that are marginalised or unheard in public discourse (Batterbury 2008; Crate 2012; Magistro and Roncoli 2001). Successful adaptations to extreme environmental conditions – including arid, hot, freezing, watery or wet – provide a spectrum of possibilities to cope with the climate challenges of the future. The biodiversity loss that is already occurring is a harbinger of greater ecological calamities to come. Communities that are heavily dependent on local natural resources for their survival are astute observers of the biophysical minutiae of environmental change, which may complement or conflict with climatological models at larger scales (Marin 2010; Nichols *et al.* 2004). The implications of these changes go well beyond the domain of natural resource management problems. Indigenous cosmologies incorporate the whole of existence into their conceptions of an ordered and continuing universe, such that loss of elemental features has world shattering implications. Quechua people in the Peruvian Andes, faced with the retreat of glaciers, told the anthropologist: 'When all the snow is gone from the mountaintops, the end of the world as we know it is near, because there is no life without water' (Bolin 2009: 228).

In the view of many anthropologists, the place-based ethnographic analysis that is at the heart of many studies must be fortified with more proactive and policy-oriented approaches. A forum in 2007 in the newsletter of the American Anthropological Association, in a reflective period after the release of the IPCC Fourth Assessment Report, presented a series of short, programmatic critiques highlighting why 'anthropology has been especially absent at the climate change table' compared to other social sciences (Finan 2007: 10). Contributors pointed to the discipline's preoccupation with the social analysed mainly through the study of local groups (Lahsen 2007: 9), the dominance of anti-science 'postmodernist dogma ... celebrated at the annual meetings in arcane language and cabalistic ritual befitting the most isolated of societies' (Finan 2007: 11), lack of engagement with other disciplines in the vast field of human-environment relations (Galvin 2007: 12) and the failure to embrace research agendas that focus on the future (Nelson 2007: 13).

This anthropological angst has been tempered as practitioners have moved more actively into the mainstream of climate change research. Simon Batterbury envisages a new agenda for anthropology: 'For me, anthropology *without* a sense of urgency about global warming is unthinkable' (2008: 66). Richard Wilk finds a new potency in the discipline's holistic approach to the human condition, arguing that it is time for anthropologists to: 'use our knowledge of social change and process, our synthesis of biology and culture, our command of global issues, and our holistic understanding of the economy to make a greater contribution [to climate change debates] and increase our voice' (2009: 274).

Bob Pokrant and Laura Stocker draw on their comparative analysis of vulnerability and resilience in Bangladesh and Western Australian coastal communities to advocate a movement towards more interdisciplinary and policy-relevant research in which anthropological methods and insights contribute to adaptation planning at multiple scales (2011). Editors of a recent volume on anthropology and climate change emphasise the social justice agendas that must inform research and policy, and see anthropology as an important interlocutor. They state: 'climate change is a threat multiplier. It magnifies and exacerbates existing social, economic, political, and environmental trends, problems, issues, tensions, and challenges' (Crate and Nuttall 2009: 11).

In the terms of this *Zeitgeist*, the peoples and communities long studied by anthropologists – many of whom are Indigenous, economically marginal and living in post-colonial and neo-colonial conditions – become particular targets of research by virtue of their vulnerability. As global warming threatens all aspects of human–ecosystem relationships, indigenous and small-scale subsistence livelihoods and life ways become less viable (Brondizio and Moran 2008; Ford 2009; Lipset 2013; Rudiak-Gould 2013), even while most were already traversing paths shaped by hegemonic states, corporate capitalism and consumer culture. As scientists proclaim that increased warming is inevitable, 'adaptation' is now paired with 'mitigation' in policy frameworks, although these domains of action reside in different Working Groups (II and III respectively) of the IPCC.[1] Crate and Nuttall warn that: 'Combined with institutional and legal barriers to adaptation, the ability to respond to climate change is severely constrained for many people around the globe' (2009: 10). In this looming emergency they contend that the roles of anthropologists as 'advocates, communicators, educators, practitioners, and activists' (Crate and Nuttall 2009: 10) – in fact a normative expectation to act as public intellectuals and change agents – should be canvassed, not without, however, probing the ethical and methodological dilemmas at the heart of any collaborative process.

In fact, as practitioners of 'climate anthropology' make clear, climate change may be one of the least pressing life crises, not only for the poor and disenfranchised, but for all people who attend most closely to immediate threats that they perceive to their livelihood, health and happiness. The bland conclusions of the IPCC AR5 Impacts, Adaptation and Vulnerability Working Group II (2014: 7) hold no surprises for social scientists:

People who are socially, economically, culturally, politically, institutionally, or otherwise marginalized are especially vulnerable to climate change and also to some adaptation and mitigation responses (*medium evidence, high agreement*). This heightened vulnerability is rarely due to a single cause. Rather, it is the product of intersecting social processes that result in inequalities in socioeconomic status and income, as well as in exposure.

(italics in the original)

In adverse circumstances climate change may be well below the horizon of public awareness. Whether usurped by other life challenges (Toussaint 2008) or dampened by an active process of denial (Norgaard 2011), worrying about climate change requires an allocation of attention that is usually not applied to abstract future contingencies (Weber 2010). One of the findings of an analysis of recent surveys of global climate change concern in the US by Brulle and colleagues was that 'in a society with a limited amount of "issue space", unemployment, economic prosperity, and involvement in wars all compete with climate change for public concern' (2012: 185).

'Critical anthropologists' address the suppressed problem of climate change by focusing on the structural features of contemporary capitalism that drive carbon-intensive economies. The title of a short essay by Hans Baer, *Global Warming as a By-product of the Capitalist Treadmill of Production and Consumption – The Need for an Alternative Global System* (2008) gives a sense of the theoretical direction of critical anthropology approaches. In a recent study of climate activism, Rosewarne *et al.* outline the cost of corporate capitalism's growth imperative: 'The accumulation of capital directly produces the accumulation of greenhouse gases, and drives climate change' (2014: 2). They go on to describe the 'metabolic rift' that capitalism's domination of nature causes, which they argue is ultimately self-destructive. All these authors identify the living earth's destruction from climate change as a systemic outcome of capitalist accumulation, but one that also engenders a collective impetus towards radical social transformation, identified with a broadly conceived 'global climate movement'. The actions and organisations of the climate movement, in diverse locations and contexts around the world, have become the subject of ethnographic study by anthropologists, complementing research by other disciplines such as political science and sociology (Baer and Singer 2014; Burgmann and Baer 2012; Rosewarne *et al.* 2014). This work will be considered in more detail in Chapter 5.

Territorialising the future? Ethnographic research on climate change

Ethnographic coverage of humans in a warming biosphere is necessarily uneven, given the small scale of many studies and the large scale of the changes occurring. Ecological zones under the most severe threat of climate change impacts have become a major focus of applied research funding from international, national and non-government organisations. Many of these locations are part of the global South, inhabited by people in post-colonial situations in rural or remote areas where resources are limited. The implied rationale for interventions is that these zones are the 'climate change canaries', the places where the real effects of climate change will be tested, providing an 'expendable' example of how the rest of the world might follow, much like the canary released into the coal mine to determine the presence of noxious gasses (Farbotko 2010: 53–4).

There are different stories to tell about highly climate-exposed communities. Long-standing records of anthropological research predate the selection of sacrificial zones as spectres for the global North's climate change fears. A more nuanced understanding of humans in the biosphere suggests that these regions are part of 'the majority world' (Connell 2007), which Comaroff and Comaroff (2012: 115) have referred to as 'the suppressed underside of the North' – the places and peoples with minority power in international affairs and capitalist accumulation that make up a majority of the world's population living on the greater part of the earth's surface – Asia, Latin America, Africa, Oceania and the Circumpolar North. Anthropology is the only discipline that has a methodology for holistically studying an important fraction of this majority – remote, small-scale and sometimes radically divergent manifestations of human sociality – with the aim of discovering the full extent of humanity's existential condition and potential for biosphere adaptation. While Northern sociologists have discovered the intellectual force of Southern thinkers in creating new understandings of global North hegemony (Connell 2007), this other important vantage point from the South – the voices and understandings of those living in the 'hot spots' – is largely left to anthropology, a responsibility that some scholars regrettably no longer count among 'core concerns', but rather a hangover from the discipline's colonial origins.

The discussion of ethnographic accounts in this chapter pursues the anthropological purpose of deploying the comparative method to 'de-territorialize the exotic: any people or practice is potentially exotic to any other' (Kapferer 2013: 823). Anthropology also provides a means of territorialising the future: in a warming world, the range of human adaptation in extreme or unusual locations becomes a resource for thinking about life worlds in biosphere conditions – heatwaves, drought, extreme weather events, species loss, food shortages – that all humans may encounter in the near future.

Two contrasting regions of the Earth are considered here, both with high biophysical sensitivity to climatic changes. The Circumpolar North and the South Pacific are places where the effects of global warming are already sharply experienced by people who live on ancestral lands in close interaction with their surrounding environments. Both these regions share commonalities with other ecological zones. Islands (excluding Australia and Antarctica) make up one-sixth of the earth's surface and one-tenth of the world's population (Baldacchino 2006: 3). The circumpolar glaciers now exhibit the accelerated melting that can be found in other glacier zones of the world, including Central Asia and South America, causing already socio-economically marginalised groups, including many First Nations, extreme difficulty in day-to-day life. In the Circumpolar North, defined by high latitudes, severe climates and long-established presence of hunters and herders, ice is melting, hunting is more dangerous, subsistence food is scarcer and local knowledge is less reliable. While circumpolar people are embedded in larger nation-states, the post-colonial politics of Indigeneity in the face of climate change – around land and water rights, livelihoods and traditional knowledge – have come to prominence in international forums and are relevant to the situation of many other First Nation peoples.

The Asia Pacific region encompasses the world's largest ocean as well as some of the biggest GHG emitters in highly fossil fuel intensive economies like Australia and China. Spread across the southern waters of the Pacific Ocean, residents of low-lying islands in Melanesia, Polynesia and Micronesia face sinking land masses, diminishing natural resources and the prospect of relocation. The South Pacific is a focus of attention in Australia because of geographic contiguity, well-established migration networks and public perceptions that inundated islands will result in waves of climate change refugees. The inhabitants of the South Pacific are not generally classified among the Indigenous people of the world but they participate in the international arena as citizens of autonomous states, most in the UN-recognised category of 'Small Island Developing States'.

Environmental change: unstable sentience

The diverse ways humans come to experience their worlds are part and parcel of epistemologies and ontologies that are active in ecosystems large and small. Ways of experiencing environmental change in the majority world are constructed through human dwelling as part of an ecocosmos that incorporates non-humans who may share purpose and agency with humans. Ways of being may call into question dualistic ontologies of Western modernity, such as human subject/natural object distinctions, and corollaries in the framing of sentient and non-sentient realities. Anthropologists have charted the social nature of these connections, attempting to move beyond the 'nature–culture divide' (Cruikshank 2005; Descola 2013; Ingold 2011; Latour 1991; Milton 1996). Ethnographic research with Indigenous and non-Western peoples has discerned or collaboratively generated various framings of culturally specific place and landscape knowledge, including traditional ecological knowledge (TEK), Indigenous knowledge (IK), local knowledge (LK), *Inuit Qaujimatuqangit* (IQ – 'Inuit knowledge') (Leduc 2012) or simply traditional knowledge (TK). Proponents argue that these knowledges should be in dialogue with other understandings as a political tool for people who have become more integrated into state bureaucratic regimes, conservation regulation, science discourse and modes of capitalist accumulation, especially resource extraction and tourism, with accompanying environmental damage.

It is not surprising that much of the conceptualisation of TEK has originated from research in the rapidly warming Circumpolar North. Anthropologists have documented how historically based understandings of shifting ecological zones have always been a feature of Arctic people's landscape knowledge. Julie

Cruikshank, who has studied the people and icefields of the St Elias Mountains in Alaska and the Yukon, evokes images of a sentient glacial landscape that is part of Tlingit and Athapaskan speakers' experience of climatic change over hundreds of years of the Little Ice Age (1550–1900) through to the contemporary era (Cruikshank 2001, 2005). For Indigenous communities, glaciers are agents 'within a deeply moral universe where natural-cultural histories are always entangled' (2005: 243). For generations of explorers, scientists and surveyors, glaciers are sites of inquiry, measurement and boundary making, threaded with narratives of experiences that have been in different ways inspirational, instructive, terrifying and transformative. Cruikshank argues for a more balanced consideration of inhabitants' and scientific narratives, presenting them as equally subjective. She portrays local understandings, particularly as they refer to glaciers, as symbolically and practically rich. She reflects that local people are quite likely to characterise science in terms often used by outsiders to describe TEK – as 'illusory, vague, subjective, context-dependent ... open to multiple interpretations, and as embedded in social institutions ... as socially valueless' (2001: 15).

Further north, Timothy Leduc (2007) writes of the forces that imbue the Inuit cosmos with life in IQ, expressed in ideas about Sila. According to one Inuit shaman encountered by the Danish explorer Knud Rasmussen in his 1921 expedition from Greenland to Siberia:

> Sila [is] a strong spirit, the upholder of the universe, of the weather, in fact all life on earth – so mighty that his speech to man comes not through ordinary words, but through storms, snowfall, rain showers, the sea, through all the forces that man fears, or through sunshine, calm seas or small, innocent children.
>
> (Ostermann 1952: 97–8, cited in Leduc 2007: 241–2)

Other Inuit encountered by Leduc rejected this anthropomorphic and gendered construction of Sila but acknowledged it as a sentient force that is immanent in the flux of all existence, resistant to Western and colonial reductionisms of 'weather', 'deity' or 'energy' (2012: 26–30). The spiritual and ethical dimensions that imbue Inuit experience, Leduc speculates, may sensitise them to the changing conditions of survival of all living things in their Arctic surroundings.

Anthropologists of Arctic societies like Cruikshank and Leduc strive to attend more carefully than other interlocutors to Indigenous ways of knowing, while recognising the highly politicised ways in which all knowledge claims, Indigenous and otherwise, are implicated in struggles over resources and conservation. Researchers illuminate inhabitants' understandings, including their perceptions of decline in a new epoch of environmental change. One Inuit man complained to Leduc that Inuit knowledge didn't 'work' any more: '... weather has so changed that IQ is pretty much gone, it can no longer predict because of the change in climate' (hunter Andre Tautu, in Leduc 2012: 1).

A similar experience is expressed in Jolly *et al.* (2010), in the words of an Inuvialuit (Western Arctic Inuit) resident:

The weather didn't change that much years ago. It was always cold. Not like today. Now, you can't even tell when the weather is going to change. Mild weather – means it is going to be a storm coming, and we get ready for it. But today it changes so much – we are expecting a big storm and next day, clear as can be. I can't predict the weather anymore like we used to years ago.
(Peter Esau, Sachs Harbour 1999, in Jolly *et al.* 2010: 95)

Cruikshank observes that traditional ways of knowing are a resource in dealing with the vicissitudes of extreme weather events. She writes, 'Stories that are useful in times of crisis concern proper relations with land and crystallise quick and timely social responses' (2005: 250). This knowledge cannot be reduced to the terms of scientific materialism and she asserts, more optimistically than Leduc and his informants, that it remains a resource, embedded as tacit knowledge in everyday modes of coping with situations of change (2005: 256). However, Cruikshank, Leduc and many other anthropologists (see Krupnik and Jolly 2010) have recorded the laments of Indigenous peoples that the vitality and authority of their knowledge is fading because of alienation from ancestral places that makes transmission to new generations almost impossible. There are many forms of dispossession. For the Mt Elias Mountains inhabitants where Cruikshank worked, it has been the boundary making of national and international organisations that exclude First Nations from declared conservation areas and 'wilderness' areas that by definition are devoid of human occupancy. People lose their economic sustenance from living on the land; new generations have no immersion in the landscape that nourished traditional knowledge and cultural identity. An ironic consequence of land rights agreements, writes Cruikshank, is that 'Indigenous people are now being asked to document their "traditional knowledge" about places from which they were evicted sixty years earlier' (2005: 257), an observation that could also be made about Indigenous people in Australia under Native Title legislation.

In subarctic regions of Central and North Asia, inhabitants deal with warmer and wetter climates drawing on local knowledge that prefigures scientific predictions of climate change. From Andrei Marin's work with pastoral nomads in the desert-steppe region of Mongolia, it is evident that herders' knowledge of their environment often differs from the evidence of meteorological records. They distinguish *tsag agar* (weather, or literally 'hour air') and *uur amilsga* (climate, literally 'steam breath'). Marin observes that: 'The herders perceive themselves as being constantly "under the weather"; the realisation that nature in general and weather in particular control their lives is ubiquitous and explicitly formulated' (2010: 164).

The herders' spirituality combines Buddhist and shamanic elements, whereby 'masters of the land' (*gazarin ezed*), of whom a deified sky (Tenger) is paramount, bestow good weather or vengefully inflict drought or pestilence. Land use by humans falls under a spiritually sanctioned moral code. Damage to the land is seen as the 'wrong use of nature', and transgressions have wider consequences for weather and the well-being of the natural world (Marin 2009: 1). Marin suggests that climate science is important in understanding subarctic Mongolian land-scapes, but should not take superiority over herders' knowledge. He observes that local ideas about climate are sensitive to changes at smaller spatial scales that are not anticipated in larger-scale scientific predictions (2010: 163). During his field research in 2006, herders complained of dust storms being more intense and protracted than anything they had known previously. Grazing plants were destroyed, and one person said: '…the sheep cannot carry their weight anymore from all the dust in their wool'. Year after year of late rains mean loss of plants that 'usually flower twice each year, now they only flower once' (Marin 2010: 167–8).

Further north, in the permafrost region of Northeastern Siberia, Susan Crate has documented dramatic experiences of climate change among Sakha horse and cattle breeders living in the Viliui River watershed. They have now experienced years of milder winters (which allow *more* snow to fall), and unusually wet, humid summers. Their animals cannot reach the winter grass under the thick snow; the summer potatoes rot in the damp ground; the summer hay harvested for winter does not dry; insects previously only found in warmer latitudes are demolishing the plant life. One female elder commented: 'As Sakha people, we need strong cold here. It is how our lives are organized and how nature works here. The big cold is good' (Crate 2009: 142).

Sakha cosmology personifies winter in the figure of the 'Bull of Winter', a white bull with blue spots, huge horns and frosty breath (Crate 2009: 139). The Bull of Winter keeps the land cold in winter, but his horns start to melt in January, as spring approaches. His arrival again with the winter is communally celebrated, as is his disappearance in the spring. This cycle of cosmic regenera-tion is central to how Sakha people orient their seasonal activities and cultural identity. They feel at home in a dry, frozen landscape that supports valued forms of embodied well-being and sociality. They worry about the permafrost melting and becoming a 'permanent swamp'. The freezing cold destroys diseases, but now warmer winters bring sickness, and humid summers enervate and deplete living things (Crate 2009: 142). Breakdowns in social relationships are linked to ecological deterioration. As one woman put it, 'The way people are so violent these days I think is connected to the change in air and climate' (Crate 2009: 143).

Studies such as these document the adaptability of Northern people to varia-tions in climate and other forms of environmental change over many generations during which they have flourished in a harsh environment. But as Jolly *et al.* (2010: 107) point out, there are limits to human adaptability, and community resilience is being tested by the experience of frequent extreme weather events, increased variability and unpredictable changes to expected patterns. As one Inuit man put it:

> Just a comment about global warming, you hear it all the time on radio and TV and I don't think it makes much difference in some places if the temper-ature rises two degrees, but if our temperature up here rises two degrees or

something, the fact that we live on the ice and snow, I don't know what would happen to us. If we ever saw a real change, a real quick change, I don't know how we'd deal with the impacts of something like that, I don't know how we'd react to it, we'd have a hard hard time.

(Nairn, Labrador, in Furgal and Gosselin 2010: 267)

While Arctic and subarctic peoples have survived by adapting to the surging and waning of glaciers and the vicissitudes of ice and permafrost, Pacific Islanders have ways of knowing land and sea that incorporate millenia of climate change experiences, including the cyclical variation in surface ocean temperatures, called the El Niño-Southern Oscillation, that connects the western seaboard of South America with the Australian continent and the ocean in between. The inhabitants of the smaller Pacific Islands have been hostage to long-held Western tropes of small islands – vulnerable, isolated and poor, ripe for imperial-ist initiatives – now augmented by their popular reputation as natural laboratories for the extreme effects of anthropogenic climate change on human societies (Baldacchino 2008; Lazrus 2012). Counter-tropes, drawing on pre-Christian and Christian cosmologies, as well as resourceful blends of island ecological knowledge and local interpretations of climate science, give substance to islander modes of resilience and adaptation that draw on long-established ways of knowing and being in the Pacific world.

In traditional cosmologies of Micronesians and island Melanesians, humans were situated as caretakers of sacred sites generally located in close proximity to the human domain; spirit guardians that protected the fertility of the land and the clemency of the weather required ritual propitiation. Extensive missionary activity from the early nineteenth century introduced the symbolic universe of Christianity into human relations with the rest of the natural world. In these societies, oral traditions are a significant source of practical knowledge about the vicissitudes of weather and climate. Jerry Jacka (2009) documents knowledge of famines associated with El Niño droughts among the landlocked Ipili people in the Porgera Valley of highland Papua New Guinea. Jacka describes how the high altitude rain forest (*aiyandaka*) beyond the abode of humans contained an impor-tant ritual site for a guardian named Lemeane who sustained the wholeness of the world. One Ipili man said, 'we were the caretakers of Auwolo Anda [the site]. We performed the rituals to control the rain and renew the earth' (Jacka 2009: 205). 'Sky women' (*tawe wanda*) also protected the precious upper rain forest. Reciprocity through ritual was necessary to maintain the protective influence of the sky women, who wreaked vengeance by bringing drenching rain on those who wantonly destroyed the precious food trees. These days, Christianised Porgerans are more likely to draw on apocalyptic stories from the biblical Book of Revelations to interpret unusual occurrences like an earthquake and a solar eclipse (Jacka 2009: 199).

Syncretism of Christian and pre-Christian narratives of environmental change can be found throughout the heavily missionised Pacific islands, now combined with understandings of climate change from peoples' own experiences and science-derived discourse. Inhabitants of the Micronesian Marshall Islands have experienced countless cycles of El Niño weather extremes, irradiation and multiple recent relocations. In the 1940s and 1950s, residents were severely impacted by US hydrogen bomb tests. Ethnobotanists Bridges and McClatchey suggest that Marshallese oral records of climate changes prior to nuclear testing would have included 'long-term observations about "normal" variation in climate over the last several thousand years' (2009: 143), but separation from their ancestral landscape after the nuclear tests disrupted this vital flow of tradition-based knowledge.

Peter Rudiak-Gould explores ideas of environmental change among Marshall Islanders as told in different narratives of the past. He writes of pre-Christian practices that reinforced hierarchy in the social world as well as the religious domain:

> … a small pantheon of gods (*ekajab*) from the spirit island of Eb in the west, as well as other ancestral and nonancestral spirits (*anij*), were supplicated with real or symbolic offerings of food in the hopes that they would reciprocate in the form of fair weather and good harvests.
>
> (Rudiak-Gould 2013: 16)

Integration of new narratives by Marshallese can occur in many ways. One 'respected local man' on the island of Ujae brings Christianity, science and the media into one ecocosmic amalgam, speaking about a fallen coconut tree:

> It fell because the sea is higher. The waves knock the trees over – not just coconut trees but others as well … If the tide rises, it will wash all of the land and all of the trees into the ocean, and we won't be able to plant anything. God told Noah that He would never flood the earth again. But the scientists say the ocean will rise. It's hotter so the snow melts and the ocean will rise and flood the Marshall Islands. I heard this on the radio news in 2000. The ocean will rise higher than the tops of the coconut trees.
>
> (Rudiak-Gould 2013: 1)

Different understandings of climate change stem both from locals' observations and their engagement with science-derived narratives, mass media and new religions. Rudiak-Gould argues that Marshallese 'graft the scientific notion of climate change onto pre-existing narratives of Christian eschatology and cultural decline, making the global discourse intimately local' (2011: 12). Marshallese use the concept of *oktak in mejatoto* to reinterpret science-derived concepts of climate change in a broader notion that interconnects all sorts of changes in their phenomenal world, including the eating of processed 'American' foods; a solar eclipse; disease; lack of social cooperation; and the acceleration of time flow (Rudiak-Gould 2012). In a statement reminiscent of Sakha informants that Susan Crate interviewed, a Marshallese man, asked by the anthropologist if he believed scientists on climate change, replied: 'I think it may be true. Because I

see that the *mejatoto* is not very good nowadays. Life is harder. Goods are expensive. The sun is stronger. And there are improper relations between kin'
(Rudiak-Gould 2012: 51).

This linking of the 'environmental' and the 'social' (a Western-derived dual-
ism) is inherent in the very notion of *anthropogenic* climate change and may be a
salutary message for climate science, argues Rudiak-Gould (2012: 52–3). Such
holism is common across Pacific Island groups, and informs their responses to all
sorts of environmental change.

Interlocutors of environmental change: Agency and action

Different ways of thinking about climate change are important when we consider
the role of myth in motivating people to action. Jonathan Marshall (2009: xxii)
writes:

> if we don't explore how humans go about imagining global warming, the
> environment and catastrophe generally, then we will not have much hope of
> producing the psychological and behavioural changes which are necessary
> for us to adapt to and mitigate ecological problems. Without this under-
> standing we may try to produce change in people by strategies which are
> counterproductive or leave them feeling overwhelmed and inclined to
> retreat from the problem, and thus make things worse. We need new, useful
> and meaningful myths to live by.

While circumpolar and South Pacific people express some fears about environmental change, forebodings of apocalypse and annihilation are more prominent
in Western discourses of climate change to which they are now exposed. These
discourses draw their power from the cosmology of scientific materialism – the
ultimate realisation of a world where humanity is cut off from the resources of the
natural world it exploits and destroys, and where there is no meaningful human
relationship with other forms of life. Scientific bodies like the IPCC amplify the
disaster rhetoric with predictions of GHG effects on the planet's climate system:
accelerated warming of ocean and atmosphere, ocean acidification, shrinking of
glaciers and sea ice, reduction of permafrost and sea-level rise (IPCC 2013:
5–17). The pluralistic cosmologies of land- and water-based peoples and their
apprehensions of vulnerability are in dialogue with outsiders' constructions of
hazard and risk in highly exposed ecological zones of the planet, such as those
discussed in this chapter. Indigenous ways of knowing are often posited as
science's other, in romantic constructions of the 'ecologically noble savage'
(Hames 2007). But people living off the land and waters in regions already highly
impacted by global warming are reworking their own ways of knowing and being:
they are interlocutors in a time of environmental change, not passive recipients
nor innocent bystanders.

The unequal relationships of scientific, colonial and in-dwelling people's
knowledge of environmental change, frequently analysed in ethnographic

studies, find their logical development in the recommendations that emerge in policy solutions of government and non-government bodies. The initiatives of the UNFCCC have failed to come up with an effective international agreement to stabilise greenhouse emissions, and reductions (while urgently necessary) will not ameliorate the already manifest impacts on the more sensitive areas of the planet. Analysis of climate change impacts on humans, if reduced to vulnerability, often lead to recommendations for action centred on adaptations such as resettlement, relocation and migration that may undermine local livelihoods and ways of being in ancestral places. Attempts to press for other forms of remedial assistance by affected populations, whether as nation-states lobbying in international arenas or as Indigenous peoples like the Inuit within nations or cross-national regions, have not had much success, reflecting the post-colonial and transnational politics that hamper action on climate change more generally. Anthropological studies shed some light on the impediments to ameliorating impacts in the areas that form the focus of this chapter.

The evidence for vulnerability of circumpolar peoples' lives to the effects of global warming is now abundantly clear. Environmental change is not new to inhabitants of these areas, however, the rapid rate of change makes the weather and other biophysical phenomena increasingly unpredictable. The small coastal Inupiaq Eskimo village of Shishmaref in Alaska has been called one of the first 'climate refugee' areas, 'as the community has chosen to move their village further inland as sea ice rapidly retreats and increasing storm surges and coastal erosion eat away their land' (McNeeley and Huntington 2007: 146). There is now a corpus of collaborative studies between researchers and Indigenous experts in Arctic communities that have documented the melting of inland glacial ice and sea ice in their localities, disrupting hunting, fishing and other subsistence activities on which people have always depended (e.g. Nichols *et al.* 2004; Nuttall 2010). In the volume *The Earth is Faster Now* (Krupnik and Jolly 2010), scientists engage with Indigenous people of the Arctic to achieve place-based understandings of the complex social-ecological system in which they are experiencing global warming effects. The enormous repositories of ecological knowledge that are part of the ways of being of circumpolar peoples are found to be dynamic and responsive, up to a point, to the growing variability and unpredictability of weather patterns, and local impacts such as glacier retreat, permafrost thaw and inundation.

Changes wrought by global warming are only one dimension of changes to environment and livelihood being experienced in these communities, some triggered by the melting landscape. These changes include intensified commercial extraction of oil and gas, mining, hydroelectric developments, declaration of nature conservation 'wilderness' areas and in general a greater integration into a cash economy and commodity goods (Berkes 2010; Cruikshank 2005; Ford 2009). Indigenous people in this region are living in a post-colonial world of intensive capital accumulation. The damage to their lives and livelihoods from global warming is an exacerbation of long-existing forms of exploitation by the settler societies in which they are embedded. Marybeth Long Martello, for example, found that the 2004 Arctic Climate Impact Assessment portrayed Inuit visually and textually as 'exotic, expert, and endangered' (2008: 353). Scholars engaged in collaborative projects have noted the tendency to reduce Indigenous ecological knowledge to the terms of Western science, rupturing the ecocosmic field in which this knowledge has meaning and efficacy (Berkes 2010; Cruikshank 2005). In a similar vein, Emilie Cameron (2012: 103–4) depicts the burgeoning institutional domain of arctic climate policy as a continuation of colonial governmentality:

> The dominant academic, governmental, and political institutions at play in the Arctic – from the Arctic Council to various Inuit associations to federal and territorial governments to the network of scholars brought together through International Polar Year – now routinely refer to, and attempt to document, assess, and respond to, the 'human dimensions' of climatic change.

She argues that the terms on which Inuit have a voice in the framing of local vulnerability and its remediation are restricted, with the outcomes slanted towards increasing 'governmental interest in reshaping the conduct of Inuit conduct', an extension of projects of colonial governmentality. Increasing dependence of Inuit communities – on fossil fuels, wage labour, state services, imported commodities – are both an effect and a driver of these governmental projects.

Circumpolar peoples take a proactive role in climate change negotiations at national and transnational forums through organisations such as the Arctic Council (Henshaw 2009: 153; Leduc 2012). This is reflected in the emphasis on 'co-production of more robust solutions that combine science and technology with indigenous knowledge' in the 2014 IPCC WG2 AR5 report on 'impacts, adaptation and vulnerability' in polar regions (IPCC 2014). But 'unbalanced encounters' still pervade peoples' relations with the states that encapsulate and attempt to control them (Cruikshank 2005). In Subarctic Mongolia for instance, initiatives and government policies aimed at maintaining herder productivity in a warming climate have both enhanced and undermined communities in different ways. While Chinese aid and investment has increased some technological and informational capacities, the need for introduced livestock species and the difficulty of continuing to migrate over large (now climate change-affected) areas, has decreased herder communities' adaptability and mobility (Wang *et al.* 2013: 1682).

Mining, oil and gas developments by corporations ever eager to exploit new fossil fuel resources have encountered strong resistance in communities that value the perpetuity of sacred sites and traditional hunting grounds over monetary wealth. In 2012, Tahltan people in the Northwest of Canada won their legal battle to stop Royal Dutch Shell Corporation drilling for methane gas in their sacred headwaters in the Klappan Valley (Forest Ethics 2014). In 2013 they engaged in a battle with American-based resource company Fortune Minerals to stop a coal mining development in the same region (Terrace Standard 2014) and in September 2014 the British Columbia government announced a temporary hold on all coal exploration permits in the area (*Globe and Mail* 2014). The government then bought the 61 coal permits in the region, and in 2015, is in talks with mineral companies and the Tahltan people about next steps (Lazenby 2015).

Nunavut groups in the Canadian Arctic are fighting seismic testing for offshore oil and gas in Baffin Bay and Davis Strait that threatens to destroy marine life. The testing has been approved by the National Energy Board, and allows seismic ships to travel through the area, towing air guns that release 230 decibel shots (90 more decibels than a human can hear without getting permanent hearing loss) into the ocean every 13 to 15 seconds, 24 hours a day. The local Nunavut people are worried about the impacts of the testing on their food sources and culture. The mayor of Clyde River, Jerry Natanine expressed concern that:

> Inuit have lived off of this land and these waters for over 4,000 years … The marine mammals in these waters are central to our way of life. They are our food and are integral to our culture. If the oil companies take that away, we'll have nothing left.
>
> (*Arctic Journal* 2014)

The melting of ice caps and glaciers and thawing of permafrost have set in train a race to exploit reserves of rare-earth minerals, gold, iron ore, rubies, uranium, oil and gas, with significant ramifications for local and Indigenous peoples. Two Australian mining companies, Tanbreez Mining and Greenland Minerals and Energy, are proposing large mines in Greenland, one in a mountain that Tanbreez says holds the world's biggest rare-earth deposit, and which would greatly affect the town of Narsaq at the foot of the mountain, while the other mine includes uranium, the mining of which was banned in Greenland until recently. Narsaq local Avaaraq Olsen recalls the day the ban was overturned: "'I was very sad, I was crying," she says. "I'm ashamed of being a Greenlander. If this mine is starting here in Narsaq, we will be moving away, not just from Narsaq, but from Greenland'" (Fletcher 2014). Bringing both employment opportunities as well as fears of environmental damage, pollution and influxes of foreign workers, the fervour around mining development is at an all time high in Greenland, with the desire on the part of some groups for more jobs and economic benefits, while others express concern about pollution, radioactivity and other adverse effects of mining on their lives (see Fletcher 2014). Climate change is playing a key role in Greenland's resource extraction: as the ice melts and permafrost thaws, minerals are more accessible and mining developments more cost efficient (Fletcher 2014).

Awareness of climate change can promote new forms of thinking about ecocosmic relationships and political responsibilities of Indigenous people. George Noongwook, a Yupik man in Alaska, told Igor Krupnik:

we cannot change nature, our past, and other people for that matter, but we can control our own thoughts and actions and participate in global efforts to cope with these global climate changes. That I think is the most empowering thing we can do as individuals.

(Krupnik 2010: 189)

This ideal of global cooperation may be compromised, however, as Indigenous people confront the impact of intensified resource extraction by powerful transnational corporations in their changing lands.

The island nations of the South Pacific are often represented as the paradigmatic case of vulnerability in the industrialised world's forebodings about climate change. Attention focuses on these islands as 'geographic objects' – their scarce natural resources, fragile ecologies and rising sea levels (Barnett and Campbell 2010). The people who inhabit these islands, their agency, modes of survival and potential for adaptive responses to climate change impact, are often overshadowed by dominant discourses of small island vulnerability. But island environments have always been dynamic, and deep time records of geology and archaeology show patterns of human adaptation to previous changes in climate and sea levels, as well as many other forms of environmental change (Barnett and Campbell 2010: 184; Lazrus 2012). In the Marshall Islands, for example, Bridges and McClatchey describe the taro pit as a fresh-water reservoir that has been adapted over time to maximally conserve available water by creating microclimates of humidity. This is an ancient technology that will adapt or decline as rising seas impinge on the pits' depth and volume (2009: 142). As is the case for the Indigenous people of Arctic regions, many forms of environmental damage in the Pacific Islands can be related to colonial and post-colonial exploitation: French, British and US nuclear testing, mining, deforestation and over-fishing.

While atoll islands such as Tuvalu and the Marshalls often appear in Western representations as small, isolated and vulnerable – the planet's climate change laboratories – the new climate change awareness of Pacific Islanders builds on alternative imaginings of networks of connectedness, romanticised as an 'oceanic community' of island voyagers (Hau'ofa et al. 1993) forged over many millennia. Pacific Islander mobility has transformed and expanded as new generations seek livelihoods as transnational migrants in the more affluent Pacific Rim countries of Australia, New Zealand and the USA. Local economies are increasingly dependent on remittances that enable high levels of integration into cash economies and commodity markets. In this context, as Farbotko and Lazrus have observed of Tuvaluans, 'inherently mobile' Pacific people are not threatened by the prospect of migration in itself, '... rather it is the prospect of permanent loss of land and self-determination, particularly if there is no forthcoming remedy for these losses from those who caused the damage' (2012: 388).

Transnational climate activism was strikingly evident in a visit of Pacific Islanders to Australia in 2014. The Pacific Climate Warriors, a group of 30 individuals from 12 Pacific Island countries, visited climate change hotspots including the Port of Newcastle to protest Australia's expanding export coal industry. A Warrior from Tokelau talked of the importance of direct action and self-determination in protecting their lands:

> It is very important for us to take direct actions against climate change because it is threatening our lives and our islands. Our land is the most valuable treasure in our lives and the impacts of climate change will destroy it. We don't want this to happen and we will not allow it to happen.
>
> (Quoted in Kelly 2014)

In Pacific homelands, there is a vigorous climate politics particularly around issues of resettlement to other countries. Carol Farbotko and Heather Lazrus found conflicting views on the environmental impacts of climate change and their predicted social consequences in Tuvalu. Often predicted as the world's first nation of climate refugees, Tuvaluans show an understandable antipathy to such powerfully loaded language (Farbotko and Lazrus 2012). They challenge science and international agency narratives of victimhood that ignore place-based knowledge and practices. Local understandings of the problem are inspiring a range of government-sponsored adaptation measures. Tuvaluans object to the hopelessness surrounding the refugee scenario, and want more lasting policies to strengthen existing communities rather than simply waiting for an inevitable exodus (Farbotko and Lazrus 2012: 386). They contest the fatalism of apocalyptic media discourses of 'disappearing islands' in many ways, from assertive delegations at international climate change conventions to vigorous debates on online forums (Farbotko 2010).

The Republic of Kiribati under the leadership of President Anote Tong has taken a different stance in international forums, foreshadowing a relocation of the populace to enclaves in neighbouring areas – what Tong calls a 'migration with dignity' policy (Lagan 2013). This future is strongly contested in Kiribati, among a people deeply connected to their 'God given' land, including highly influential community members, especially those within the church (Barnett and O'Neill 2012; Lagan 2013). Many argue that focusing on resettlement ignores more pressing concerns, such as 'severe overcrowding, proliferation of informal housing and unplanned settlement, inadequate water supply, poor sanitation and solid waste disposal, pollution and conflict over land ownership' that is happening on the Tarawa atoll (IPCC 2014). As Barnett and O'Neill point out, 'planned resettlement may significantly undermine adaptation and the sustainable use of islands, because if there is no future for people in the places in which they live then there is no reason to manage those places sustainably' (2012: 10). Rising sea levels is one threat among many. They argue that migration needs to be removed as an option, so that the more short-to-medium-term threats of fresh water shortages and living standards can be addressed more effectively (Barnett and O'Neill 2012; Storey and Hunter 2010). Relying on the narrative of climate change refugee resettlement 'forecloses on all other adaptation options', when 'the full gamut of adaptation responses, and their barriers and limits, has not been adequately assessed' (Barnett and O'Neill 2012: 10).

In the Marshall Islands, Rudiak-Gould's ethnographic research has documented the debates and policy positions that have developed as people come to terms with the vulnerabilities of their atolls. As in Tuvalu and Kiribati, there is no consensus that resettlement is inevitable, and Marshall Islanders have also been a strong voice in international forums for robust mitigation efforts and adaptation assistance for small islands by means of UNFCCC agreements. Rudiak-Gould argues that the majority of Marshall Islanders roundly reject relocation as a climate change response, with abandoning their homeland often espoused as less favourable than drowning (2013: 152–5). Despite being confronted with apocalyptic consequences of climate change, and possessing adequate knowledge about the various aspects of global warming, Marshall Islanders – from government officials to young teenagers – adamantly reject the 'climate refugee' discourse and the possibility of migration. As one person told the anthropologist, '… I'd rather die with this island than go elsewhere … because I feel this place is part of me and I'm part of it' (Rudiak-Gould 2013: 153).

Far more than in the Arctic, where new resource extraction opportunities have drawn settlers from outside, external organisations not uncommonly propose resettlement as the inevitable culmination of climate change adaptation of smaller Pacific Island populations whose sovereignty, like their size, may seem insignificant to the world of large nation-states. As Godfrey Baldacchino (2008) has argued, in a robust challenge to the 'small is insignificant' political discourse, referring to islands as small reinforces colonial objectifications, and gives the incorrect impression that islands share a homogenous smallness and 'strangeness', whereas they actually vary greatly in population and size. There are in fact more 'smaller' nations globally than there are 'larger' – of the 237 jurisdictions in the world in 2006, 158 had populations of less than 10 million (CIA: 2006) and of the 21,000 islands in the world with a land area larger than 1 square km, less than 300 have land masses over 100 square km, making small in fact the norm and large the 'anomaly' (Baldacchino 2008: 39–40). As Lazrus reminds us, islands are open communities that are often 'deeply globally connected' in multiple ways (2012: 286). The image of the small island, argues Baldacchino, also often conjures up images of small, warm paradises, which can minimise or ignore the problems faced by many islanders, such as 'under-employment, aid dependency, loss of talent, waste mountains, eutrophied coasts and lagoons, sewage overflows' etc. (Baldacchino 2008: 42).

Pacific Island nations make up about 40 per cent of the Small Island Developing States (SIDS), most of which form a negotiating bloc of countries within the United Nations. The Pacific Island members of SIDS have been vocal participants in the annual conferences sponsored by the UNFCCC, striving to exert moral and political suasion to facilitate the enforcement of Article 4.8, which affirms the parties' commitment to assisting small island states' adaptation to the impacts of global warming, which these states have done nothing to create (Barnett and Campbell 2010: 87–97).

The international response has been a flow of aid agency and non-government organisation funding on a regional or country-specific basis, but despite the expressed preferences of Pacific Island countries, only a small percentage of this has gone to the practical implementation of adaptation projects in communities, with a much greater proportion going to research, financing and technical assistance (Barnett and Campbell 2010: 114–19). Felicity Prance's (2016) critical analysis of the World Bank's National Consultations in the Republic of Kiribati is an example of these shortcomings. She found that the aim of developing culturally appropriate climate change adaptation initiatives was not achieved. Obstacles included use of English instead of I-Kiribati language in community meetings, lack of sensitivity to gender, age and status hierarchies in group discussions, failure to take into account cultural priority on short-term survival rather than long-term planning, misunderstanding of how traditional knowledge was individually owned rather than publicly disseminated, and a focus on physical infrastructure at the expense of behavioural change and social support strategies.

In their roles as close observers and advisers in climate change and development projects in the Pacific, Jon Barnett and John Campbell have identified recurring features of successful projects and a series of shifts towards more useful, community-based initiatives. They note that there have been encouraging shifts:

> in scale – from regional to local; in focus – from impacts assessments to adaptation; in nature – from processes driven by experts from outside of the region, to processes driven by people within the region; and in cost – from expensive big projects to relatively cheaper smaller ones.
>
> (Barnett and Campbell 2010: 136)

Successful projects actively engaged communities in the vulnerability assessment phase as well as in adaptation activities, taking into account local capacity and the many pressures people face from other sources of environmental change, economic hardship and poor access to services and education. The specificity of local social organisation, such as land tenure, kinship, community decision-making structures and customary law, as well as performance traditions like dance, song and story-telling, were incorporated into project goals and activities.

More often though the prospect of displacement due to rising sea levels and increased storm inundation, and the consequent need for resettlement of diverse populations, raises a host of intractable problems that challenge the generic adaptation discourses of national governments and international bodies. David Lipset documents such an effort to internally resettle a population of about 3,500 Murik people who live in five settlements along coastal lakes of the Sepik River estuary in Papua New Guinea – a people whose mangrove-based fishing livelihoods are increasingly vulnerable to storm inundation linked with sea-level rise (Lipset 2013: 147). Despite support for a government-funded resettlement project from the prime minister, himself a Murik man, ambivalence and resistance to this move characterised local discourses. During a field trip in 2008, Lipset documented the complexities of local dispositions towards the plan to resettle the three most exposed villages a short distance inland. Men's discussions in the Male Cult House cast resettlement as emasculating and cowardly, a betrayal of primordial ties: "'How many times" he [a senior man] asked, "has the sea taken the village? What did your ancestors do? Run away?"' (Lipset 2013: 150).

Gardening, an unfamiliar form of subsistence activity for Murik but now possible in the resettlement site, was seen as unattractive compared to fishing in their own waters: 'Another senior man extolled the pleasures of home when he vowed to "stay on the beach where the wind is good and the fish are plentiful. A lot of people share my view. They say, 'Buy the land, we can garden on it!' But we will stay on the beach"' (Lipset 2013: 150).

These reservations were compounded by fears of conflict with the horticultural neighbours of the resettlement site – long-term trading partners with whom the Murik had an uneasy interdependence. They feared conflict over the land transfers necessary for the project to proceed – arrangements that they worried would not hold up to future challenges under customary land tenure rights. Moreover there was some prospect of oil exploration under their own lands, raising concerns that the resettlement project was a government plot to deprive residents of royalties (Lipset 2013: 151). These views fed into a general disenchantment with the modern state, which villagers perceived had failed to provide them with services, security or justice. On return trips, Lipset recorded the complete collapse of the government resettlement project by 2010 amid allegations of corruption. In 2011 after a tsunami that severely damaged villages and the lakes ecosystem, many villagers initiated their own resettlement plans, without government support or intervention, but which 'were devised, entirely in terms of ethnohistory, hereditary trading partnerships, and lineage, i.e., entirely in sub-state, or local, terms' (Lipset 2013: 154).

The failed Murik relocation bears out the argument made by Barnett and O'Neill that forced resettlement policies have a high risk of maladaptation in the Pacific Islands, especially when rushed in anticipation of climate change impacts. People resettled in this way face higher risks of 'landlessness, unemployment, homelessness, social marginalization, food insecurity, reduced access to common-property resources and increased morbidity' (2012: 9). Adaptive strategies initiated by people themselves, and other migration options such as 'voluntary labour mobility' provide more effective options, both socially and economically. Resettlement is perceived as a loss of local agency and ultimately sovereignty.

Parables of change

Climate change viewed through the lens of anthropological studies has an unstable existence. Its scientific foreground of modelling and risk analysis dissolves into a hazy background, displaced by other realities that confront people everywhere: the experience of immediate threats to local environments, health, safety and livelihoods. Global warming may be perceived by land- and sea-based peoples as a Western 'environmentalist parable' (Cruikshank 2005: 259), whose moral truth has little relevance in the face of territorial appropriation, loss of local food supply, objectification of traditional knowledge and conservationist politics. There is an incompatibility of scale, whereby the global scale of climate change models cannot easily accommodate the anomalies of local experience, which disappear in the coarser grain of climate models.

Calls for a more integrative approach to Indigenous/traditional knowledge and Western science is a common theme in anthropological studies of environmental change. Programmatic statements about the value of integration in achieving more resilient ecological systems must grapple not only with distortions of scale but also with the problems of reconciling discordant epistemologies, and the accompanying social contexts and politics of knowledge (Bohensky and Maru 2011). Land- and sea-based peoples have ways of experiencing environmental change with knowledge developed from close interdependence with natural forces that are understood as having their own sentient powers. These powers are embedded in cosmologies that imbue the rhythms of daily life as well as crisis situations. The circumpolar and Pacific examples discussed in this chapter suggest that people's inclusive understandings integrate new forms of environmental change as phenomena that span many dimensions of human experience and institutionalised practices, permeating the whole ecocosmos. This holism may resist or misrecognise climate change reality but may also be a potentially constructive response to its complexities.

Note

1   In the IPCC's Fifth Assessment report, 'adaptation' is defined as a process of adjustment to actual or expected climate and its effects. It can seek to moderate harm and exploit beneficial opportunities, or facilitate adjustment to the climate. 'Mitigation' refers to the human intervention to reduce the sources or enhance the removal of GHGs (IPCC 2014).

References

Arctic Journal 2014. 'Nunavut community groups mount legal challenge against seismic testing'. Press release from Ruby Shiller Chan Hasan, Barristers. July 28. Available at http://arcticjournal.com/press-releases/832/nunavut-community-groups-mount-legal-challenge-against-seismic-testing (accessed 8 August 2014).

Baer, H. 2008. 'Global Warming as a By-product of the Capitalist Treadmill of Production and Consumption: The Need for an Alternative Global System'. *The Australian Journal of Anthropology* 19 (1): 58.

Baer, H. and Singer, M. 2014. *The Anthropology of Climate Change: An Integrated Critical Perspective.* New York: Routledge, Earthscan.

Baldacchino, G. 2006. 'Islands, Island Studies, Island Studies Journal'. *Island Studies Journal* 1 (1): 3–18.

Baldacchino, G. 2008. 'Studying Islands: On Whose Terms? Some epistemological and methodological challenges to the pursuit of island studies'. *Island Studies Journal* 3 (1): 37–56.

Barnett, J. and Campbell, J. 2010. *Climate Change and Small Island States: Power, Knowledge and the South Pacific.* London: Earthscan.

Barnett, J. and O'Neill, S. 2012. 'Islands, Resettlement and Adaptation'. *Nature Climate Change* 2 (January): 8–10.

Batterbury, S. 2008. 'Anthropology and Global Warming: The Need for Environmental Engagement'. *The Aus Journal of Anth* 19 (1): 62–68.

Berkes, F. 2010. 'Epilogue: Making Sense of Arctic Environmental Change?'. In: *The Earth is Faster Now: Indigenous Observations of Arctic Environmental Change*. Krupnik, I. and Jolly, D. (eds). Fairbanks, Alaska: Arctic Research Consortium of the United States.

Bohensky, E. L. and Maru, Y. 2011. 'Indigenous Knowledge, Science, and Resilience: What have we learned from a decade of international literature on "integration"?'. *Ecology and Society* 16 (4): 6.

Bolin, I. 2009. 'The Glaciers of the Andes are Melting: Indigenous and anthropological knowledge merge in restoring water resources'. In: *Anthropology and Climate Change: From encounters to actions*. S. Crate and M. Nuttall (eds). Walnut Cree, Ca.: Left Coast Press.

Bridges, K. W. and McClatchey, W. C. 2009. 'Living on the Margin: Ethnoecological insights from Marshall Islanders at Rongelap atoll'. *Global Environmental Change* 19 (2): 140–146.

Brondizio, E. S. and Moran, E. F. 2008. 'Human Dimensions of Climate Change: The vulnerability of small farmers in the Amazon'. *Philosoph. Trans. Royal Soc.* 363: 1803–1809.

Brulle, R. J. 2013. 'Institutionalizing Delay: Foundation funding and the creation of U.S. climate change counter-movement organizations'. *Climatic Change* 122 (4): 681–694.

Brulle, R. J., Carmichael, J. and Jenkins, J. H. 2012. 'Shifting Public Opinion on Climate Change: An empirical assessment of factors influencing concern over climate change in the US, 2002–2010'. *Clim Change* 114 (2): 169–188.

Burgmann, V. and Baer, H. 2012. *Climate Politics and the Climate Movement in Australia*. Melbourne: Melbourne University Press.

Cameron, E. 2012. 'Securing Indigenous Politics: A critique of the vulnerability and adaptation approach to the human dimensions of climate change in the Canadian Arctic'. *Global Environmental Change* 22: 103–114.

CIA (Central Intelligence Agency) 2006. *CIA World Factbook 2006*. Central Intelligence Agency, United States of America.

Comaroff, J. and Comaroff, J. L. 2012. 'Theory from the South: Or, how Euro-America is evolving toward Africa'. *Anthropological Forum* 22 (2): 113–131.

Connell, R. 2007. 'The Northern Theory of Globalization'. *Sociological Theory* 25 (4): 368–385.

Crate, S. A. 2009. 'Gone the Bull of Winter? Contemplating climate change's cultural implications in northeaster Siberia, Russia'. In: *Anthropology and Climate Change: From encounters to actions*. Crate, S and Nuttall, M. Walnut Cree, Ca.: Left Coast Press.

Crate, S. A. 2012. 'Climate and Culture: Anthropology in the Era of Contemporary Climate Change'. *Annual Review of Anthropology* 40: 175–194.

Crate, S. A. and Nuttall, M. 2009. *Anthropology and Climate Change: From Encounters to Actions*. Walnut Cree, Ca: Left Coast Press Inc.

Cruikshank, J. 2001. 'Glaciers and climate change: perspectives from oral tradition [of Athapaskan and Tinglit elders]'. *Arctic* 54 (4): 377–393.

Cruikshank, J. 2005. *Do Glaciers Listen? Local Knowledge, Colonial Encounters and Social Imagination*. Vancouver and Seattle: UBC Press and University of Washington Press.

Curran, G. 2009. 'Ecological Modernisation and Climate Change in Australia'. *Environmental Politics* 18 (2): 201–217.

Descola, P. 2013. *Beyond Nature and Culture*. Chicago, IL: University of Chicago Press.

Dryzek, J., Norgaard, R. and Schlosberg, D. 2013. *Climate-Challenged Society*. Oxford: Oxford University Press.

Fagan, B. 2005. *The Long Summer: How climate changed civilization*. New York: Basic Books.

Farbotko, C. 2010. 'Wishful sinking: Disappearing islands, climate refugees and cosmopolitan experimentation'. *Asia Pacific Viewpoint* 51 (1): 47–60.

Farbotko, C. and Lazrus, H. 2012. 'The First Climate Refugees? Contesting global narratives of climate change in Tuvalu'. *Global Environmental Change* 22: 382–390.

Finan, T. J. 2007. 'Is "Official" Anthropology Ready for Climate Change?'. *Anthropology News* December: 10–11.

Fletcher, J. 2014. *Mining in Greenland – A country divided*. Available at www.bbc.com/news/magazine-25421967 (accessed 8 August 2014).

Ford, J. D. 2009. 'Dangerous Climate Change and the Importance of Adaptation for The Arctic's Inuit Population'. *Environmental Research Letters* 4: 1–9.

Forest Ethics 2014. 'How we got Shell out of the Sacred Headwaters'. Available at http://forestethics.org/sacred-headwaters-timeline (accessed 30 July 2014).

Fuller, S. 2016. 'When Climate Change is not The Concern: Realities and futures of environmental change in village Nepal'. In: *Environmental Change and the World's Futures: Ecologies, Ontologies, Mythologies*. Marshall, J. P. and Connor, L. H. (eds). London: Routledge.

Furgal, C, M. D. and Gosselin, P. 2010. 'Climate Change and Health in Nunavik and Labrador: Lessons from Inuit Knowledge'. In *The Earth is Faster Now: Indigenous Observations of Arctic Environmental Change* (2nd ed) Krupnik, I and Jolly, D (eds). Fairbanks, Alaska: Arctic Research Consortium of the United States.

Galvin, K. A. 2007. 'Adding the Human Component to Global Environmental Change Research'. *Anthropology News* December: 11–12.

Globe and Mail 2014. 'Coal exploration permits on hold in Klappan while B.C. government, First Nation talk'. September 8. Available at www.theglobeandmail.com/news/british-columbia/coal-exploration-permits-on-hold-in-klappan-while-bc-government-first-nation-talk/article20487180/ (accessed 10 February 2015).

Hames, R. 2007. 'The Ecologically Noble Savage Debate'. *Annual Review of Anthropology* 36: 177–190.

Harris, M. 1979. *Materialism: The Struggle for a Science of Culture*. New York: Random House.

Hau'ofa, E., Waddell, E. and Naidu, V. 1993. *A New Oceania: Rediscovering our sea of islands*. Suva: University of the South Pacific.

Henshaw, A. 2009. 'Sea Ice: The Sociocultural dimensions of a melting environment in the Arctic'. In: *Anthropology and Climate Change: From Encounters to Actions*. Crate, S and Nuttall, M (eds). California: Left Coast Press.

Ingold, T. 2011. *The Perception of the Environment: Essays on Livelihood, Dwelling and Skill*. London: Routledge.

IPCC (Intergovernmental Panel on Climate Change) 2007. *Fourth Assessment Report: Climate Change 2007, Vol. 2006*. Available at www.ipcc.ch/activity/ar.htm (accessed 20 July 2008).

IPCC 2013. 'Summary for Policymakers'. In: *Climate Change 2013: The Physical Science Basis. Contribution of Working Group I to the Fifth Assessment Report of the Intergovernmental Panel on Climate Change* [Stocker, T.F., D. Qin, G.-K. Plattner, M. Tignor, S.K. Allen, J. Boschung, A. Nauels, Y. Xia, V. Bex and P.M. Midgley (eds)]. Cambridge University Press, Cambridge, United Kingdom and New York, NY, USA.

IPCC 2014. *Impacts, Adaptation and Vulnerability. AR5, Working Group II.* Available at www.ipcc.ch/report/ar5/wg2/ (accessed 2 November 2014).

International Energy Association 2012. *World Energy Outlook 2012.* Paris: International Energy Association.

Jacka, J. K. 2009. 'Global Averages, Local Extremes: The Subtleties and complexities of climate change in Papua New Guinea'. In *Anthropology and Climate Change: From Encounters to Actions*, S. Crate and M. Nuttall (eds). Walnut Grove, CA: Left Coast Press.

Jolly, D., Berkes, F., Castleden, J., Nichols, T. and the community of Sachs Harbour 2010. 'We can't predict the weather like we used to: Inuvialuit observations of climate change, Sachs Harbour, Western Canadian Arctic'. In *The Earth is Faster Now: Indigenous Observations of Arctic Environmental Change* (2nd ed). Krupnik, I. and Jolly, D. (eds). Fairbanks, Alaska: Arctic Research Consortium of the United States.

Kapferer, B. 2013. 'How Anthropologists Think: Configurations of the exotic'. *Journal of the Royal Anthropological Institute* 19: 813–836.

Kelly, M. 2014. 'Pacific Climate Warriors block ships in Newcastle harbour protest'. *Newcastle Herald*, October 17. Available at www.theherald.com.au/story/2631698/ newcastle-harbour-blockade-delays-ship-photos-video/?cs=310 archived by WebCite at www.webcitation.org/6TnKA6aQU (accessed 3 November 2014).

Krupnik, I. 2010. 'Watching Ice and Weather Our Way: Some lessons from Yupik observations of sea ice and weather on St. lawrence Island, Alaska'. In *The Earth is Faster Now: Indigenous Observations of Arctic Environmental Change* (2nd ed). Krupnik, I. and Jolly, D. (eds). Fairbanks, Alaska: Arctic Research Consortium of the United States.

Krupnik, I. and Jolly, D. (eds) 2010. *The Earth is Faster Now: Indigenous Observations of Arctic Environmental Change* (2nd ed.). Fairbanks, Alaska: Arctic Research Consortium of the United States.

Lagan, B. 2013. *Kiribati: A Nation Going Under. The Global Mail*, April 15. Available at www.theglobalmail.org/feature/kiribati-a-nation-going-under/590/ archived by WebCite at www.webcitation.org/596Ofc541vep (accessed 8 April 2014).

Lahsen, M. 2007. 'Anthropology and the Trouble of Risk Society'. *Anthropology News* December: 9–10.

Latour, B. 1991. *We Have Never Been Modern.* Simon and Schuster: UK.

Latour, B. 2004. *Politics of Nature.* Harvard: Harvard University Press.

Lazenby, H. 2015. *BC government buys Klappan coal licences to spur Aboriginal parleys.* May 6. Available at www.miningweekly.com/article/bc-government-buys-klappan-coal-licences-to-spur-aboriginal-parleys-2015-05-06 (accessed 30 August 2015).

Lazrus, H. 2012. 'Sea Change: Island Communities and Climate Change'. *Annual Review of Anthropology* 41: 285–301.

Leahy, T., Bowden, V. and Threadgold, S. 2010. 'Stumbling Towards Collapse: Coming to terms with the climate crisis'. *Environmental Politics* 19 (6): 851–868.

Leduc, T. B. 2007. 'Sila Dialogues on Climate Change: Inuit wisdom for a cross-cultural interdisciplinarity'. *Climatic Change* 85: 237–250.

Leduc, T. B. 2012. *Climate, Culture, Change: Inuit and Western dialogues with a warming North.* Ottawa: University of Ottawa Press.

Lipset, D. 2013. 'The New State of Nature: Rising sea-levels, climate justice, and community-based adaptation in Papua New Guinea (2003–2011)'. *Conservation and Society* 11 (2): 144–157.

Long Martello, M. 2008. 'Indigenous peoples as representations and representatives of climate change'. *Social Studies of Science* 38 (3): 351–376.

Magistro, J. and Roncoli, C. 2001. 'Introduction: Anthropological perspectives and policy implications of climate change research'. *Climate Research* 19: 91–96.

Malinowski, B. 1944. *A Scientific Theory of Culture and Other Essays*. Chapel Hill: University of North Carolina Press.

Marin, A. 2009. 'Angry Spirits of the Land: Cultural and ethical elements of climate change adaptation among Mongolian pastoralist nomads'. *IOP Conference Series: Earth and Environmental Science* 6.

Marin, A. 2010. 'Riders Under Storms: Contributions of nomadic herders observations to analysing climate change in Mongolia'. *Global Environmental Change* 20: 162–176.

Marshall, J. 2009. *Depth Psychology: Disorder and Climate Change*. Sydney: Jung Downunder Books.

McNeeley, S. and Huntington, H. 2007. 'Postcards from the (not so) Frozen North: Talking about climate change in Alaska'. In: *Creating a Climate for Change: Communicating climate change and facilitating social change*. Moser, S. and Dilling, L. (eds). Cambridge: Cambridge. University Press.

Milton, K. 1996. *Environmentalism and Cultural Theory: Exploring the role of Anthropology in Environmental Discourse*. London: Routledge.

Milton, K. 2008. 'Anthropological Perspectives on Climate Change'. *The Australian Journal of Anthropology* 19: 57–58.

Nelson, D. 2007. 'Expanding the Climate Change Research Agenda'. *Anthropology News* December: 12–13.

Nichols, T., Berkes, F., Jolly, D., Snow, N. B. and the Community of Sachs Harbour 2004. 'Climate Change and Sea Ice: Local observations from the Canadian western Arctic'. *Arctic* 57 (1): 68–79.

Norgaard, K. 2011. *Living in Denial: Climate Change, Emotions and Everyday Life*. Cambridge: MIT Press.

Nuttall, M. 2010. 'Anticipation, Climate Change, and Movement in Greenland'. *Études Inuit Studies* 34 (1): 21–37.

Paterson, M. and Newell, P. 2010. *Climate Capitalism: Global warming and the transformation of the global economy*. Cambridge: Cambridge University Press.

Pokrant, B, and Stocker, L. 2011. 'Anthropology, Climate Change and Coastal Planning'. In *Environmental Anthropology Today*. Kopnina, H. and Shoreman-Ouimet, E. (eds). London and New York: Routledge.

Prance, F. 2016. 'Indigenous Ontologies and Developmentalism: Analysis of the National Consultations for the Kiribati Adaptation Program'. In: *Environmental Change and the World's Futures: Ecologies, Ontologies, Mythologies*. Marshall, J. P. and Connor, L. H. (eds). London: Routledge.

Rayner, S. and Malone, E. L. 1998. *Human Choice and Climate Change*. Columbus, MO: Battelle.

Rosewarne, S., Goodman, J. and Pearse, R. 2014. *Climate Action Upsurge: The ethnography of climate movement politics*. London and New York: Routledge.

Rudiak-Gould, P. 2011. 'Climate Change and Anthropology: The importance of reception studies'. *Anthropology Today* 27 (2): 9–12.

Rudiak-Gould, P. 2012. 'Promiscuous Corroboration and Climate Change Translation: A case study from the Marshall Islands'. *Global Environmental Change* 22 (1): 46–54.

Rudiak-Gould, P. 2013. *Climate Change and Tradition in a Small Island State: The rising tide*. New York: Routledge.

Steward, J. 1973. *Theory of Culture Change: Methodology of Multilinear Evolution*. Urbana: University of Illinois Press.

Storey, D, and Hunter, S. 2010. 'Kiribati: An environmental "perfect storm".' *Australian Geographer* 41 (2): 167–181.

Terrace Standard 2014. 'Tahltan forbid mining company from entering their land without permission'. Available at www.terracestandard.com/news/253289581.html (accessed 8 August 2014).

Toussaint, S. 2008. 'Climate Change, Global Warming and Too Much Sorry Business'. *The Australian Journal of Anthropology* 19 (1): 84.

Wang, J., Brown, D. G. and Agrawal, A. 2013. 'Climate adaptation, local institutions, and rural livelihoods: A comparative study of herder communities in Mongolia and Inner Mongolia, China'. *Global Environmental Change* 23: 1673–1683.

Weber, E. U. 2010. 'What Shapes Perceptions of Climate Change?'. *Wiley Interdisciplinary Reviews: Climate Change* 1 (3): 332–342.

White, L. 1949. *The Science of Culture: A study of man and civilization*. New York: Farrar, Strauss.

Wilk, R. 2009. 'Consuming Ourselves to Death: The anthropology of consumer culture and climate change'. In: *Anthropology and Climate Change: From encounters to actions*. S. Crate and Nuttall, M. (eds). Walnut Cree, Ca.: Left Coast Press.

Wolf, J. and. Moser, S. C. 2011. 'Individual Understandings, Perceptions, and Engagement with Climate Change: Insights from in-depth studies across the world'. *Wiley Interdisciplinary Reviews: Climate Change* 2: 547–569.

World Bank 2013. 'Toward a sustainable energy future for all: directions for the World Bank Group's Energy Sector'. Available at www-wds.worldbank.org/external/ default/ WDSContentServer/WDSP/IB/2013/07/17/000456286_20130717103746/Rendered/ PDF/795970SST0SecM00box377380B00PUBLIC0.pdf (accessed 5 January 2014).

2 Life and time in a carboniferous zone

Ecocosmic realities connect geophysics, biosphere and anthropos in the planet's processes of deep time transformations. Circumpolar people surveyed in the previous chapter live in landscapes of ice and snow, formed over the successive glaciations of the Quaternary period. The tropical ambience of South Pacific islanders is dominated by the flow of oceanic currents and monsoon cycles around volcanic islands and atolls formed over hotspots in the ocean floor, originating from a breakup of the Panthalassic Ocean hundreds of millions of years ago. Vibrant mythopoetics constitute places of human dwelling. Ancestral humans lived in sentient terrains where living things and landscape features were active in human affairs, where glaciers, for example, could not only listen, but also 'take action and respond to their surroundings' (Cruikshank 2005: 3). Non-human personages included beings, labelled in the European naturalist tradition as 'spirits' and 'deities', which were contacted and influenced through purposeful human activity. Occult techniques could animate otherwise neutral substances through sorcery and witchcraft. While tempered by missionary monotheism and Western and scientific epistemologies in recent generations, these ontologies remain deeply embodied among people who still live in ancestral places. They are part of contemporary human experiences of significant environmental change in many parts of the world, as the examples in the preceding chapter illustrate.

How can we apprehend the ecocosmos of a different place, a type of location both more familiar to readers from the global North, and yet still strange as an object of anthropology? The Hunter Valley, a region situated on the populous eastern seaboard of Australia, presents a striking case for inquiry into forms of being, knowing and doing in relation to climatic changes, anthropos and the time flows of modernity. This chapter begins with a consideration of the deep time transformations, life forms and modes of being that distinguish the Hunter Valley. I draw on Aboriginal, settler, historians' and others' accounts to seek some insights about the worlds of first people here, including the rupture of ties with country, demographic collapse, shattered social organisation after 1788 and forms of adaptation in a settler state. The regional story of colonisation and agrarian settlement is briefly analysed through the lens of climate and coal: both elemental forces of ecocosmic transformation. The chapter concludes with an intimation of the Hunter Valley as a *topos* – a place that has been densely encountered, created, experienced and imagined – now firmly anchored in the epochal conjuncture of Holocene and Anthropocene, which is the time and circumstance for the book's ethnographic study.

Creation events: Gondwanaland to Coquun

The Hunter Valley presents a series of conjunctures that take us from continent creation to hunter-gatherer worlds and into the industrial era of fossil fuel dependence, corporate capitalism and global warming. In geological terms the Australian landmass has been part of all ancient supercontinents, emerging from the oceans several billion years ago. The origins of the Hunter Valley and the Sydney Basin of which it forms a part are found in the Devonian period (about 380 million years ago) when Australia still formed part of the supercontinent of Gondwanaland. In the Carboniferous period that followed, the abundant plant life in swamps and bogs created the conditions for rich coal deposits that formed during the Permian period. The plants grew, died and were preserved in the swampy anaerobic environment of a huge warming marine basin that was subjected to advancing and receding sea levels created by the heat and pressure of volcanic activity and tectonic plate movements. These preserved plants, repositories of millions of years of stored solar energy, became the coal measures that are contained as strata within the Permian period sedimentary rocks in the Sydney Basin, a vast depression stretching northwest to southeast from coast to inland mountains with the city of Sydney roughly at the centre (Drysdale *et al.* 2000: 18–24). Along the coast, coal seams are clearly visible in the southern headland cliff faces, on coastal rock platforms, and the peculiar island of volcanic tuff noted by Captain Cook, which is now Nobby's Head (see Figure 2.1).

In the late Jurassic period, the Australian continental landmass started to separate and move northwards. The landmass now known as Australia separated from the southern supercontinent of Gondwanaland over a hundred million years ago. By this time the rich Permian period coal measures of the Sydney Basin had formed, setting the scene for the very different types of landscape change by humans that eventuated millions of years later. The landmass separation caused new atmospheric and ocean patterns in the Cretaceous period, including warming temperatures and sea level rise (Fluteau *et al.* 2007). The Cretaceous is known as the time of flowering plants and also of early mammal evolution – abundant resources in a later period for the first people of the continent.

The ancient bedrock channel of the Hunter River goes back more than 65 million years to the beginning of the Tertiary (Paleogene) period. Surface flows and estuary area grew and receded in line with sea level fluctuations associated with the freezing and melting conditions of glacial and interglacial periods. Intensely fluctuating climate conditions and sea levels characterise the Quaternary period, the most recent 'ice age' covering the last 1.8 million years, when the river and its tributaries evolved into their current form (Drysdale *et al.* 2000: 31). As recently as 18,000 years ago, at the end of the Last Glacial

Figure 2.1 Coal seam at Glenrock lagoon, south of Newcastle
Source: Carrol Cummings, Cartoscope Pty Ltd

Maximum, the Hunter coastline extended 25 km into the sea from the current location, and the river incised its channel over steeper gradients. As the planet started warming in the later part of the Pleistocene epoch, melting ice sheets transferred millions of cubic metres of water into the oceans (Smith 2005). Approximately 6,000 years ago, the sea level stabilised and the extensive estuary was infilled with upstream sediment (Drysdale *et al.* 2000: 33–5). The inundation of seawater at this time decisively shaped the regional topography, creating the modern coastline and river estuary as well as the large lake that is now known as Lake Macquarie (Kidd and Timms 2000: 94).

The Aboriginal people of the Hunter Valley probably arrived during the latter Pleistocene epoch of the Quaternary period, when sea levels were lower and megafauna were abundant, as elsewhere in the world. Generations of Aboriginal people experienced the consequences of the greatest global climate change in the era of modern humans: post-glacial sea level rise. Approximately 3 million square km of coastal land between Tasmania and New Guinea was inundated, obliterating country on which Aboriginal people had been living for thousands of years, transforming ecosystems and weather patterns and necessitating major adaptations for survival (Smith 2005). Aboriginal groups also adapted to the most striking climatic condition that has affected the Australian continent for many millennia: the El Niño current and Southern Oscillation (ENSO). This is an atypically warm ocean current in the eastern equatorial Pacific Ocean, associated with a feedback loop between ocean and atmosphere that creates higher air temperatures, causing heavy rainfall and storms on the South America Pacific coast and parts of North America, and scarce rainfall, monsoon failure and droughts in the lands to the west of the Pacific Ocean: Australia, Indonesia, South Asia and parts of Africa. El Niños typically occur every four to seven years (Bureau of Meteorology 2015). The most severe can have global effects and last for several years (Grove 2005: 128). La Niña is the alternate phase: cooler equatorial currents bringing wetter conditions to the lands west of the Pacific.

Archaeological sites provide evidence of human habitation for the last 5,000 to 10,000 years in the Hunter region (Moore 1969). Earlier sites are hard to find in this long-settled, mining-disturbed and geomorphically unstable landscape, but in the Penrith area northwest of Sydney, evidence of humans goes back more than 40,000 years, and archaeologists presume that Aboriginal occupation was widespread in the favourable east coast environment, including the Hunter Valley (Hughes and Spooner 2010; Hiscock, pers. comm. June 2013).

The river system and estuary were sources of sustenance for the tribes living in the catchment. The large catchment of the Hunter River is the most prominent geographic feature of the Hunter region, extending over 300 km from the coastal estuary deep into the inland mountain range (see Figure 2.2), and with a drainage area of 22,000 square km. The river's headwaters rise high in the northwest of the range, from which it flows through hills and fertile floodplains of the broad middle valley, joined by many tributaries before fanning out to an estuary scattered with tidal islands, intertidal river flats and sandbars.

Aboriginal groups had various names for the main river, such as Coquun, Myan and Coonanbarra. It figured largely in the place Dreaming of the different groups, and provided a rich diet of seafood and game, with different names for many species of oysters, crustaceans and fish, birds, reptiles and mammals (Albrecht 2000). The Awabakal lived in the lower reaches of the Coquun/Hunter River, as well as the estuary (Mulunbinbah – 'place of edible ferns') and the saltwater lake (Awaba), now known as Lake Macquarie. The Wanaruah[1] lived in the northwest region, while the Geawagal lived along the northernmost tributaries. Other groups include the Worimi, around the Great Lakes and Port Stephens down to Stockton Bight, and the Darkinung, Kamilaroi and Birpai (see Figure 2.3). Although it is difficult to estimate pre-contact population size, each tribal group had distinct forms of social organisation, Dreaming stories and distinctive languages, with hundreds or even thousands of speakers each.

The first people of the region know it as an ancient land demarcated by tribal boundaries that are linked by the journeys of Dreaming ancestors who created the landscape and all the beings in it. Contemporary Hunter Aboriginal scholars have written about the Dreaming:

> Prior to the creation period the Hunter Valley like the continent at large was a vast empty flat plain devoid of any living thing. The creation ancestors rose up from their slumber beneath the plain to invoke the creation period.

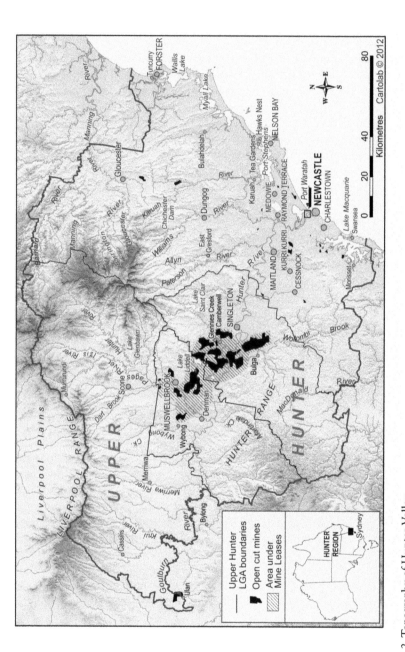

Figure 2.2 Topography of Hunter Valley

Source: O. H. Rey Lescure 2012

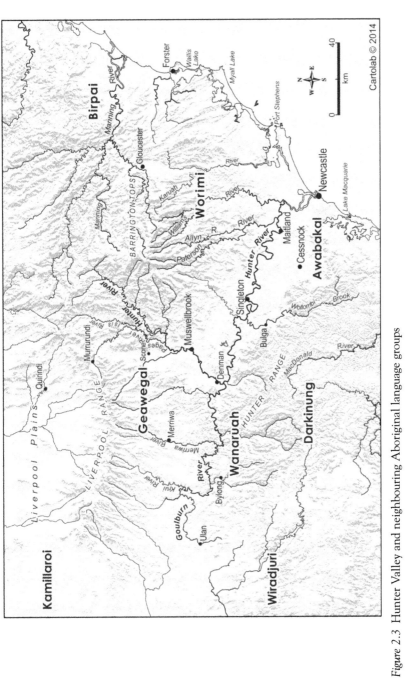

Figure 2.3 Hunter Valley and neighbouring Aboriginal language groups

Source: O. H. Rey Lescure 2014

In doing so they left their indelible imprint – mountains, rivers, lakes, rocks, flora, fauna and man/woman. Every geographical feature and living thing on the land bore the mark of the Creative Ancestors.

(Blyton *et al.* 2004: 13)

The early traveller John Dunmore Lang commented on this richly named land-scape: 'Indeed, every remarkable point of land, every hill and valley in the territory, has its native name, given, as far as can be ascertained from particular instances, from some remarkable feature of the particular locality' (Lang 1834: 87, cited in Albrecht 2000). Some names refer to places of water and food sources important to the survival of hunter-gatherer groups, while others encap-sulate the stories of Creative Ancestors who moved across the land. The Awabakal have a story of the creation of the Coquun when a greedy frog, Tittalik, drank all the ground water, depriving other creatures of this life-giving fluid. When provoked to laugh by the antics of a platypus, all the water came tumbling out in a huge torrent that gouged the river's course across the land (Maynard 2004: 51–2). In another place Dreaming, Whibay-Gamba (known to early Europeans as Nobby's Island), a striking landform off the southern entrance to the harbour, is associated with a story of a giant kangaroo who fled there to escape flocks of wallaby pursuers after sexually assaulting one of their number. His periodic movements make the land tremble. This story gained attention as a sort of environmental warning after the Newcastle earthquake of 1989 (Maynard 2004: 49).

For people living in a region so abundantly supplied with coal, creation stories about this dark matter are rare. Maynard (2004: 50) recounts an Awabakal Dreaming story about the origin of *nikkin* (coal), which may be centred on a prehistoric eruption that has left its traces in the plug (named Kintirabin by Awabakal) of a small volcano near the present-day coastal suburb of Redhead. The story recounts that a black hole suddenly formed in the mountain, blocking the light and bringing silence and fear to the living beings of the land:

Men, women and children dug up rocks and sand and broke down foliage from trees and bushes to cover up the thick darkness, which was breaking through the surface of the earth. The people feared that the ever-burning fires deep in the ground would release the darkness again. After the darkness was covered over, generations passed, in which the people walked on the ground pressing the darkness and flames together under the earth to become *nikkin*, or coal. Now, whenever coal is burned, the spirit of the ancient fire is again released.

(Maynard 2004: 50–1)

In Wanaruah country of the upper Hunter, there is an ancient seam of burning coal at a place still known as Wingen, from the Wanaruah word for 'fire'. In geological time, the fire from Permian coal deposits was formed 300 million years ago deep in the ground and may have been burning for as long as 15,000 years at the rate of 1–2 meters per year. Smoke filters up through numerous crevasses where the hot ground, sulphurous fumes and oxides kill all vegetation. Local people recount a Wanaruah Dreaming story about a group of neighbouring Kamilaroi men who planned to steal Wanaruah women. Their menfolk, on learning of this, set off to quell the attack, but one was mortally wounded and did not return. His grieving wife, waiting high on the mountaintop, asked Baiame, the powerful creation ancestor, to end her life of sorrow, but he turned her to stone instead. As she changed, her flow of tears turned to fire that created the burning seam all down the mountain. The profile of the mountain reveals her seated form today, known by locals as the Wingen Maid.

This fertile river catchment supported hunter-gatherer societies for many generations until the invasion of Europeans. The energy needs of the Aboriginal populations were low, and ultimately derived from renewable energy from the sun: human labour power fuelled by food, and wood for fires. They suffered the vicissitudes of climate extremes, especially the droughts of ENSO, but with low population density and high potential for mobility, small-scale social groups could survive.

Figure 2.4 'Natives fishing in a bark canoe'. Richard Browne, ca 1813–1819

Source: State Library of New South Wales – DGA 3/1

Coal irruption

From Dreaming stories still known today, it appears that Hunter-based Aboriginal groups viewed coal as a dangerous substance associated with an unstable, fiery and grieving landscape. The archaeological record provides no evidence that coal was ever used as a fuel by Aboriginal people anywhere in Australia (Philip Hughes, pers. comm. June 2013; Peter White, pers. comm. June 2013). Nor is there any evidence in colonial accounts for Aboriginal use of coal. From the scant evidence available, it seems that coal featured only minutely in the Dreaming of the Hunter tribes, dangerously flammable but lying dormant.

With the arrival of the colonists coal irrupted as a force in a new ecocosmos in which the black rock played a heroic role in the advance of Western civilisation. The settlers were early beneficiaries of the industrial age, and were among the first generations of humans to depend heavily on fossil fuels that generated steam power for the machinery used in transport and many forms of production. The move from one coal-rich land in the northern hemisphere to another in the Antipodes favoured the ready adoption of industrial innovations such as steam transport, industrial production and agriculture. This stimulated dynamic economic growth and by the mid-nineteenth century many in the Australian colonies had achieved standards of living that outstripped any other country (Macintyre 2004: 107).

Coal and colonialism went together in the eighteenth and nineteenth centuries. From its inception, the colony of New South Wales was locked into the industrial scale of energy consumption powered by coal. The settlers came from a small island country with a burgeoning population and depleted reserves of wood, which (apart from the sun) had been *homo sapiens'* main energy source since the discovery of fire in the Palaeolithic era by hominin ancestors. The deforestation of England, especially near the cities, was evident from the fourteenth century, and the island's abundant reserves of coal were the most expedient and cheapest fuel option, despite its acrid, toxic smoke and sooty fallout (Freese 2003: 26). The use of coal for energy freed up land for growing food for an expanding urban population, land that hitherto had been used to grow less efficient wood fuel. By the late eighteenth century, England's industrial economy, powered by coal, was well underway. James Watt's coal-fired steam engines were in operation by the mid-1770s, pumping water out of mines and blowing iron foundry bellows. Baked coal processed into coke made advances in iron production possible (Freese 2003: 63–6). Steam power from coal turned the machinery of British factories; there was a coal 'resource boom' with an exponential expansion of mines in the first half of the nineteenth century (Freese 2003: 67).

The availability of large quantities of high-grade black coal in Sydney's northern hinterland was probably more important than anything else in securing the success of the struggling colony in its early days. The first colonial official to set foot on Awabakal country was the English naval officer, Lieutenant John Shortland, who entered the estuary of the Coquun in 1797 on his way north to Port Stephens, pursuing runaway convicts who had seized a large boat.

Figure 2.5 Nobby's Island and Pier, '*Newcastle, 1820*' (watercolour by unknown artist)
Source: State Library of New South Wales – DG SV1B/10

Lieutenant Shortland's letter home to his father expressed no doubt about the benefits to the colony of the coal, the river and the harbour:

> My Dear Father,
> About a twelvemonth since I went on an expedition in the Governor's whaleboat as far as Port Stephens, which lies 100 miles to the northward of this place. In my passage down I discovered a very fine coal river, which I named after Governor Hunter. The enclosed I send you, being an eye-sketch which I took the little time I was there. Vessels from 60 to 250 tons may load there with great ease, and completely landlocked. I dare say, in a little time, this river will be a great acquisition to this settlement.
>
> (Shortland 1798)

The commodification of coal proceeded apace. After Shortland's reports to the governor, small traders began to take advantage of the fuel, sending parties to collect coal by hand in baskets to be shipped back for sale in Sydney (Johnson 2009: 54). Thirteenth-century Britons called these lumps of coal on the shore, fallen from the cliff or washed up from underwater seams, 'sea coal' (Cantril 1914). Sea coal is still common on Hunter beaches today (see Figure 2.6). In 1801 Governor King sent an exploratory party led by Lieutenant James Grant and Lieutenant-Colonel Paterson to survey the Hunter River and investigate 'where the most eligible place would be to form a settlement, both with respect to procuring coals and for agricultural purposes' (Bladen 1896: 391). The party returned to Sydney to report on the discovery of alluvial land that was excellent for forming an agricultural settlement (Bladen 1896: 414–16), as well as the strata of coal in Nobby's Island, 'running from side to side of the mountain of various qualities and degrees of thickness' (Grant cited in Johnson 2009: 54). Grant also wrote 'the Colony of New South Wales cannot fail of reaping great advantage from a mine of coals so near to it, and so easy to be worked' (cited in Johnson 2009: 54). When Governor King established the settlement of Newcastle (named after England's coal port) at the river mouth as a place of secondary punishment for Sydney's convicts, these 'desperate characters' and 'choice rogues' (Schaefer and Watt 2006: 132) laboured in a web of tunnels that underlay the city.[2]

It was not long before the resources of the Hunter region attracted entrepreneurs. The colonial government opened it up for free trade and settlement in the 1820s, while the penal settlement was moved further north. The first commercial coal operation was undertaken by the Australian Agricultural Company (AAC), formed by a stock issue in Britain in 1824.[3] AAC was granted a virtual coal monopoly for 31 years from 1828, triggered by the government's assessment that private enterprise could produce coal more efficiently than government mines worked by convict labour. A land grant of almost 2,000 acres of coal rich land in Newcastle was conditional on a guaranteed cost price supply to government, but conflict over prices and contract conditions ensued almost immediately (Turner 1972: 240–1). The Company's profits were substantial but within a decade challenges to the monopoly arose.[4] Under pressure from a spate of legal challenges, the company relinquished its monopoly in 1847.

Figure 2.6 Sea coal on Redhead Beach

Source: Linda H. Connor, 2015

The settlers were hungry for the black rock that allowed the colony to expand: for building construction, iron foundries, factories and transport. The first coal-powered steam railway from Sydney to Parramatta, a distance of 22 km, was opened by the New South Wales (NSW) government in 1855. A few years before that a coal-hauling railway traversed a tunnel from mines south of Newcastle to the port (Scanlon 2013). The Newcastle–Maitland passenger line opened in 1857. Coal gas lamps spread through the city of Sydney from 1841 and gasworks sprung up in the city to supply heat and light to a growing population (Pearse *et al.* 2013).

Freed from dependence on wood fuel, there was ample land to support a growing population and economy. The colony's settler population had increased from a few thousand to a recorded 187,000 by 1850. The flood of immigration associated with the NSW and Victoria gold rushes of the early 1850s swelled NSW settler population to 350,000 by 1860 (Marsden 1998: 178) and increased the demand for coal. By the mid-1850s, a few years after the AAC's monopoly officially ended, Hunter mines were producing almost 60,000 tonnes of saleable coal, including exports to the booming gold rush economies of Victoria and California (Martin *et al.* 1993: 8; Marsden 1998: 178–9).

Ecocosmos destruction

Awabakal people living in the river estuary were already experiencing the brunt of colonisation in the early decades of the nineteenth century as the Newcastle settlement expanded to meet Sydney's demand for coal, timber, salt and lime (Turner 1973: 27). In the upper reaches of the Hunter/Coquun, the hunter-gatherer livelihoods that Wanaruah and surrounding groups had established within their environment over many millennia were rapidly destroyed as government-claimed 'Crown land' was allocated for pastoral settlement in the 1820s. Connections to totemic sites and through them to creation heroes like Baiame and Koin were severed as people were dispossessed of their country (Blyton *et al.* 2004). Populations collapsed as disease, massacres, land appropriation and environmental destruction took their toll (Blyton *et al.* 2004: 15–17). In 1837, one missionary wrote of the situation in the southeast: 'the measles, the Hooping cough, and the Influenza, have stretched the Black victims in hundreds on the earth, until, in some places, scarcely a Tribe can be found' (Threlkeld in Gunson 1974a: 137). The cataclysm was indicative of conditions across the continent. Charles Rowley, one of the first scholars to write about the destruction wrought by white settlement throughout Australia, commented that the Aboriginal people's 'more subtle relationship with his country was either ignored or not understood' (1972: 14). Attempting to reconstruct an Aboriginal perspective, Tony Swain (1995: 59) writes: 'A new kind of human without land-spirit ties had arrived to conquer Aboriginal lands. They were an amoral people by Aboriginal standards, who, unlike Melanesians and Indonesians, were unreachable even by equitable trade exchanges'.

Compared to British dominion in other lands, where first peoples like Native

Americans or New Zealand Maoris could base negotiations on familiar forms of territorial social organisation like villages, hierarchy and organised warfare, in the Australian colonies 'no treaties concerning land were ever signed or rights recognised' (Rowley 1972: 12). Aboriginal societies did not engage in territorial wars, and as the historian Henry Reynolds has observed, 'If blacks often did not react to the initial invasion of their country it was because they were not aware that it had taken place' (2006: 71). In any event, the demographic collapse of Aboriginal populations made large-scale resistance impossible. A year after the Sydney colony was established, tens of thousands of Aboriginal people (of an estimated total of 250,000 in the southeast) had died from a smallpox epidemic, and by 1850 the majority was dead from disease and settler violence (Swain 1995: 57).

As in other colonised lands, Christian missionaries were early arrivals, bringing their doctrines of universal morality stemming from a single transcendent God who loves all people and all places equally. Such ideas stood in stark opposition to the Dreaming cosmology based on conditions of connection, identity and responsibility for particular sites and beings through kinship and totemic relationships. Missionaries focused on protecting Aboriginal people, but this was coupled with a conversion agenda that left no place for the Dreaming. Missionaries of all denominations 'peppered the continent' by 1850 (Swain 1995: 82). Their messages of Divine love, coupled with regimented mission station routines and welfare, engendered both resistance and accommodation, as ruptures to land, Dreaming and kin relationships proceeded apace (Swain 1995: 49–77). Conversions were rare, and in general Aboriginal people went to the missions because 'they wanted food, especially in times of drought; they wanted neither religious instruction nor work' (Rowley 1972: 246).

Foremost among the missionaries in the Hunter region was the Reverend Lancelot Threlkeld, a congregationalist minister who took up a post in 1824, creating a mission on the eastern side of Lake Macquarie, under the auspices of the London Missionary Society (LMS). Threlkeld's combative personality and financial woes often brought him into conflict with the LMS, but in contrast to the dominant European settlers' views about Aboriginal racial inferiority, depravity and inevitable extinction, he held progressive ideas for the day on the equal capacities of Aboriginal intellect (but not the worth of their religious practices), and was quick to deplore and challenge the many forms of cruelty by settlers that afflicted the lives of Hunter Valley tribes (Gunson 1974a). He gained the trust and friendship of the Awabakal leader Biraban/McGill, became a proficient speaker of the language and wrote extensively about aspects of the social life, material culture and language of the Awabakal. His reminiscences and letters provide raw accounts of the contact situation in Newcastle and Lake Macquarie from the 1820s to 1840s (see Gunson 1974a, 1974b).

Only two decades after the first settlement in Newcastle, Threlkeld's reports to the LMS were documenting the despair and degradation of the Awabakal people of Lake Macquarie. By this time there were more than 1,200 Europeans in Newcastle. In 1823, Port Macquarie – in Dhan-gadi, Birpai and Ngamba country – was decreed as the new penal colony, and the number of convicts in Newcastle started to decline (Heath 1998: 50). The 'official class' of the colony took a broadly humanitarian approach to the Aboriginal populations, fuelled no doubt by the conviction that they were doomed to extinction (Gunson 1974a: 9). But there were many reasons the Aboriginal people feared the Europeans: settlers engaged in violent reprisals against perceived transgression, convicts were notorious for kidnapping and raping women, and macabre entrepreneurs killed or disinterred bodies in order to obtain skulls that were in demand by phrenologists to prove their theories about racial degeneracy. In his 1825 report to the LMS, Threlkeld recounts that he was invited to the traditional burial ceremony of a young Awabakal woman. He writes:

> The interment being over, a female came to me, and in broken English begged that I would not tell any person where the body was laid. Enquiring the reasons of this injunction, they replied they were fearful that white fellow come and take away her head. The public exposure of New Zealanders' heads for sale is, no doubt, one of the causes of their fear.
> (Threlkeld in Gunson 1974b: 190)

People exposed to new diseases and deprived of traditional hunting and gathering grounds by colonial settlement were sick and hungry. Although some skills of Aboriginal people were recognised by the settlers – as guides and trackers, for instance – there was no substantial employment available in the Newcastle settlement in the early days, where the dirty, heavy labour was carried out by convicts. Nor was Threlkeld's small farming enterprise associated with the Ebenezer mission at Lake Macquarie able to provide regular wages or food to the Awabakal people he was charged to convert.

The process of dispossession on the coast was characterised less by bloodshed and violence and more by disease and depopulation, in contrast to the expanding pastoral frontier. Here, Aboriginal resistance to European encroachment in the early nineteenth century took the form of guerrilla actions like spearing individuals as well as stealing sheep, cattle and crops to fend off starvation (Reynolds 2006: 72). In 1824 martial law was declared in NSW because of threats to growing numbers of rural settlers including the 'wild blacks' of the upper river tribes (Gunson 1974a: 5). Threlkeld, who was frequently called in as interpreter and chronicled many instances of frontier violence, was a vocal critic of the manifold injustices they suffered at the hands of Europeans.

> Under present circumstances the guilty escape, and human justice can only announce the Law as it exists, which bars the door of Equity against the Blacks, and leaves them to public vengeance, or, to the private revenge of injured Europeans, which steady to its purpose, will surely, secretly, and speedily annihilate the Aborigines from the face of this land.
> (Threlkeld *et al.* 1837: 4)

European incursions into the upper river valley began a couple of decades later than at the coast. Between 1818 and 1821 exploration parties led by Benjamin Singleton and John Howe, under the aegis of the colonial government, took them into the grasslands and forests of Wanaruah country (Blyton *et al.* 2004: 15). A report from Benjamin Singleton evokes the colonists' fear of Aboriginal people at the time:

> Deep Gully's to the westward to get Water Halted the Night about 8 o'clock Disturbed by the Voice of Natives Cracking of Sticks an Rolling By the Stones Down towards us every man of us arose and fled from the fire secreting ourselves behind trees with our guns.
>
> (Cited in Blyton *et al.* 2004: 15)

In 1824, a survey party of five men was reportedly forced to withdraw after being attacked by approximately 150 Aboriginal men. As reported at the time by *The Australian*, 'they met with a large body of natives ... by whom they were attacked unawares: one of their party having been struck by a spear in the head' (Blyton *et al.* 2004: 16).

As settler numbers expanded and the expropriation of land for pastoralism increased, they responded with organised massacres of Aboriginal people (Heath 1998: 56–7). Reverend Threlkeld documented the 'up country' resistance to the settlers and the settlers' hostility to his Aboriginal mission, soon after his arrival in Newcastle:

> But Alas! the blood of the Blacks begin to flow, we are in state of warfare up the country here – two stockmen have been speared in retaliation for the 4 natives who were deliberately shot without any trial or form whatever. Martial Law is the cry of the Settlers and there be many who are grieved that a man is come to seek the welfare of the Aborigines.
>
> (Gunson 1974b: 213)

Despite fierce resistance, the Wanaruah and other Aboriginal tribes of the upper valley could not protect their way of life or country during their early encounters with Europeans. As Blyton *et al.* (2004) note, it was in the settlers' interests to play up Aboriginal barbarity as a means of sanctioning their own terror campaigns. A petition presented by upper Hunter River landholders to Governor Ralph Darling in 1826 included the following excerpts:

> We, the undersigned, Landholders at Hunter's River, beg leave most respectfully to represent to Your Excellency the present very disturbed state of the country by the incursions of the numerous Tribes of Black Natives, armed and threatening death to our Servants, and destruction to our property ... we most humbly trust Your Excellency will take this into Your consideration, either by ordering others to take their places, or by suspending the order to recall to Newcastle, until the threats and murderous designs of the Natives

shall have subsided; for, in the event of our losing the protection of the Troops, our property will be exposed to revenge and depredation of these infuriated and savage people.

(cited in Blyton *et al.* 2004: 20)

Conflict between settlers and Aboriginal people continued vigorously throughout the upper valley until the 1830s, when fighting eased as the colonists gained ascendency through force. Only in the uppermost reaches of the valley toward what is now the New England region does evidence suggest regular conflict continued past this time (Blyton *et al.* 2004: 23–4). In 1854 Edward Ogilvie returned to the upper Hunter to revisit his childhood home, where he met up with an old childhood friend, an Aboriginal man named Coolan, who told him of the demise of his people. Ogilvie writes of the conversation:

Not one of the tribes above enumerated [by Coolan] had ever come into hostile collision with the white intruders, but had from the first occupation of their country, remained on terms of the most perfect amity with the strangers. Yet all have been swept away, as though to destroy and exterminate had been the aim of the new comers, instead of the human desire to preserve and support their dark-skinned brethren ever evinced by the settlers in this locality.

(cited in Blyton *et al.* 2004: 30)

Many Wanaruah people survived, but the decline of their social organisation and hunter-gatherer life was severe for the Wanaruah and surrounding groups. In less than 20 years, they lost their hold on their country, and a regime of welfare and seasonal work was already in motion. Blyton *et al.* (2004: 26) write:

with their food supply diminished Aboriginal people turned to the sheep, cattle and crops of the colonists to survive, but … this brought retribution from the colonists who reacted with violent force to what they saw as 'incursions' of their property. Without food the health of Aboriginal people naturally deteriorated and a reliance on the handouts of the colonists was precarious … Aboriginal people did work of a seasonal nature by assisting in the harvest of crops in return for food … but too often the payments included addictive substances such as alcohol and tobacco.

New forms of communal life evolved in the face of these dire circumstances. As Morris remarked of the settlement some years later in the Macleay Valley further north, the Dhan-gadi people were not totally dispossessed and nor were they devoid of agency. Modes of autonomy and accommodation were expressed in different ways in the coastal settlement and the pastoral zones. They 'had their own expectations and priorities which determined their involvement' with the settlers (Morris 1989: 31). In Newcastle and Lake Macquarie, interactions with settlers were diverse in scope and purpose. For example, in 1823 we find an account of the Awabakal people staging a corroboree after a banquet for the visiting governor of the colony (Heath 1998: 50). Some ceremonial life was maintained for decades, and much of the information assembled by Threlkeld was focused on the ritual life and survival techniques of very mobile groups. He wrote that their 'rambling dispositions' meant that in order to learn the language he had to accompany them as they moved around their country seeking food and performing ceremonies. From the early days he found that the Aboriginal people would only come to the mission if food and the loan of fishing boats were offered; schooling or religious instruction were not sufficient incentives (Gunson 1974a: 118–19). By 1840, however, there were hardly any Awabakal people left on traditional lands near the Mission. The social life, employment opportunities and 'vices of the town' were a powerful attraction. Threlkeld's annual report records:

> The blacks have nearly forsaken this Lake, having found at Newcastle employment suitable to their habits; some being engaged in fishing, some as water carriers, messengers, servants, and some on board the numerous vessels, according as their services are required … they [find] their wants supplied at Newcastle, and loving society, they congregate there, and have done for some time past. But it is to be deplored, that whilst they are, in many instances, usefully employed, spirits too often are the wages for their services in that town, and consequently drunkenness is a daily occurrence.
>
> (Gunson, 1974a: 166–7)

Threlkeld observed that Aboriginal people disdained agricultural employments 'excepting such as are connected with stock requiring horsemanship' (Gunson 1974a: 166). In the hinterland, as their resistance to the graziers was quelled, Wanaruah and surrounding groups quickly developed the skills – horse mustering, breaking and riding, droving, shearing, fencing (in addition to the tracking and bush skills on which explorers depended) – that enabled them to occupy a place in the growing pastoral economy. Gaynor Macdonald has documented a similar process among the Wiradjuri people further to the northwest, writing that they 'became more engaged with the activities of pastoralism as their economic options closed off with more intense land use' (2010: 55). Aboriginal workers also found a valued place in the horse-breeding industry. The first horse studs were established in the 1820s, and racing became a vibrant part of settler life in the regional towns. The high-quality horses and the rugged, inaccessible stretches of high country also attracted bushrangers to the districts, and the exploits of characters like Captain Thunderbolt and his Wanaruah common-law wife Mary-Anne Bugg are still a mainstay of local history today (Blyton *et al.* 2004).

Rural production

In the early years of the colony, Aboriginal people living on country were effaced from explorers' descriptions of the verdant landscape in the hinterland of the Hunter. Ancestral country became settler land grants and the colonists waxed lyrical about fine grazing land. In 1819 the explorer John Howe wrote: 'It is the finest sheep land I have seen since I left England ... The grass on the low ground equals a meadow in England and will grow as good a swath and is like the native grass where old stockyards have been' (cited in Blyton *et al.* 2004: 16).

Early British visitors to the region also appreciated the wild beauty of the river and the abundance of animal and plant life that it supported, but not apparently the human inhabitants. The clergyman and historian John Dunmore Lang exhorted his reader to:

> figure to himself a noble river, as wide as the Thames in the lower part of its course, winding slowly towards the ocean, among forests that have never felt the stroke of an axe ... on either bank, the lofty gum tree or eucalyptus shoots up its white naked stem to a height of 150 feet from the rich alluvial soil, while underwood of most luxuriant growth completely covers the ground; and numerous wild vines, as the flowering shrubs and parasitical plants of the alluvial land are indiscriminately called by the settlers, dip their long branches covered with white flowers into the very water.
>
> (Lang 1834, cited in Albrecht 2000: 5)

Despite such favorable reports, the upper valley remained unexploited for more than a decade. In 1818, the commander of Newcastle, Captain James Wallis, placed 11 well-behaved prisoners on the alluvial flats between Wallis Creek and the Hunter River (now West Maitland), and a few others along the Paterson River. These convicts were to work as farmers, providing supplies to the settlement at Newcastle, and the fertile land meant they were able to successfully produce maize, butter, poultry and eggs for the military and civil officers stationed at Newcastle (Hartley 1995: 9). Wheat growing was another early success:

> As well as wheat, maize and tobacco were also grown along the Hunter ... Robert Dawson expressed the opinion that "The Hunter River is by far the richest and most important in the Colony: it may truly be said to be the garden as well as the grainary [sic] of New South Wales" [1831].
>
> (Hartley 1995: 15)

The colony's agricultural economy expanded in the 1820s, and the lush Hunter Valley landscape and fertile soil attracted settlers, who were readily able to establish successful farms in a European population explosion. Henry Dangar, a colonist ordered by Governor Brisbane to survey the lands along the Hunter River, recorded that in 1825 the rural Hunter River district had a population of 792 Europeans who had taken up land grants of 372,141 acres, with a further 232,164 acres reserved for church, school and Crown use (Goold 1981, cited in Heath 1998: 50).

The early settlers, like farmers today, were subject to the cycles of the El Niño-La Niña Southern Oscillation, whose extreme flood and drought conditions have been a dominant feature of climate in the Holocene epoch. Historical documents suggest some very severe El Niños occurred in past centuries, affecting food production and decimating populations in many places. Eastern Australia is particularly vulnerable to severe ENSO events (Grove 2005: 128). The worst El Niño on record appears to be the 'Great El Niño' of 1788–1795, with far reaching effects around the world, including famine and political unrest (Grove 2005). In NSW, this event had a devastating effect on the new colonial settlement under the governorship of Arthur Phillip, who recorded crop failures due to drought and the drying up of water supplies in Sydney. Phillip remarked in 1791, 'I do not think it probable that so dry a season often occurs' (cited in Grove 2005: 129). While Aboriginal people had adapted their gathering and hunting practices to the unpredictable conditions and hard dry conditions over countless seasons, the settlers accustomed to Great Britain's steadier seasons and different climate had no ancestral knowledge on which to draw.

In 1829 drought conditions were again harsh, and the Hunter Valley was described as 'a scene of wretchedness – the grass withered up to the root and the wheat and barley shrivelled up and the settlers were almost broken-hearted' (Hartley 1995: 25–6). Another drought from 1838–1839 caused dramatically falling prices for agricultural produce and farmers suffered, 'with sheep and cattle on inland properties reduced to eating loppings from trees, the herbage being completely destroyed' (Hartley 1995: 19). El Niño droughts continued to plague the Australian colonies throughout the nineteenth century, and the 'Federation drought' in the first years of the twentieth century is one of the worst on record.[5]

By 1840, coal-fired steam power was providing the means to get food to the growing city of Sydney, already with a population of almost 30,000 (Australian Data Archive 2012). The ships of the Hunter River Steam Navigation Company carried Hunter Valley stock, grain and other produce from the port of Morpeth near Maitland to Newcastle and down the coast to Sydney (Hartley 1995: 29). The steamers travelled almost the entire 56 km of navigable river, from the busy wharves, dockyards and factories of Newcastle harbour to the vegetable gardens, orchards and dairies situated among cleared forests along the lower river, and thence to the broadacre grain farms, vineyards, cattle and sheep ranges in higher reaches. An early traveller, John Askew, painted a vivid picture of the verdant settled landscape near the flourishing river town of Morpeth:

> In some places luxuriant crops of yellow grain were growing down to the water's edge. In others were rich orchards and vineyards, noble mansions and picturesque villas with broad walks leading to the river, and pleasure-boats painted in gay colours, resting near the water-gates, for the denizens of these delightful abodes to disport themselves upon their stream.
>
> (Askew 1857: 244–5)

Wine production and horse breeding were established early, with Dr Henry Lindeman, founder of the still renowned wine label Lindeman's, first planting vines on his land grant property on the Paterson river in 1843 (O'Neill 2000:

159). By the 1830s many settlers moved to the Hunter Valley to establish studs in country that was considered the best quality in NSW for this purpose, and the number of stallions in the Hunter tripled between 1830 and 1840 (McManus and Connor 2013: 99). One of the first and most influential horse studs was established in 1823 on a land grant to Robert and Helenus Scott. They developed a thoroughbred stud called Glendon on the banks of the Hunter River about 16 km from Singleton and their horses dominated the lively racing scene in both the Hunter and throughout the colony, setting the stage for future Upper Hunter dominance in Australian thoroughbred breeding (Guilford 1985: 67–8).

Into the Anthropocene

The European colonisation of the coastal and upper Hunter Valley had different trajectories in the first hundred years. In the hinterland, the rich alluvial soils of the river and its tributaries provided food, wool and other commodities. The town of Maitland and river port of Morpeth were the hub of the rural economy during the middle decades of the nineteenth century, eventually marginalised by the growth of rail transport and the maritime port at Newcastle (Marsden 1998: 179). The growing urban and industrial centre of Newcastle was dominated early on by coal mining, manufacturing and maritime activity (Marsden 1998: 178). Occupational groups formed close-knit communities, with strong traditions of mutual support forged in the harsh working conditions of nineteenth-century Britain. Survival depended on collective institutions like consumer cooperatives, mutual aid associations that sponsored hospitals, ambulance services and libraries, and eventually trade unions (Lucas 1998; Metcalfe 1988). Through the nineteenth century, the nucleated mining villages merged into suburban aggregations, and as coal resources dwindled, 'expanding rings' of coalmines moved westward and northward into newly discovered coal measures further inland. Old coal towns near the coast drew new economic sustenance from the port, urban administrative centre activities, railways and engineering industries (Hartig and Holmes 2000: 189).

The Aboriginal people of the Hunter Valley survived, dispossessed and depopulated. These dynamic and resilient societies had endured through the extremes of post-glacial inundation and harsh El Niño seasons in the many millennia prior to colonisation. Their worlds collided violently with settler society, constituting a state of warfare over several generations that has never been declared as such in Australian history. They were marginalised spatially, socially and economically, but maintained forms of autonomy through those connections – to country and kin – that could not be obliterated by settler society. Many found viable livelihoods as valued workers in the pastoral industry and rural homesteads. The conditions of life for Aboriginal people deteriorated in the late nineteenth century, with diminishing civil rights after Federation in 1901. In NSW, legally enforced subdivision of the large pastoral properties enabled denser white settlement of a growing population. Government increasingly intervened in the conditions of Aboriginal lives, with the establishment of statutory boards that regulated Aboriginal occupation of reserved lands (Macdonald 2010: 56–7).

The economic character of the region that would continue for the rest of the century was set by the mid-1800s. With the notable exception of the big NSW and Victorian gold rushes mid-century, the colonies hitched their fortunes to a single commodity, wool, and the vagaries of international markets. The Australian economy rode, sometimes precariously, on the sheep's back – there were 13 million sheep in NSW in 1850 and wool constituted 90 per cent of all exports from the Australian colonies to their main market of Britain (Macintyre 2004: 57). Colonial wealth was gained at great cost. Expropriation of Aboriginal land, never acknowledged as owned, proceeded apace, as did rampant environmental degradation as hard hooves compacted the earth, deep-rooted native grasses were eaten out, trees were felled, fragile soils cracked and dust clouds rolled across the land in the El Niño droughts that recurred every few years.

The long-term and as yet invisible cost of this wealth was the dependence on coal to drive the processes of appropriation – of labour, land and potentially all living things – as well as production and its supporting infrastructure – roads, rail, shipping, mechanical equipment, manufacturing, electricity, gas. Some energy was replaced by another lighter, more portable fossil fuel, oil, in the early decades of the twentieth century, but the abundant coal seams of the Hunter Valley remained an indispensable foundation of wealth production as the towns and farms prospered and grew. Coal provided the basis for locating an important new industry in Newcastle in the early twentieth century – the Broken Hill Proprietary Company (BHP) steelworks opened its first blast furnace in 1915. Over the next 80 years, BHP was a major employer in the region and the steel-making industry defined the identity of Newcastle and several generations of workers. This was a society that was propelling itself into the Anthropocene.

Notes

1   There are variant spellings of Wanaruah. I use 'Wanaruah', which is the NSW Aboriginal Land Council spelling, except where other spellings are used in quoted or cited material.

2   Another job, the burning of oyster shells for lime was saved for the worst reoffenders, who suffered burns to eyes and hands from the strongly alkaline quicklime. Work logging the cedar stands was also exceptionally hard and miserable toil (Johnson 2009: 55).

3   The company rose to prominence on profits from wool exports, benefiting from a 1 million acre NSW government land grant and a growing colonial labour force, which included Aboriginal people who 'worked as shepherds (sheep), stockkeepers (cattle), surveyors, hutkeepers, messengers, envoys, constables, boat rowers and builders' (Hannah 2002: 17).

4   These included Reverend Threlkeld's Ebenezer mine on the shores of Lake Macquarie, opened in 1839, and James Brown's mine at East Maitland, opened in 1843 (Turner 1972).

5   Severe El Niño droughts occurred periodically through the twentieth century, in the 1910s, 1940s, 1960s, 1980s and late 1990s. The 2015 El Niño season is forecast to be the worst on record (Hannam 2015).

References

Albrecht, G. 2000. 'Rediscovering the Coquun: Towards an Environmental History of the Hunter River'. *River Forum 2000*.

Askew, J. 1857. *A voyage to Australia and New Zealand including a visit to Adelaide, Melbourne, Sydney, Hunter's River, Newcastle, Maitland, and Auckland; with a summary of the progress and discoveries made in each colony from its founding to the present time*. London: Simpkin, Marshall, & Co.

Australian Data Archive. 2012. *NSW 1841 Census*. Available at http://hccda.ada.edu.au/pages/NSW-1841-census-01_1 (accessed 2 September 2013).

Bladen, F. M. 1896. *Historical records of NSW*. Volume 4. Sydney: Government Printer.

Blyton, G., Heitmeyer, D. and Maynard, J. 2004. *Wannin Thanbarran: A history of Aboriginal and European contact in Muswellbrook and the Upper Hunter Valley*. Muswellbrook: Muswellbrook Shire Aboriginal Reconciliation Committee.

Bureau of Meteorology. 2015. 'Risk management and El Niño and La Niña'. Available at www.bom.gov.au/watl/about-weather-and-climate/risk/risk-enso.shtml archived by WebCite at <www.webcitation.org/6WXm0BnSz (accessed 16 February 2015).

Cantril, T. C. 1914. *Coal Mining*. Cambridge: Cambridge University Press.

Cruikshank, J. 2005. *Do Glaciers Listen? Local Knowledge, Colonial Encounters and Social Imagination*. Vancouver and Seattle: UBC Press and University of Washington Press.

Drysdale, R., Shimeld, P. and Loughran, R. 2000. 'The physical landscape of the Hunter Valley'. In: *Journeys: The Making of the Hunter Valley*. McManus, P., O'Neill, P. and Loughran, R. (eds). Sydney: Allen & Unwin.

Fluteau, F., Ramstein, G., Besse J., Guiraud, R. and Masse, J. P. 2007. 'Impacts of palaeo-geography and sea level changes on Mid-Cretaceous climate'. *Palaeogeography, Palaeoclimatology, Palaeoecology* 247: 357–381.

Freese, B. 2003. *Coal: A human history*. New York: Penguin Books.

Grove, R. 2005. 'Revolutionary weather: The climatic and economic crisis of 1788–1795 and the discovery of El Niño'. In: *A Change in the Weather: Climate and culture in Australia*. Sherratt, T., Griffiths, T. and Robin, L. A. (eds). Canberra: National Museum of Australia.

Guilford, E. 1985. 'The Glendon Stud of Robert and Helenus Scott, and the beginning of the thoroughbred breeding industry in the Hunter Valley'. *Journal of Hunter Valley History* 1 (1): 63–106.

Gunson, N. 1974a. *Australian Reminiscences & Papers of L. E. Threlkeld, Missionary to the Aborigines, 1824–1859*. Vol I. Canberra: Australian Institute of Aboriginal Studies.

Gunson, N. 1974b. *Australian Reminiscences & Papers of L. E. Threlkeld, Missionary to the Aborigines, 1824–1859*. Vol II. Canberra: Australian Institute of Aboriginal Studies.

Hannah, M. 2002. 'Aboriginal workers in the Australian Agricultural Company, 1824–1857'. *Labour History* 82 (May 2002): 17–33.

Hannam, P. 2015. 'El Nino strongest since super event of 1997-98 and intensifying, BoM says'. *The Sydney Morning Herald*. September 2. Available at www.smh.com.au/nsw/el-nino-strongest-since-super-event-of-199798-and-intensifying-bom-says-20150901-gjcmdi.html archived by WebCite at www.webcitation.org/6bHLEWm4h (accessed 3 September 2015).

Hartig, K. and Holmes, J. 2000. 'Whatever happened to Coaltown?'. In: *Journeys: The making of the Hunter region*. McManus, P., O'Neill, P. and Loughran, R. (eds). St Leonards: Allen & Unwin.

Hartley, D. 1995. *Men of Their Time: Pioneers of the Hunter River*. North Arm Cove: Aquila Agribusiness Pty Limited.

Heath, J. 1998. 'Muloobinbah'. In: *Riverchange: Six new histories of the Hunter (Celebrating the 1997 Bicentenary)*. Hunter, C. (ed.). Newcastle: Newcastle Region Public Library.

Hughes, P. and Spooner, N. 2010. *Landscape History in the Hunter Valley, NSW: Why there is a multitude of Holocene archaeological sites but so few Pleistocene sites*. Prepared for the Australian Archaeological Association Annual Conference, Batemans Bay, 9–13 December 2010.

Johnson, R. 2009. *Newcastle on the Hunter*. Available at www.heritageaustralia.com.au/ titles.php:www.heritageaustralia.com.au/pdfs/Heritage%200309_Newcastle.pdf (accessed 30 June 2014).

Kidd, R. and Timms, B. 2000. 'Of waves and tide'. In: *Journeys: The making of the Hunter region*. McManus, P., O'Neill, P. and Loughran, R. (eds). St Leonards: Allen & Unwin.

Lucas, E. 1998. 'Hear my song'. In: *Riverchange: Six new histories of the Hunter (Celebrating the 1997 Bicentenary)*. Hunter, C (ed.). Newcastle: Newcastle Region Public Library.

Macdonald, G. 2010. 'Colonizing Processes, the Reach of the State and Ontological Violence: Historicizing Aboriginal Australian experience'. *Anthropologica* 52 (1): 49–66.

Macintyre, S. 2004. *A Concise History of Australia*, 2nd ed. Cambridge: Cambridge University Press.

Marsden, S. 1998. 'Waterfront alive'. In: *Riverchange: Six new histories of the Hunter (Celebrating the 1997 Bicentenary)*. Hunter, C (ed.). Newcastle: Newcastle Region Public Library.

Martin, C. H., Hargraves, A. J., Kininmonth, R. J. and Saywell, S. M. C. 1993. *History of Coal Mining in Australia*. Monograph 21, Parkville Victoria: The Australasian institute of mining and metallurgy.

Maynard, J. 2004. *Awabakal Word Finder: An Aboriginal dictionary and dreaming stories companion*. Southport, QLD: Keeaira Press.

McManus, P. and Connor, L. 2013. 'What's Mine is Mine(d): Contests over marginalisation of rural life in the Upper Hunter, NSW'. *Rural Society* 22 (2): 166–183.

Metcalfe, A. 1988. *For Freedom and Dignity: Historical agency and class structures in the coalfields of NSW*. North Sydney: Allen & Unwin.

Moore, D. R. 1969. 'The prehistory of the Hunter River Valley'. *Australian Natural History* March: 166–171.

Morris, B. 1989. *Domesticating Resistance: The Dhan-gadi Aborigines and the Australian state*. Oxford, New York: St. Martin's Press.

O'Neill, P. 2000. 'The gastronomic landscape'. In: *Journeys: The making of the Hunter region*. McManus, P., O'Neill, P. and Loughran, R. (eds). St Leonards: Allen & Unwin.

Pearse, G., McKnight, D. and Burton, B. 2013. *Big Coal: Australia's dirtiest habit*. Sydney: New South Publishing.

Reynolds, H. 2006. *The Other Side of the Frontier: Aboriginal resistance to the European invasion of Australia*. Sydney: University of New South Wales Press.

Rowley, C. 1972. *The Destruction of Aboriginal Society*. Harmondsworth: Penguin Books Ltd.

Scanlon, M. 2013. 'History beneath the hill'. *Newcastle Herald*, 22 March. Available at www.theherald.com.au/story/1380986/history-beneath-the-hill/ (accessed 12 June 2013).

Schaefer, K. and Watt, D. 2006. 'Nobby's Newcastle: Place, history, heritage, identity and performance'. In: *Unstable Ground: Performance and the Politics of Place*. McAuley, G (ed.). Brussels: P. I. E. Peter Lang.

Shortland, J. 1798. *Geological History of Hunter Region*. Available at http://coalriver.word-press.com/history/ (accessed 2 June 2013).

Smith, M. A. 2005. 'Paleoclimates: An archaeology of climate change;. In: *A Change in the Weather: Climate and culture in Australia*. Sherratt, T., Griffiths T. and Robin, L. A. (eds). Canberra: National Museum of Australia.

Swain, T. 1995. 'Australia'. In: *The Religions of Oceania*. Swain, T. and Trompf, G (eds). London & New York: Routledge.

Threlkeld, L. E., Wason, W. and Gunther, J. 1837. *New South Wales Aborigines. Reports of the Mission to the Aborigines at Lake Macquarie and at Wellington Valley*. Digitized and transcribed by Gionni Di Gravio, Archives Rare Books and Special Collections, Auchmuty Library, University of Newcastle, March 2005.

Turner, J. W. 1972. 'The Entry of the Australian Agricultural Company in the New South Wales Coal Industry'. *Journal of the Royal Australian Historical Society* 58 (4): 233–246.

Turner, J. W. 1973. *Newcastle as a Convict Settlement: The evidence before J. T Bigge in 1819–1821*. Newcastle: Newcastle Public Library in association with the Newcastle and Hunter District Historical Society.

Part II
Quotidian worlds

3 Being in the weather

Anthropological research retains much of its distinctiveness and value through its core activity of participant observation, which opens up the complexity of people's lived experience in whatever 'sites' or situations are selected for study. The challenge for a multi-sited or regional study is to find ways of understanding quotidian worlds – the worlds of practices that are common, routine and habitual, or what Bronislaw Malinowski famously called 'the imponderabilia of actual life' (1922: 18) – so that these worlds do not recede from view in the larger scale purview of multiplicity. Part II of this book sets out to elucidate some aspects of Hunter Valley residents' quotidian worlds that are relevant to the sorts of environmental changes they are experiencing and their understandings of climate change, and to consider these in relation to evidence from other studies. This chapter focuses on weather and climate as a crucial part of social being and environmental understanding. Peterson and Broad observe, 'Climate or weather – to varying degrees – link all scales of human activity, objects, and ideas' (2009: 80).

The chapter begins with a broad-brush account of contemporary Hunter Valley economy and demographic indicators, following on from the social historical narrative in Chapter 2. The extractive economy of coal, while not the most prominent contributor to the regional economy, is a critical context for public discourse on climate change and environmental degradation, and an agent of structural violence in the lives of many residents. I then consider the by now well-aired topic of 'climate change concern', drawing on survey data from the region and beyond. Vicissitudes of concern are explored in the Australian context through residents' struggles with coal industry expansion, in media coverage and in party politics. This brings the Hunter Valley ethnography into focus, engaging with residents' dynamic understandings of the phenomena of climate change, environment, nature and weather, including their mythical and ontological significance as expressed in casual 'weather talk' and in reflective commentaries. An important part of this discussion is consideration of the psychological and cultural dimensions of climate change risk, worry and scepticism that residents sustain in daily routines and ways of talking and that are articulated in civil society discourse. The discussion draws on materials from a range of research methods used during the course of the Hunter research project, including participant observation, analysis of mass media and social media, and interviews. Especially valuable were the results of a population-based survey that sampled the views of a large number of residents that would not be encountered in more localised field research, and that provide a basis for generalisations across subregions. The chapter concludes with a discussion of the 'touchiness' of climate change in conversation. It is a topic about which people often feel diffident and which they may suppress or ignore unless it is summoned by researchers' enquiries.

Regional transitions

In the early decades of the twenty-first century, the human residents of the Hunter Valley live in a flourishing region where land and life is still nourished by the Hunter River and its tributaries, now a dammed, regulated and depleted system of water supply to agriculture, mines, households, industry and environmental flows. Visitors, who typically enter from the south, are beguiled by the natural beauty of what they see. Commuter planes fly low and close to the coast along wide sandy beaches, or over Lake Macquarie's myriad bays and inlets, while road and rail travellers are afforded vistas of ocean and lake through bushland on either side of the southern approaches. Leisure travellers head inland to 'Hunter wine country', a major weekend hospitality destination for Sydneysiders, where open cut coal mines stop short of the vineyards, hobby farms, holiday accommodation, restaurants and gourmet food outlets that dot the countryside.

Figure 3.1 Lake Macquarie
Source: Lake Aerial Photo, 2015

The region that residents usually identify as 'The Hunter' roughly corresponds to the catchment of the Hunter River, and is commonly divided into two broad subregions, 'Upper' and 'Lower'.[1] The Lower/Upper division embraces demographic and socio-economic differences as well as geographic. About 50,000 people reside in the Upper Hunter, where coal mining and agriculture predominate (Australian Bureau of Statistics 2012), and where mine workers commute each day to work. The bulk of the population (about 275,000 people) lives in the Lower Hunter, in town centres like Newcastle, Maitland and Charlestown, and the comfortable suburban clusters that surround them. The first and oldest settlement, Newcastle (or 'Newie' in the vernacular) in particular attracts loyal support from its 'Novocastrian' residents (and newspaper editors) as a 'truly great world city', as well as discontent that 'On a per capita or economic basis, we simply haven't received our "fair share"' for urban renewal and other civic projects (Crawford 2014). Such complaints persist despite the fact that Newcastle enjoyed its heyday during the twentieth century. With the global shift of heavy manufacturing to East Asia and the closure of the BHP steelworks in 1999, population growth in the expanding suburbs of Maitland and Charlestown local government areas (LGAs) has outpaced the city (Deeming 2014; NSW Department of Planning 2012: 30).

The subregional division also corresponds to voting patterns and political party affiliation. Upper Hunter voters generally favour the rural-focused National Party at both state and federal government levels, while Lower Hunter voters, with their historical working-class base in underground coal mining, steel-making and other manufacturing industries, have traditionally favoured the Labor Party. In recent decades, more volatile voting patterns have upset these established loyalties to some degree. Voter discontent with the favour enjoyed by Sydney electorates is reflected in frequent public commentary about politicians' disregard for the economic contributions made by the Hunter coal industry. In an opinion piece in the *Newcastle Herald*, Wayne McAndrew aired the common sentiment that 'the mining communities who pour their sweat and blood into the industry rarely see that wealth flowing back to them' (McAndrew 2014). An editorial complained, 'This city deserves better. We might be the second biggest and the second oldest in the state, but we don't have to settle for second rate' (*Newcastle Herald* 2014a).

As in most of Australia, the majority of the region's working population is now employed in services, retail and manufacturing, especially in the more urbanised Lower Hunter. Coal mining has never been a large source of employment, providing jobs for about 7.7 per cent of the Hunter workforce in 2011 (Australian Bureau of Statistics 2012). More than 2,000 jobs have been lost since 2012, as a result of the economic decline of the industry (Lannin 2014). Lower Hunter employment suffered with the closure of the huge BHP steelworks in 1999, but the company developed a successful transition plan, promoting retraining and alternative employment to ameliorate the impacts, with unions and state government. One economic analysis characterised the Hunter Valley as 'Australia's most diverse, skilled, well-endowed and socially cohesive region' (O'Neill and Green 2000: 109), which was able to weather Australia's recessionary economy of the 1990s including a major downturn in export demand for coal and 30 per cent job losses in the industry. The Lower Hunter diversified dramatically after the closure of the steelworks, with job growth focused in the labour-intensive retail and services sectors. In the Upper Hunter in 2011,[2] 12.7 per cent of people were employed in 'agriculture, forestry and fishing'. The coal industry in the Upper Hunter employed 16.5 per cent of the workforce at the height of 'boom' conditions in 2011 (Australian Bureau of Statistics 2012) but these figures have declined markedly since then, with many mines going into care and maintenance or scaling back operations. The Upper Hunter is diversified across the rural sector. There are about 70 thoroughbred horse studs, with 'the most expensive stallions and broodmares in Australia ... located in the region' (McManus and Connor 2013: 168). Viticulture is a significant employer, with many wineries linked to tourism and hospitality businesses (Hunter Valley Wine Industry Association and the Hunter Valley Protection Alliance 2012: 9). Dairying, once a dominant feature of the regional economy, has been in decline since the New South Wales (NSW) government deregulated the industry in the 1990s. Gone are the days when 'if you had a family dairy, you could raise four children comfortably', as one dairy farmer remarked to the researchers. More recently, factors such as the growth of 'factory farm' dairies further south and supermarket wars have forced down farm gate prices for Hunter producers although there is optimism about growth of export demand from affluent consumers in Asia (NSW Department of Primary Industries 2013). Wool, lamb and beef production are significant sources of employment in the Upper Hunter, and in the past two decades there has been a diversification of rural enterprises, including poultry, olive groves and horticulture (McManus and Connor 2013: 169).

The economic and demographic divisions of earlier centuries between the Upper Hunter districts characterised by rural production and the more densely populated towns and suburbs near the coast still prevail, but an important change has occurred that has affected the lives of all residents, directly or indirectly. The abundant quantities of high-quality black coal have fulfilled the potent imaginings of the eighteenth-century colonists who literally stumbled upon it, providing a profligate supply of energy from the converted and stored sunlight of the Carboniferous and Permian periods hundreds of millions of years ago. The small underground mines of earlier years are now dwarfed by huge open cut cavities in the landscape. Multinational corporations have ownership of the vast majority of the mines, and account for 90 per cent of saleable production by volume (Campbell 2014: 13). They export most of the coal to industrialised East Asian nations. The infrastructure of the Hunter Valley coal chain reaches from bulk container ships queuing offshore in the Pacific Ocean to the stackers, reclaimers and loaders of the Port of Newcastle (celebrated by industry as 'the world's largest coal-exporting port') to the ever-expanding rail lines. Diesel engines pull long wagon trains day and night through the villages and towns from the coast to the Upper Hunter, extending to the slopes and fertile farmland on the western side of the Great Dividing Range where the Gunnedah Coalfield also contains rich coal seams and greenfield mine projects.

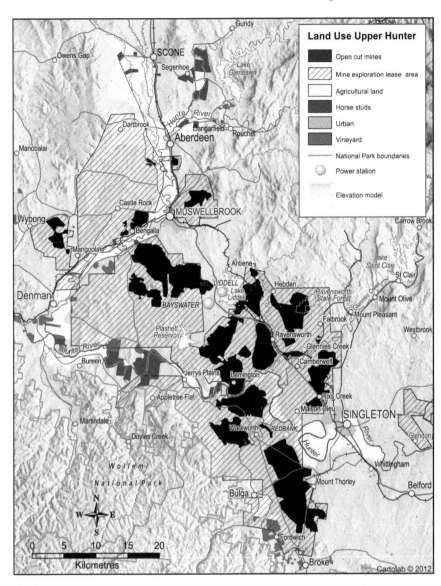

Figure 3.2 Upper Hunter land use
Source: O. H. Rey Lescure, 2012

Open cut coal mine excavation occupies more than 16 per cent of the Upper Hunter Valley floor, with another 64 per cent of land under exploration leases (McManus and Connor 2013). In 2014 there were approximately 40 open cut pits and 15 underground works operating in the Hunter, which together with 7

Gunnedah Coalfield mines have an approved annual maximum production capacity of more than 200 million tonnes per annum (Mtpa) of saleable coal.[3] About 75 per cent of the coal produced in the Hunter Valley coal chain is exported, amounting to 159 million tonnes (Mt) in 2014 (NSW Department of Industry 2014). Emissions from burning exported coal are not counted in the National Greenhouse Accounts, a source of continued criticism from opponents of government climate policies. The Australia Institute reported in 2014, 'Burning a tonne of Hunter Valley coal generates around 2.4 tonnes of carbon dioxide equivalent, meaning that the coal exported through Newcastle generates around 334 million tonnes of emissions' (Campbell 2014). By comparison, Australia's greenhouse gas (GHG) emissions in 2012–2013 from all domestic sources were recorded as 557 million tonnes (Campbell 2014). The escalating damage from coal mining, burning and export (and more recently, coal seam gas drilling) is a tangible reality for many residents and a known future risk for others.

Trajectories of climate change concern

The Hunter is a region where residents value and often sing the praises of the 'environmental amenity' of their region – the proximity of beautiful coast, lake and riverine landscapes and the abundant native flora and fauna that all can enjoy. All sorts of groups exist to protect loved places and outdoor activities in natural settings: Hunter Bird Observers, Hunter Koala Preservation Society, Hunter Cycling Network, Hunter Region Landcare, Citizens against Kooragang Abuses, Newcastle Orienteering Club, North East Forest Alliance, Parks and Playground Movement, Surfrider Foundation Hunter, Sugarloaf and Districts Action Group and dozens more. By contrast, the process of anthropogenic global warming has not inspired broad-based citizen organisations.

While attitudes of scepticism and denial are not uncommon among Hunter residents, in survey responses between 60 and 80 per cent of people express 'concern' about climate change, comparable to attitudes recorded in Australia-wide surveys (Leviston and Walker 2010; Lowy Institute 2012; Reser et al. 2012; The Climate Institute 2010). In survey research, the rather unspecific term 'concern' (sometimes replaced by 'worry') is used to enquire in general terms about respondents' psychological responses and feeling states with regard to climate change, in contrast to questions about particular risk perceptions or appraisals. Reser et al. argue that 'environmental concern is a sensitive and mean-ingful psychological indicator in the context of psychosocial impact assessment and reflects an important dimension of broader public issue perceptions and understandings' (2012: 43).

In Australia and other Western countries, surveyed public concern about global warming peaked in 2006–2008. Climate change first surfaced as a signifi-cant policy issue in Australia in the 1990s, when United Nations Framework Convention on Climate Change (UNFCCC)-sponsored discussions to achieve an international agreement to reduce human-induced GHG emissions culminated in the establishment of the Kyoto Protocol at the third 'Conference of Parties' in Kyoto. The conservative (Liberal National coalition) government in Australia signed the Protocol in 1998, but it was not ratified until the Labor government came to power in 2007. Much policy debate and media coverage in the preceding years was driven by the conservative government's stand on minimising Australia's commitments, and its position that Australia could not sign until all countries made a 'fair' contribution, making climate change a divisive political issue although hardly a 'crisis' from the general public's point of view (Rosewarne *et al.* 2014: 10–11). In 2006, a constellation of events occurred to bring this specialised body of knowledge to wider public attention, especially in Australia. These included: the draft of the much heralded fourth Intergovernmental Panel on Climate Change (IPCC) report (2007); the well-publicised Al Gore film *An Inconvenient Truth*; and the UK government-sponsored Stern report on the economic effects of climate change (Stern 2006). In Australia there was an enduring and serious drought for more than a decade, termed the Millennium Drought, associated with severe El Niño conditions. For some people, the widespread *experience* of drought, always a politically salient event in Australia, became part of a *phenomenology* of climate change.

By 2006, scientific research had accumulated a diverse and compelling evidence base for assertions of human caused global warming, and there was increasing government funding support, as well as stronger moves towards international cooperation and policy initiatives. A broad array of non-government organisations, multilateral bodies and political affiliations coalesced around this vital challenge of the twenty-first century. Between 2005 and 2007 mass public demonstrations occurred around the world. The Global Day of Action on Climate Change launched in 2005 with 30 countries hosting demonstrations coinciding with climate talks in Montreal. In 2007 marches were held in 50 countries to coincide with United Nations climate talks in Bali (BBC News 2007). In Australia, an estimated 100,000 people in 60 cities took part in Walk Against Warming marches in November 2007 (ABC News 2007).

For those concerned to combat anthropogenic climate change, the conjunction of scientific evidence, environmentalist concern, broad public support and apparently proactive government and multilateral stances offered optimism for the future. These circumstances explain why attitudinal surveys of 2006–2007 show a peak of climate change concern amongst broadly based Australian population samples (see Department of Climate Change 2009; Hunter Valley Research Foundation 2009; Lowy Institute 2009). Climate change was a new phenomenon: it dominated the news cycle, and it met the criteria for a crisis. This energised policy responses, in Australia and internationally, with various renewable energy projects and carbon pricing schemes developed or strengthened. The international culmination that became a 'reality-check' was the UN-sponsored Copenhagen Climate Summit in 2009, now recorded in the annals of history as a spectacular failure in multilateral cooperation on an issue of global urgency.

The Hunter Valley Research Foundation annual Environmental Attitudes Survey of the Hunter region for 2006 found 80 per cent of respondents agreed with the statement 'Climate change will have a direct impact on your life in the next 20 years' and 76 per cent agreed they would be prepared to pay more for electricity generated from renewable sources (Hunter Valley Research Foundation 2006). Similarly, the 2006 Lowy Institute Annual Poll on Australian Attitudes toward Global Warming reported 68 per cent of respondents agreed that 'Global warming is a serious and pressing problem' (see Tables 3.1 and 3.2).

By the end of 2008, concerned attitudes receded, possibly because climate change no longer met public and news cycle expectations of a crisis – it had been going on too long, had few visible catastrophes clearly associated with it, and an 'easy' solution was not in sight. The new global crisis became the global financial crisis – the GFC as it was called in Australia.

Table 3.1 Hunter Valley Research Foundation Environmental Attitudes Survey Data, 2006–2012: percentage agreement with statement

	HVRF findings 2006[a]	HVRF findings 2008–2009[b]	HVRF findings 2009–2010[c]	HVRF findings 2012[d]
Climate change will have a direct impact on your life in the next 20 years	80% [UH] 80% [H]	61% [UH] 64% [H]	61%	61%

Notes: [a] The HVRF 2006 and 2008–2009 surveys divided the Hunter into Upper Hunter (the LGAs of Singleton, Muswellbrook and Upper Hunter Shire [UH]) and Hunter regions (Hunter Region Statistical Division NSW [H]). [b] Survey sample was 323 randomly selected people (UH) and 300 people (H) over the age of 18 throughout the survey areas from households with landline telephone connections. [c] 300 randomly selected Hunter residents with landlines. [d] Budgetary restraints meant the Foundation could not complete the survey with a full report. They surveyed 300 residents and give basic results in a small summary report.

Table 3.2 Lowy Institute Environmental Attitudes Surveys, Australia, 2006–2015: percentage agreement with statement

	Lowy Institute 2006	Lowy Institute 2009	Lowy Institute 2012[a]	Lowy Institute 2014[b]	Lowy Institute 2015
Global warming is a serious and pressing problem	68%	48%	36%	45%	50%

Notes: [a] 1,005 Australian adults using mobile and landline telephones. [b] 1,150 Australian adults using mobile and landline telephones. Answer options are: 'Global warming is a serious and pressing problem. We should begin taking steps now even if this involves significant costs' (45%). 'The problem of global warming should be addressed, but its effects will be gradual, so we can deal with the problem gradually by taking steps that are low in cost' (38% agree). 'Until we are sure that global warming is really a problem, we should not take any steps that would have economic costs' (15%). Answer options are the same in each Lowy Poll.

The more recent results for these two surveys are telling: the 2008–2009 Hunter Valley survey declined from 80 per cent to 64 per cent affirming that climate change would have a direct impact on their lives in the next 20 years, and fell a further 3 per cent in 2012. Willingness to pay more for electricity from renewable sources declined substantially to 56 per cent agreeing in 2009. The Lowy national attitude item about seriousness of global warming dropped 20 per cent in 2009; only 48 per cent of respondents saw it as a pressing problem. It fell further in 2012 but climbed to 50 per cent in 2015. At this latest poll, the majority supported Australian government commitment to significant emissions reductions. The weak policies of the current government were given a low score on 'managing the issue of climate change' in the survey's 'report card' (Lowy Institute 2015).

The American Gallup polls (with more confronting questions) show similar trends, but are uniformly lower. They peaked in 2007 with 40 per cent agreeing that global warming 'will pose a serious threat to way of life in your lifetime', and are currently at 36 per cent (Jones 2014). An international survey on climate change attitudes showed that Americans were far less likely to view climate change as a serious threat than most other surveyed countries, ranking 33rd most concerned out of 39 countries (Pew Research Center 2013).

Cross-national surveys indicate that Australian respondents who express concern about climate change are less prone than other country's citizens to view climate change as only a distant threat. They are familiar with environmental hazards such as cyclical droughts, floods, heatwaves and bushfires as recurring, nearby events. For example, when presented with the statement 'climate change will affect areas far away from here', 32 per cent of a British national sample agreed, compared to only 8.5 per cent of Australians. A majority of Australian respondents (61 per cent) agreed that 'My local area is likely to be affected by climate change', compared to 52.6 per cent of the British sample (Reser *et al.* 2012: 62).

Hunter Valley surveys of public concern about anthropogenic climate change have consistently shown significant age and gender differences. Women and younger age groups are more likely to agree that human activities are contributing to climate change. For example, in the December 2009 survey of residents by the Hunter Valley Research Foundation, 65.2 per cent of women agreed that 'human activities are causing significant changes to the earth's climate' while only 54.2 per cent of men agreed. By age, 75.5 per cent of 18–34 year olds agreed with the statement, contrasted with 49 per cent in the 65 plus age group (Hunter Valley Research Foundation 2009). Gender differences are also found in Australia-wide studies (Lowy Institute 2014; Leviston *et al.* 2011), while age differences are less consistent (Leviston *et al.* 2011). However, one study reported that respondents aged 55 and over were more likely to think climate change was the result of natural causes and that nothing could be done (Leviston *et al.* 2011). Reser and colleagues' national surveys of large British and Australian samples found women to be more concerned than men, and younger people more concerned than older (2012: 48). Lorraine Whitmarsh found that both older and rural-dwelling people in the UK were more likely to be sceptical about the human causes of climate change (Whitmarsh 2011: 695).

Surveys of climate change concern and risk perceptions provide valuable results about trends in several Western nations over more than a decade, as well as differences among specific population categories. These results suggest that views about climate change may be part of resilient schematisations of experience in social groups, or what anthropologists refer to as ontologies (Descola 2013: 405). Attempts to understand climate-change thinking in quotidian worlds through structured survey responses have limitations as this research does not observe the very substance of these worlds: forms of embodied social activity such as talk, and the situations of economic and political power in which they are embedded, to which I now turn.

The contested landscape of concern

It seems paradoxical that most people in the carboniferous zone of the Hunter Valley do not readily talk about anthropogenic climate change, 'the environment in general' or carbon footprints. One of the few ethnographic studies undertaken in a comparable setting to the Hunter Valley, although conducted some years before the peak of climate-change concern in Western countries, found a similar lack of expressed concern. Kari Norgaard summed up a well-established disposition towards denial that she found in a rural Norway community during 2000–2001: 'public response to global warming is *produced* through cultural practices of everyday life' (2011: 207, emphasis in original). It is, she argues, a response of 'socially organized denial' that normalises climate change. The well-educated and affluent people of the small town of Bygdaby: 'are paralyzed in the face of not only climate change, but the many problems of the modern world, from human suffering in the form of disease, warfare and human rights abuse to ecological deterioration' (2011: 208).

Norgaard suggests that this paralysis occurs because of the contradictions between the fossil fuel dependent affluence that residents enjoy and the environmental critique of their political economic realities, plus the emotionally disturbing nature of messages about climate change, all of which keep it out of the frame of everyday life in a collective and systemic way (2011: 210–11). In Hunter communities it would be more apt to say that residents are not paralysed but rather do not rank climate change among their most salient problems. Adverse changes to familiar land, air and waterscapes are a persistent feature of everyday experience. Many residents are confronted with the harsh realities of the Hunter's resource-extractive economy: proliferating coal mine developments, coal seam gas drilling, port expansion, increasing coal train movements, traffic congestion, air pollution and damage to water sources, as well as poorly planned rural subdivisions and suburban sprawl. In this context, lack of concern about climate change may be at least partly understood as a problem of attention – which, as Elke Weber argues, can be 'a very scarce cognitive resource' (2010: 334). Substantiating this proposition, one longitudinal survey of 25,000 people in 51 countries found that decline in climate change concern was associated with higher concern about other environmental issues like pollution and water shortage (Nielsen 2011 cited in Reser *et al.* 2012: 49–50).

In the Hunter Valley, local sources of negative environmental change, with greater immediate impact on residents, win their attention and stimulate various types of actions. Many of these changes arise because of coal mining: the structural violence and physical immediacy of this form of industrial activity has a disordering effect on residents' lives, distracting them from other civic concerns and threatening livelihoods and well-being. A typical example is the current dispute between multinational coal company Peabody Resources and resident Ron Fenwick in the Upper Hunter village of Wambo where Peabody is proposing to extend an underground longwall mine that will cause damage to two creeks on Mr Fenwick's land. The company have justified the extension by arguing that the creeks had already been 'undermined' by mining and fracturing in the 1990s and that the extra damage would be minimal. Mr Fenwick, who owns a cattle farm adjoining the longwall proposal, says 'They seem to have taken the position that they've stuffed the creeks, so what does it matter if they stuff them any more?' (McCarthy 2015). He has fought Peabody previously, in 2011, when it blocked his right of way. The court ruled in favour of Mr Fenwick, ordering Peabody to reinstate a formal crossing, which they did to a minimal standard:

> Since 2011 Mr Fenwick has been able to cross South Wambo Creek – but only in a 4WD vehicle, at least several hundred metres from where the court was told the crossing should be, and not on a reinstated, properly constructed, approved crossing, as required by the court.
>
> (McCarthy 2015)

Mr Fenwick expresses his reluctance to go back to court, but his willingness and confidence to do so should it be necessary. He stated, 'I think I've shown them I'm prepared to stand up for my rights' (McCarthy 2015), a sentiment writ large in the mobilisations against coal operations discussed in the next chapter. While for Peabody this is just another tactical skirmish in the relentless quest for profit, for the Fenwick family it is a cataclysmic situation that has now dominated their lives and obliterated amenity rights to their property for several years, despite legal requirements that the company has ignored. Circumstances like these tend to overshadow the changes in climatic indicators that many rural residents perceive.

Residents like Ron Fenwick are 'reluctant activists' in local conflicts about the damage caused by coal mining in the Hunter Valley, when company operations threaten residents' health, livelihoods and quality of life: 'grass roots environmental activists *are made*, they are *brought into being*, by external forces and agencies which impinge on their normal life worlds unexpectedly and hegemonically' (Peace *et al.* 2012: 219, emphasis in original).

Individuals are drawn into these conflicts not through a political commitment to 'environmentalism', which as Kay Milton has described, in popular understanding 'typically refers to a concern that the environment should be protected, particularly from the harmful effects of human activities' (1996: 27). Mr Fenwick is standing up for his rights as a property owner who is experiencing the marginalised position of rural residents whose livelihoods are threatened by extractive industries that have captured state regulatory regimes. He is caught in a contact zone where the rules of engagement – between state and corporate fossil fuel interests and private citizens – result in a war of attrition that residents rarely win.

In Australia's parliamentary democracy, the 'landscape of concern' about climate change is a contested terrain in which long-term planetary protection is a marginal or minority issue in a short-term electoral cycle. State elites committed to 'business as usual' models of capitalist growth and neoliberal doctrines of deficit reduction work against raising awareness of the increasing risks of human-caused climate change and the urgent need for policies to address it (Rosewarne *et al.* 2014). Many politicians in the current conservative government are sceptics, and the prime minister when in opposition declared the science 'absolute crap' (Rintoul 2009), mounting a successful campaign to abolish the Labor government's carbon tax when attaining government. This sceptical stance

Figure 3.3 Upper Hunter 'lunar landscape'

Source: Peter Lewis, *Newcastle Herald*, 2009

becomes evident when political leaders dismiss any connection between extreme weather-related events and climate change, as illustrated in the prime minister's comments on bushfires. In the last few years, extended periods of very hot weather have been associated with catastrophic wildfires on suburban fringes and farmlands in several Australian states, with severe loss of human and animal life, property and landscape. At the time of writing, major bushfires are occurring in South Australia and Victoria. In the Adelaide Hills 32 homes have been destroyed with 19 communities forced to evacuate and 12,500 hectares burnt, while dozens of fire warnings continue to be issued across Victoria, with over 2,000 firefighters called upon to fight the blazes (news.com.au 2015; Watson 2015). After severe bushfires in the Blue Mountains suburbs and nature reserves west of Sydney in the spring of 2013, the season of high bushfire danger was extended to earlier in the year. The prime minister dismissed any causal connection to climate change, saying that the link was 'complete hogwash', and adding 'I suppose you might say they are desperate to find anything that they think might pass as ammunition for their cause' (Parkinson 2013), with the identity of 'they' left unspecified. By contrast, senior officials with responsibility for fire control were emphatic in their warnings, such as NSW Rural Fire Service Commissioner Shane Fitzsimmons who said:

> If our window of opportunity continues to shrink, in order to get those really important pre-season activities underway then, yes, there's a broader argument that needs to be had around matters of climate change and its effect on fire management and fire seasons.
>
> (Phillips and Malone 2014)

Robert Brulle and colleagues' (2012) review of the factors affecting public concern about climate change in the US, drawing on 74 surveys from 2001–2010, found that 'elite cues', particularly partisan political debates, inhibited the growth of consensus in public concern about climate change. This has occurred in Australian politics, with a federal government largely made up of sceptics supported by the anti-climate change agenda of the News Limited outlets that dominate Australian mass media (Chubb and Nash 2012; Manne 2011) and cohorts of 'celebrity sceptics': journalists, academics, talk-back radio hosts and the like (Connor 2010). The influence of anti-climate change lobby groups on Australian government has been well documented by Guy Pearse in his 'greenhouse mafia' thesis (2007), and still occurs.

The sceptical messages from conservative politicians were briefly overshadowed when in November 2014 US President Barack Obama visited Australia for the annual G20 summit and put climate change at the forefront of his concerns. He spoke about Australia's vulnerability to climate change and called on young Australians to pressure politicians to resist 'entrenched interests' and 'to keep raising their voices', singling out threats to the 'incredible natural glory of the Great Barrier Reef' (Bourke 2014). He also announced a US$3 billion contribution to the UN's Green Climate Fund to help developing countries tackle climate change, a fund that the Australian government at that time declined to support. Debates continued around the risks of dredging and dumping tens of millions of tonnes of seabed dredge spoils in the Great Barrier Reef to open up pathways for coal and gas industry ships (Fight for the Reef 2014). Mr Obama's words prompted a diplomatically unusual rebuke from the foreign minister who said that he 'might have overlooked' aspects of her government's commitment to conserving the Great Barrier Reef and did not reflect the facts in his speech (*Sydney Morning Herald* 2014).

While citizens are drawn into disputes with resource corporations whose operations directly harm their property and persons, conservative governments and corporate interests in harness to a fossil fuel growth economy engage in persistent efforts to minimise the threat of anthropogenic climate change on society's future well-being. Governments exclude climate-change considerations from key programmes and policies, develop tokenistic or weak policies (such as the current 'Direct Action Plan') or deny its severity. Private citizens attempt to defend themselves against industrial harms, while state elites pursue the conditions for favourable capital accumulation and electoral success. Environmental concern, in the sense of protecting the surrounding world from harmful human activities like unrestrained economic growth and its climatic consequences, is marginal or segmented into special interest groups for particular species, places and amenities.

Weather talk

The weather, in contrast to 'the environment', is a phenomenon of daily concern for most people. Ordered weather provides foundational security; disordered weather is a physical and existential challenge. Weather is a topic of civic interest, linking collective experiences of the past with imagination and expectations of the future, in a discursive domain accessible to ethnographic research and of considerable relevance to climate change. In their cross-cultural review, anthropologists Sarah Strauss and Ben Orlove note the importance of *talk* in people's understandings of the weather (2003: 6). Weather talk belongs in the quotidian world, where weather is always a problem; we do not control it. As Mark Twain once remarked, 'Everyone talks about the weather, but nobody does anything about it' (cited in Golinski 2003: 29).

In the quotidian world of contemporary Hunter Valley residents, talk about the weather animates many of the encounters people have in their rounds of chores, work and leisure. Conversations about weekend and holiday plans often start with hopeful statements about 'good weather'. It would be rare in a country town or village not to make a comment about the weather when meeting even the merest acquaintance. Indeed weather talk may be the only conversation one has with acquaintances: 'hot enough for you?', 'nice weather for ducks', 'a scorcher of a day', or the more colourful 'brass monkey weather' (that is, cold enough to 'freeze the balls off a brass monkey') and 'pissing down', heard in pub chatter. In the suburbs, retail workers trapped in air-conditioned malls ask their customers 'What's the weather like out there?', often eliciting a lengthy reply.

Extreme weather along with natural disasters stimulates conversations between strangers in supermarket checkout queues, bus stops and other sites of accidental social proximity. In rural areas suffering from drought, no one talks about anything much *except* the weather and when the rains will come. In 2014, much of the Upper Hunter region was again facing drought conditions and week by week local media stories covered 'drought-stricken farmers', the politics of 'drought assistance packages', the impact on agricultural commodity prices, the mental health of farmers, and occasionally the 'toll on wildlife' (*Newcastle Herald* 2014b). For farmers, avoidance strategies may be an important way of coping, as the following comments to researchers reveal: 'I've stopped going out to the paddock myself. I went down on the weekend and I wish I hadn't gone'; 'You just sort of think "oh well, there's clouds out there …" My son said to me yesterday, he said "no Mum, it's never going to rain again" you know, so he's just made up his mind that it's never going to rain' (Sartore *et al.* 2008). Severe droughts are remembered, and named, providing a touchstone in personal and civic histories as well as a framework for evaluating scientific knowledge. The Millennium Drought from the mid-1990s until 2009 is reputed to be the worst on record for Southeast Australia (van Dijk *et al.* 2013).[4]

Importantly, daily weather talk revolves around *locally* experienced conditions. There is an endless mass media spectacle of extreme weather images from around the world flowing onto TV screens and newspaper pages – cyclones in Bangladesh, typhoons in the Philippines, hurricanes in the US (all personally named but not tamed under conventions of the World Meteorological Organization); floods in Thailand; heatwaves in Europe and Russia; and so on. Only the geopolitically nearer of these events – such as the 'Boxing Day Tsunami' of 2004, the 2011 earthquake and tsunami in Japan with its nuclear aftermath, and of course Australian weather disasters such as 2011 Cyclone Yasi in Queensland – intrude into daily intercourse, often associated with humanitarian fundraising efforts. Some events become national lead stories because they are emotionally near, such as the death of a two-year old boy whose suburban home was hit by a falling tree during a severe storm near Melbourne in February 2015 (ABC News 2015). For the most part, the weather events that Hunter residents are most concerned about are those in their own vicinity, often expressed in the idiom of 'wild weather' – a frequent headline element in the *Newcastle Herald*. In 2014, there were more than 20 stories headlined 'wild weather' over nine months of the year:

Wild weather to hit NSW (19 February 2014)
Huge swells and wild weather predicted for Hunter (19 July 2014)
Wild weather makes presence felt (3 September 2014)

Wild weather 'hits', 'lashes', 'reigns' and 'causes havoc' and is an agent of the tragic and the bizarre, as well as a source of excitement:

Wild weather hits Sydney, leaves one dead on freeway (30 May 2011)
'Tornado' wows residents off Stockton Beach (13 February 2012)
Hunter's big swell unearths dead whale (5 June 2012)
Wild weather delights storm chasers (4 March 2014)

In the world of mass media, wild weather and its aftermath have become spectacles (Rayner 2003: 281). Newspapers invite readers to submit their photos, which are used to illustrate stories or published in online 'galleries' (*Newcastle Herald* 2014c): lightning in purple skies, flooded creeks and roads, black clouds looming over children's sports fields. The really dark side of wild weather – massive floods and wind damage with major loss of life and property – is absent from these celebrations of nature's wildness. The 'Maitland Floods' of 1955 are still memorialised and serve as a touchstone of wild weather for an older generation. La Niña conditions caused a monsoonal depression resulting in the highest 24-hour rainfall on record, with Hunter River levels rising to over 12 metres (from an average of about 3 metres) at Maitland, on the undammed river. A total of 25 lives were lost and 103 homes were destroyed, among much other damage (Berry 2013).

The apex of wild weather in the recent experience of Hunter residents was the 'one in a hundred year' flood in June 2007. Exceeding the intensity of previous storms in living memory, this east coast low pressure system 'battered', 'caused

Figure 3.4 Pasha Bulker coal carrier aground on Newcastle beach after June 2007 storm
Source: Allan Chawner, 2007

havoc', 'devastated' (Scully *et al.* 2007) and 'ravaged' (Cook 2007) the area around Newcastle. The NSW premier declared it a natural disaster after 36 hours of extreme weather caused flooding, loss of life, property and infrastructure damage. The spectacular grounding of a 225-metre long bulk carrier on a Newcastle beach gave the storm its name: the 'Pasha Bulker Storm'. In total, ten people died, and over 10,000 emergency calls were made to the State Emergency Service. One municipal coordinator said, 'I don't think really the shock's set in yet. On Saturday people were wandering around a bit dazed; on Sunday everybody just pitched in and got rid of as much rubbish as possible; obviously today we've got a few more doing that' (Bates and Scully 2007). Such events evoke visceral responses that are long remembered. After a family of four was killed when the flood-damaged Pacific Highway they were travelling on collapsed beneath them, one resident who is a regular user of that road told the local media:

> I had to sit down when I heard about the latest tragedy because I knew exactly where it was on the road. I thought, it could so easily have been me … No one who has anything to do with roads, local or state, should walk away from this without a sense of blood on their hands.
>
> (Cook 2007)

Other sorts of extreme weather are rarely described as wild. Heatwaves[5] are 'sweltering', 'scorching' and 'blistering'. They are threatening but their insidious onset is not wild. New maximum temperature records make major news stories, and sometimes trigger warnings about climate change (which sceptical online comments invariably refute):

Upper Hunter heatwave days to soar as climate change bites (6 December 2014)
We must respond as heatwaves worsen (18 February 2014)

Heatwave predictions from meteorologists and health warnings from doctors and veterinarians are interspersed with invitations to send photos: 'How are you keeping cool?'; 'Send your pics: Hunter heatwave' (Speight 2012). While storm photos feature wild nature, readers' heatwave photos show the human response: beach swimmers, kids and pets with hoses, glasses of frosty beer, air conditioners and the like. These light-hearted takes on an enervating situation fade into the background when dry conditions combine with extreme heat days and winds to create a high risk of bushfires. The proximity of bushland and forests to outer suburbs, rural settlements and farms in most parts of Australia means fire is a real and ever-present risk for many people during hotter weather. National news bulletins are often following numerous fire outbreaks around the country on the same day, and weather conditions are reported in minute detail. Media outlets relay information from fire fighting services; hotlines inform residents of local conditions; and experts advise on proactive and protective actions for householders to take. Text banners scroll below regular programmes on the screen of the national television broadcaster: 'WA fire warning City of Rockhingham', 'The fire is burning towards pine forest in Yanchep Road', 'Homes on Perry Road are under threat', 'For people on Nisa Road it is too late to leave. Shelter in your home'.

These public modes of communication in mass and social media – weather as 'news'– take weather into the public sphere, and into imaginings of the future, both the imminently looming future of bushfires and forecasted storms, and the distant unknowns of climate change. In other words, weather, like everything else, is a political issue, one that connects many elements of human existence. Ontologies of weather come into play in the public sphere, but have their foundations in collective life worlds.

Ontologies: weather world views

Ways of talking about weather often make assumptions about its causes and therefore responsibility for it. In discovering this knowledge, survey researchers in the behavioural sciences tend to focus on psychological constructs like 'attitudes', 'perceptions' and 'intentions'. Some of these data, valuable for the rigour of their collection if not their cultural nuances, are cited below. Anthropologists undertake ethnographic research to direct their attention to more holistic constructs that integrate self and world relationships and ideas about the cosmos – in summary, collective ways of experiencing and ordering the world, which I refer to as ontologies. Australian Aboriginal groups have built up a distinctive ontology over many millennia, characterised by an experience of their country as 'sentient, social and connective' (Rose 2005: 32). Meteorologists attempt to discover the 'timetable of nature' and thus control or at least predict it through a scientific ontology. The refinement of knowledge of ENSO has been part of this process. Science ontologies also include new geoengineering technologies directed to overcoming global warming by returning a disordered climate to human control (Marshall 2016). Christian religious traditions perpetuate views of cosmic order controlled by God that have persisted over long timespans (Donner 2011). Laypersons strive to understand the patterns of weather and climate from experiences communicated over generations. Theirs is a locality-based and embodied world view formed from living in 'weather worlds' (Ingold 2010), experiential knowledge of which has been essential to people's well-being and livelihoods through most of human history.

In his essay on climate and culture in Australia, Tim Sherratt (2005) discussed the ways Australian rural producers, the backbone of the economy for most of the nation's settlement history, struggled with first the unfamiliarity and then the extreme variability of the continent's climate. He observes: 'A new climate cannot be mapped and comprehended like a new continent. It can only be known through time, through averages and extremes, through experience and expectation' (2005: 4).

Fine-grained knowledge of climate is deeply embedded in life worlds. This knowledge is painstakingly acquired across generations of weather vicissitudes by people living from land and waters in particular places. The Hunter Valley is a region where extreme weather and its aftermaths are not unusual, and indeed can be traced back to the coastal inundations of the early Holocene era and millennia of extreme ENSO events to which this part of the eastern seaboard of Australia is particularly vulnerable. Ideas about seasonal patterns and weather causation are part of central and persistent frameworks that require systematic research in relation to climate change thinking. Some ethnographic and survey researchers suggest that people's exposure to unusual or extreme weather events increases the likelihood that they will be concerned about climate change. In the Norwegian community she studied, Norgaard reported: '[I]n that winter in Bygdaby in 2000-2001, the sense that the weather was very different from earlier times was considered "common knowledge" in the community, and comments on the unusual weather were consistently linked with the possibility of climate change' (2011: 69).

A national UK survey of 1,822 adults in 2010 by Spence and colleagues found that: 'those who report experience of flooding express more concern over climate change, see it as less uncertain and feel more confident that their actions will have an effect on climate change' (2011: 46). In their review of Australian and international surveys researching the variables associated with 'direct personal experience of climate change', Reser and colleagues observed: 'climate change appears to have particular salience, immediacy and meaning for respondents in terms of their local environment and their exposure to and experience with extreme weather events' (2012: 127).

Such generalisations raise empirical questions about the dispositions of Hunter Valley residents towards weather patterns and climate change as part of their conceptions of the cosmos. What are their distinctive understandings of weather and climate as articulated in conversations, commentaries and interviews? What is the impact of the recent public discourse on human-caused climate change? While extreme weather such as the Millennium Drought or the Pasha Bulker Storm may strengthen climate change concern, these events may also confirm *alternative* views linked to quite different cosmological understandings that challenge climate science explanations.

One of the ways the author and colleagues explored understandings of weather and climate was a telephone survey drawing a stratified sample of 1,162 randomly selected coastal suburban (Lake Macquarie) and rural (Upper Hunter) residents in 2008 who identified as 'household decision makers', with follow-up in 2011. Trained telephone interviewers informed respondents that the study was seeking 'views about climate change in Lake Macquarie and the Upper Hunter'. Respondents answered structured questions about their observations of any change in 'natural events' in their area (such as 'trees dying', 'storms', 'hotter days') as well as their views on the possibility of climate change, its risks and impacts, and any climate change related actions they were taking. At the end of the survey they were invited to make comments in their own words in response to the question, 'Would you like to make any further comments about climate change, or any other issue related to this interview?'. About half (broadly representative of the sample's demographic characteristics) made open-ended comments at the end of both survey interviews and these were recorded verbatim (for full survey details see Higginbotham *et al.* 2014).

The brief summary of beliefs about global warming in the 2011 survey in Table 3.3 conveys the mixed nature of climate change understandings based on answers to structured questions in the whole sample. This picture is detailed further in the verbatim comments. Of the 44 per cent that selected natural causes, 37 per cent of that group also thought human-produced GHGs were a contributing cause. Similarly, of the 52 per cent selecting anthropogenic sources, 31 per cent of that group thought natural causes also contributed.

Respondents themselves often say that they 'believe' or 'don't believe' in climate change. In using these words, they are referring to a subjective certainty rather than a knowledge-based observation about reality. Like the related concept of 'concern', there is an ambiguity about the term 'belief' and often, as Table 3.3 shows, an ambiguity in people's responses, but as Reser and colleagues (2012: 34) point out:

> 'Belief' in climate change is arguably a rather odd notion, given the multiple meanings and referents of 'climate change' (threat, change in greenhouse gas concentrations in atmosphere, human consequences, human causality, political party affiliation, etc) and the meaning of 'belief', but this has been the language used in both public discourse and by survey researchers to frame such questions.

Statements of belief about climate change express elements of the ontological foundations of residents' life worlds with which they come to an understanding of the deeply contested issue of future climate change threats and possible limits of human survival. Many of the open-ended survey comments provide important insights into these existential realities.

The two iterations of the survey yielded approximately 1,000 comments covering various topics raised in the survey. Themes included statements of scepticism or conviction about anthropogenic climate change, observations about local weather and wildlife, views about the carbon tax and the federal government, statements about pollution and the impact of coal mining on the environment, and many more. A frequently recurring theme in the comments drove us to undertake the initial qualitative analysis and stimulated a related focus in the ethnographic research: the idea of 'natural cycles'. In the next

Table 3.3 Residents' (N=947) percentage agreement with statements about climate change (2011 follow-up survey)

Statement	Percentage in agreement
1. Climate is not warming	25% of all respondents
2. Climate is warming	60% of all respondents
3. Human greenhouse gases causing warming	52% of all respondents
4. Any warming is due to natural causes	44% of all respondents

section, I draw on residents' comments to outline the scope of natural cycles thinking, and analyse several aspects of it that are particularly relevant to the domain of climate change – ideas about the autonomy of nature, role of the Creator and the agency of humans.

Natural cycles

Almost one-fifth of the comments were about 'natural cycles' as an idea linking weather, nature and time. A further 13 per cent of comments expressed sceptical views about anthropogenic climate change without mentioning natural cycles but often emphasising the autonomy of nature from human control. The frequency of these unsolicited comments was strikingly high for a survey of this type, suggesting a distinctive cultural perspective worthy of analysis in relation to broader questions about cosmologies, planetary futures and climate change, and also a gap in the structured survey questions that respondents wanted to rectify. As the research progressed, it became evident that the term 'natural cycles' also occurred in everyday conversation, blogs, newspaper articles and interviews. The core of the 'natural cycles' view is the idea that weather, especially extreme weather events, is a cyclical process over shorter or longer spans of time. Humans are not responsible for the weather nor can they control it. Natural cycles proponents read long-term climate patterns through their embodied experience of local weather. Nature will 'take its course'. In this view, long-term cycles of climate change are affirmed, but not the human causes of current global warming, as in the following comments:

> *I think the climate is changing but I don't think it is anything new as it seems to go in cycles.*
> (Upper Hunter resident 2008)

> *I am a sceptic. I think this is all part of a natural cycle. We should not be panicking.*
> (Lake Macquarie resident 2008)

Rural respondents often drew on their lived experience of changing weather and seasonal patterns such as droughts to justify a 'natural cycles' stance on climate change:

> *I have lived in the country all my life, 60 years, run an orchard and I don't see any significant changes to weather patterns. If anything it's improved since the 1950s.*
> (Upper Hunter resident 2008)

> *Ever since I was little there were always cycles of heat/floods/storms/droughts and I remember some years there would be no cicadas and other years they would be back. So I firmly believe that we have a long way to go before we can blame climate change on all the different things that are being blamed today.*
> (Lake Macquarie resident 2011)

The idea of natural cycles encompassed a range of views across the whole sample of survey respondents, from denial climate change is occurring, expressions of scepticism about possible human causes, indecision or 'fence-sitting', concern that changes are occurring and humans could be partly responsible, and so on. Social psychologists have identified various dimensions of public scepticism about anthropogenic climate change. A recent empirical study in the UK distinguished two main types of sceptical thought. First, 'epistemic' or 'attribution' scepticism, which questions (or denies) the scientific evidence for global warming, and second 'response' or 'impact' scepticism, which expresses doubt about the efficacy of ameliorative actions, from the individual to the policy arena (Capstick and Pidgeon 2014). The striking form of scepticism among Hunter Valley respondents was epistemic scepticism: 25 per cent of those responding to a formal survey question disagreed that global warming was occurring (Higginbotham *et al.* 2014: 709). In general, however, survey respondents' thinking was often more nuanced than dichotomous analytical categories would imply. Many respondents who favoured natural causes for climate change also acknowledged human causes could be a factor, and vice versa (see Table 3.3). Others could be characterised as undecided on the issue:

> *Climate change might be a natural occurrence. Pollution levels would add to altering weather conditions. History shows these things are cyclical.*
>
> (Lake Macquarie resident 2008)

> *I think a lot of these issues are cyclic; others are due to environmental issues due to pollution.*
>
> (Upper Hunter resident 2008)

> *I think climate change is not just Mother Nature. Maybe Mother Nature might be just trying to fix itself. We should cut out greenhouse gases anyway. It might be just natural. We don't know for sure.*
>
> (Lake Macquarie resident 2011)

Those respondents who worried about human-caused climate change tended to make brief, emphatic statements expounding the concept, rather than venturing into theoretical explanations, perhaps confident about their agreement with the dominant scientific view, and less confident about the technical details of the carbon cycle, the enhanced greenhouse effect and so on: 'I think it's a big issue'; 'I definitely agree the climate is changing'; 'I believe there is climate change'; 'I think it's a reality'; 'It is a serious problem'.

Among the commenters who espoused a strong natural cycles viewpoint, denying any human causes for climate change, the phenomenon of autonomous nature was frequently invoked. This is an optimistic cosmology, where 'nature' has the agency to heal itself:

The whole approach to climate change is overrated. Not enough unison around the world. If no one else does it what's the point? Nature will adjust itself to whatever man will do.

(Lake Macquarie resident 2008)

I think it's nature taking its natural course.

(Lake Macquarie resident 2008)

Nature will find its own cure.

(Lake Macquarie resident 2011)

Similar comments are made in blogs responding to newspaper articles about climate change. A *Newcastle Herald* piece reporting on the likelihood of more increased heatwaves due to climate change (Harris 2014) elicited many affirmative comments but also vigorous rebuttals based on historical precedents for these events:

If the weather we're experiencing now is global warming, whoops, climate change, then bring it on! Seems to me like the cycle is swinging back to what it was 25 years ago; hot days and a lovely storm in the arvo to bring some rain and cool things down. Frankly, I'm sick of the scaremongering in order to make money. We're coming out of an ice age people, it ain't rocket science. These storms every afternoon might help fight the green terrorists and their attempt to let fuel loads get to extreme levels (as well as add ozone to the atmosphere).

('Hayfarmer78')

Like 'Hayfarmer78', survey commenters presented various syntheses of science and natural history, with both older and younger respondents making reference to evolution, ice ages and cyclical change:

Needs more scientific research to see if it is cyclic to every 200 to 300 years. The planets are not in danger. In my belief it will look after itself. It's only living creatures that suffer from our actions. History has proven this, as in ice age and dinosaurs.

(Upper Hunter resident 2008)

I think it is a natural cycle that the planet goes through as we are still coming out of the last ice age and it will eventually get to a point where it will start to cool down again.

(Lake Macquarie resident 2011)

A few respondents expressed their conviction that any higher order control of nature must come from the Christian God. Simon Donner (2011) observed that the cosmological underpinnings of climate beliefs in Western societies stem from Christian doctrines that God controls the weather. This way of thinking surfaced in some comments, with a few respondents stating explicitly their conviction that God controlled cosmic order, and natural cycles are part of this order:

> *I would say that if you looked on a whole cycle of the world and how it has run in the past it is probably more like a bigger time frame cycle ... i.e. a thousand year cycle. If you read your bible you will see in Revelations that it is part of the original plan for the universe.*
>
> (Upper Hunter resident 2008)

Several commenters who agreed that anthropogenic climate change *was* a problem expressed their faith in God's protection:

> *I think that God will provide a solution.*
>
> (Lake Macquarie resident 2011)

The following woman, with similar views, also stated that biblically preordained changes did not relieve humans from 'looking after the planet':

> *Our family is confident that what we are seeing now is fulfilling bible prophecy and the Creator will ensure that things get better in the future but, as we are the care-takers of the planet, we have to look after it.*
>
> (Lake Macquarie resident 2008)

One commenter invoked the idea of climate change as God's wrath wreaked on humans, which is also a powerful narrative in the last book of the Bible, Revelation to John:

> *Things are changing. Someone up there is very angry with us. Kids will need to live with climate change.*
>
> (Lake Macquarie resident 2011)

But overall, less than ten commenters invoked these ideas that explicitly connect religion and climate change in one way or another. The structured survey questions did not ask about religious beliefs or ideas, which may provide an explanation. Many commenters emphasised the idea of human responsibility for 'looking after the planet', but did not express it in a religious idiom. In regional census results, most residents declare an affiliation with Christian denominations, suggesting that familiarity with the idea of human stewardship of God's creation, 'the planet', is quite widespread if implicit. By contrast, a USA survey of the environmental values of 142 people in five different occupational and interest groups undertaken in the mid-1990s by anthropologist Willett Kempton and colleagues asked a number of questions about God and biblical prophesy. They reported: 'We find a substantial majority agreeing with a statement justifying environmental protection by explicitly invoking God as the creator, with striking uniformity across subgroups' (Kempton *et al.* 1995: 91).

They concluded that even if not claiming membership of organised religions, the concept of biblical Creation is a way that a broad spectrum of the American population can express their understanding of the 'sacredness of nature' and their valuing of it (Kempton *et al.* 1995: 92). A similar convergence of environmentalists' and religious adherents' values in Hunter-based groups is considered in Chapter 6 of this book.

Many of the comments that supported the natural cycle view of climate change also saw human activities as a contributor. Indeed the comments suggest that it is not global warming but other forms of adverse environmental change that worry residents – caused by pollution, coal mining, bad water management and overpopulation, for example. These may or may not be contributing to climate change, but they are contributing to environmental decline. For many people, weather and climate – cyclical and largely out of human control – are not the problem. Human activities are wrecking the planet, but not through increased GHG emissions (which rarely featured in people's comments). Respondents who viewed climate change as either non-existent or due to natural cycles saw pollution as a separate problem:

> *I don't think it's the weather that is changing. What is the problem is pollution and over population. The weather has not changed; it's the cycle of nature.*
> (Upper Hunter resident 2011)

Those favouring anthropogenic views of global warming expressed similar views about the negative environmental changes caused by human activities, but tended to link these more emphatically to climate change:

> *We blame the bad things that happened in the past on cycles that are now getting worse. We have not looked after the planet and we are not serious about changing. Nobody wants to spend the money or change their ways, for example plastic bags. We still want what we want without considering the consequences.*
> (Lake Macquarie resident 2008)

> *Climate change is the deforestation of the planet as trees are the earth and we are losing too many from this planet i.e. native forests especially the Amazon. They are knocking down the trees and this is the major cause of climate change.*
> (Upper Hunter resident 2011)

These data bear out the findings of survey researchers that public education about the science is not particularly influential in shaping climate change views (Reser *et al.* 2012). Respondents' comments suggest that other experiences – such as dust, damaged water sources, air pollution, deforestation, mining – are more salient forms of environmental change that may divert concern from climate change altogether, or at least relegate it to a peripheral status. The emotive tone of some responses suggests that the subject triggered feelings of confusion and anxiety about climate change – a topic people are reluctant to talk about.

A touchy subject

Anthropogenic climate change is a difficult topic to research in quotidian worlds, for it is often a peripheral or suppressed concern, brought to awareness by the process of being a subject in a research project. An approach by researchers imbues the topic with a salience that it may not have most of the time. People are asked to report on matters that belong to a domain of discourse – the official, the scientific, the political, the future – that they may prefer to ignore but about which they may feel obliged to respond when directly approached.

The Hunter Valley research suggests many possible reasons for this. Like the people of the Circumpolar North and the Pacific Islands discussed in Chapter 1, rural residents whose livelihood is obtained from their surrounding environment are deeply knowledgeable about the conditions in their local area. This familiarity is also often found among suburban residents whose leisure pursuits – fishing, sailing, surfing, gardening, bushwalking and the like – put them in close contact with the natural world that is close by. As the responses to our survey show, people are usually confident in talking about local environmental change and long-established understandings of weather, but less willing to express opinions on scientific theories that generalise about planetary changes and ignore local conditions. Elizabeth Marino and Peter Schweitzer encountered this phenomenon in their research with Inupiaq people in northwestern Alaska, where they found: 'There exists a sharp contrast, however, between this global discourse [of climate change], imported through individual actors and media outlets, and local knowledge based on daily observations of the environment' (2009: 212).

Various conventions and taboos as well as diffidence about their knowledge inhibited Inupiaq villagers from talking about climate change, while conversations about experiences of locally changing environments were animated and informative, leading the authors to conclude that *'not talking* about climate change proved the best method for understanding local conceptions of change' (Marino and Schweitzer 2009: 210, italics in original).

Similar dynamics are at play in the Hunter, where many residents are daunted by the science of climate change, which they perceive as contested and confusing:

> *There are so many conflicting sides with the academics. Who should we believe?*
> (Upper Hunter resident 2008)

> *I just don't know. It makes it rather baffling for the novice to put a tag on it because scientists can't agree on it.*
> (Lake Macquarie resident 2011)

Other conventions against speaking out on potentially divisive topics in one's circle of friends and acquaintances are also relevant. In the polarised setting of Australian politics, climate change has become a controversial issue, engendering emotional responses on all sides. 'The greatest moral challenge of our time' said one prime minister; 'absolute crap' and 'hogwash' said another. Despite increasing evidence of mainstream support for carbon pricing and renewable energy policies, more conservative Hunter Valley residents identify public stances for climate change action with 'greenie' politics, forms of environmental activism and controversy that most people prefer to avoid:

> *It's a very touchy subject which everyone has an opinion on. There are experts for and against. We don't get into it with people.*
>
> (Lake Macquarie resident 2011)

> *It is very difficult to answer some questions as there is a lot of radicalism about climate change and I am suspicious of anything radical.*
>
> (Lake Macquarie resident 2011)

Climate change discourse also invokes themes of threatened futures and planetary destruction. Stances on such matters are seen as part of deeply held personal convictions and not the stuff of sustaining conversational routines in the everyday. Climate change beliefs, like religion, are a 'family' matter, either explicitly, as in the following comment, or implicitly, in the use of 'we' by many respondents:

> *In our family we do not necessarily think that climate change is happening. It is a fear based issue not a fact based issue.*
>
> (Lake Macquarie resident 2011)

The question of fear is an important one. The flood of information in public discourse and mass media about the threat of climate change to all forms of life on the planet constitutes a harbinger of mortality that is bound to trigger defence mechanisms. These include consciously articulated expressions of scepticism, denial and apathy, unconsciously driven carbon-profligate behaviour, as well as the embrace of ideologies and leaders who deny the science and the catastrophic consequences of climate change (Dickinson 2009). Other researchers have noted that firmly sceptical and denialist views are 'strongly held and closely associated with self-perceptions, world views and value stances' (Reser *et al.* 2012: 36) – in other words, with social ontologies of self and Other, present and future. These ways of being demonstrate some striking differences with the schema and value stances that characterise theories of human-caused climate change, resting on the hegemonic ontology of science in the modern world. Understandings of Hunter Valley residents suggest that there are different and enduring modes of being that situate humans in a cosmos where non-human nature has an ordered intentionality of its own, exerting powerful forms of agency. Although most strikingly articulated in the views of natural cycles proponents, this idea of nature, especially weather, is evident in the thinking of many residents, seemingly grounded in the particular conditions of lives and livelihoods in this region rather than the discourses of political environmentalism or climate science.

Chapter 6 will consider further the question of imagined futures and their relationship to enduring ontologies, experienced ecologies and political economies that have been charted in this chapter's exploration of Hunter Valley quotidian worlds.

Notes

1   The former includes the local government areas (LGAs) of Singleton, Muswellbrook and Upper Hunter, while the latter includes Maitland, Dungog, Cessnock, Newcastle and Lake Macquarie.
2   These statistics refer to the state electoral area boundaries for Upper Hunter.
3   Mine operators do not always reach approved annual maximum production for various reasons related to production conditions and prices.
4   The Australian Bureau of Meteorology defines drought as the 'Prolonged absence or marked deficiency of precipitation (rain)' (2015).
5   The World Meteorological Organization defines heatwave as 'Marked warming of the air, or the invasion of very warm air, over a large area; it usually lasts from a few days to a few weeks' (2015).

References

ABC News 2007. 'Tens of thousands march for climate change action'. Nov 11, *ABC News*. Available at www.abc.net.au/news/2007-11-11/tens-of-thousands-march-for-climate-change-action/722172 archived by WebCite at www.webcitation.org/6Vi0ffTOf (accessed October 2014).

ABC News 2015. 'Victorian storms: Family left shattered after 'tragic' death of toddler in wild storm'. 2 March, *ABC News*. Available at www.abc.net.au/news/2015-02-28/victorian-storms-toddler-killed-girl-taken-hospital/6271536 archived by WebCite at www.webcitation.org/6WokN3SzM (accessed 6 March 2015).

Australian Bureau of Meteorology 2015. *Glossary*. Available at www.bom.gov.au/lam/glossary/dpagegl.shtml (accessed March 2015).

Australian Bureau of Statistics 2012. *Census 2011: Census for a brighter future*. Available at www.abs.gov.au/census

Bates, J. and Scully, A. 2007. Businesses washed away by flash flooding. *1233 ABC Newcastle*. June 20. Available at www.abc.net.au/local/stories/2007/06/13/1950058.htm archived by WebCite at www.webcitation.org/6YX7IpT7T (accessed 5 February 2015).

BBC News 2007. 'Global rallies focus on climate'. 8 December, *BBC News*. Available at http://news.bbc.co.uk/2/hi/uk_news/7134060.stm (accessed 29 September 2014).

Berry, R. 2013. 'City's history of flooding'. *The Maitland Mercury*. 27 February. Available at www.maitlandmercury.com.au/story/1328053/citys-history-of-flooding/ archived by WebCite at www.webcitation.org/6YX7g6ZiX (accessed 5 February 2015).

Bourke, L. 2014. 'G20 summit: Barack Obama puts climate change at fore in speech at University of Queensland'. *Sydney Morning Herald*. Available at www.smh.com.au/federal-politics/political-news/g20-summit-barack-obama-puts-climate-change-at-fore-in-speech-at-university-of-queensland-20141115-11ndmg.html archived by WebCite at www.webcitation.org/6VskBR7No (accessed 27 January 2015).

Brulle, R. J., Carmichael, J. and Jenkins, J. H. 2012. 'Shifting Public Opinion on Climate Change: An empirical assessment of factors influencing concern over climate change in the US, 2002-2010'. *Climatic Change* 114 (2): 169–188.

Campbell, R. 2014. *Seeing Through the Dust: Coal in the Hunter Valley economy*. The Australia Institute.

Capstick, S. and Pidgeon, N. 2014. 'What *is* Climate Change Scepticism? Examination of the concept using a mixed methods study of the UK public'. *Global Environmental Change* 24: 389–401.

Chubb, P. and Nash, C. 2012. 'The politics of reporting climate change at the Australian Broadcasting Corporation'. *Media International Australia, Incorporating Culture & Policy* 144: 37–48.

Connor, L. 2010. *Climate Change and the Challenge of Immortality: Faith, denial and intimations of eternity*. Anthropology and the Ends of Worlds, University of Sydney.

Cook, T. 2007. 'Storm wreaks havoc across Australia's Hunter Valley and Central Coast'. World Socialist Web Site, June 25. Available at www.wsws.org/en/articles/2007/06/stor-j25.html archived by WebCite at www.webcitation.org/6YX7YmcVW (accessed 5 February 2015).

Crawford, E. 2014. 'OPINION: Urban renewal strategy promises to transform'. *Newcastle Herald*. Available at www.theherald.com.au/story/2178651/opinion-urban-renewal-strategy-promises-to-transform/ archived by WebCite at www.webcitation.org/6VgbVrapD (accessed July 2014).

Deeming, S. 2014. 'OPINION: Hunter yet to shift from resources'. *Newcastle Herald*. Available at www.theherald.com.au/story/2089445/opinion-hunter-yet-to-shift-from-resources-boom/?cs=308 archived by WebCite at www.webcitation.org/6VgckWXz3 (accessed August 2014).

Department of Climate Change (Australian Government) 2009. *Climate Change Household Action Campaign Evaluation Report*. Available at www.climatechange.gov.au/about/publications/pubs/think-change-evaluation-report.pdf (accessed 28 September 2009).

Descola, P. 2013. *Beyond Nature and Culture*. Chicago: Chicago University Press.

Dickinson, J. 2009. 'The People Paradox: Self-Esteem striving, immortality ideologies, and human response to climate change'. *Ecology and Society* 14: 34–53.

Donner, S. 2011. *Making the Climate a Part of the Human World*. Bulletin of the American Meteorological Society, Available at http://dx.doi.org/10.1175/2011BAMS3219.1 (accessed 30 June 2013).

Fight for the Reef 2014. *Dredging*. Available at https://fightforthereef.org.au/risks/dredging/ archived by WebCite at www.webcitation.org/6VsjlDz1o (accessed 27 January 2015).

Golinski, J. 2003. 'Time, Talk, and the Weather in Eighteenth-Century Britain'. In: *Weather, Climate, Culture*, Strauss, S. and Orlove, B (eds). Oxford: Berg.

Harris, M. 2014. 'Upper Hunter heatwave days to soar as climate change bites'. *Newcastle Herald*. Dec 6. Available at www.theherald.com.au/story/2746103/upper-hunter-scorchers-to-soar-as-climate-change-bites/ archived by WebCite at www.webcitation.org/6WCgl0My1 (accessed 6 February 2015).

Higginbotham, N., Connor, L. H. and Baker, F. 2014. 'Subregional differences in Australian climate risk perceptions: coastal versus agricultural areas of the Hunter Valley, NSW'. *Regional Environmental Change* 14 (2): 699–712.

Hunter Valley Research Foundation 2006. *Hunter Region Environmental Attitudes Survey*. Newcastle: HVRF.

Hunter Valley Research Foundation 2009. *Hunter Region Environmental Attitudes Survey 2008–9, Working Paper No. 3/09*. Newcastle: HVRF.

Hunter Valley Research Foundation 2010. *Hunter Region Environmental Attitudes Survey*

2009–10, *HVRF Working Paper No. 2/10*. Newcastle: HVRF.

Hunter Valley Research Foundation 2012. *Hunter Environmental Attitudes 2012*. Available at http://6f430d2a.enigmadigital.hosting24.com.au/regional-research-program/environmental-attitudes archived by WebCite at www.webcitation.org/6Vi1OgJfl (accessed June 2014).

Hunter Valley Wine Industry Association and the Hunter Valley Protection Alliance 2012. *Protecting the Hunter Valley from CSG mining*. White Paper, Hunter Valley, NSW.

Ingold, T. 2010. 'Footprints through the Weather-world: Walking, breathing, knowing'. *Journal of the Royal Anthropological Institute* NS: S121–S139.

IPCC (Intergovernmental Panel on Climate Change) 2007. *Fourth Assessment Report: Climate Change 2007*. Available at www.ipcc.ch/activity/ar.htm (accessed 11 February 2007).

Jones, J. M. 2014. 'In U.S., most do not see global warming as serious threat'. *Gallup Politics*, 13 March. Available at www.gallup.com/poll/167879/not-global-warming-serious-threat.aspx archived by WebCite at www.webcitation.org/6OIwgBbdy (accessed 24 March 2014).

Kempton, W., Boster, J. S. and Hartley, J. A. 1995. *Environmental Values in American Culture*. Cambridge and Massachusetts: MIT Press.

Lannin, S. 2014. 'Coal communities in NSW's Hunter Valley trying to survive the mining slowdown'. *ABC News*. Dec 15. Available at www.abc.net.au/news/2014-12-14/coal-communities-trying-to-survive-the-mining-slowdown/5966418 archived by WebCite at www.webcitation.org/6bHdxEhVo (accessed 3 September 2015).

Leviston, Z. and Walker, I. 2010. *Baseline Survey of Australian Attitudes to Climate Change: preliminary report, national research flagships climate adaptation*. Perth: CSIRO Ecosystem Sciences.

Leviston, Z., Leitch, A., Greenhill, M., Leonard, R. and Walker, I. 2011. *Australians' views of climate change*. CSIRO Report. Canberra.

Lowy Institute for International Policy 2009. *The Lowy Institute Poll 2009*. Sydney: Fergus Hanson.

Lowy Institute for International Policy 2012. *The Lowy Institute Poll 2012: Public opinion and foreign policy*. Available at www.lowyinstitute.org/files/lowy_poll_2012_web3.pdf (accessed 6 September 2012).

Lowy Institute for International Policy 2014. *The Lowy Institute Poll 2014*. Available at www.lowyinstitute.org/publications/lowy-institute-poll-2014 (accessed January 2015).

Lowy Institute for International Policy 2015. *The Lowy Institute Poll 2015*. Available at www.lowyinstitute.org/publications/lowy-institute-poll-2015 (accessed July 2015).

Malinowski, B. 1922 [1984]. *Argonauts of the Western Pacific*. Long Grove, IL: Waveland Press.

Manne, R. 2011. 'The truth is out there'. *Sydney Morning Herald*, News Review, 3–4 September, p. 22.

Marino, E. and Schweitzer, P. 2009. 'Talking and not talking about climate change in northwestern Alaska'. In: *Anthropology and Climate Change: From Encounters to Actions*. Crate, S. and Nuttall, M (eds). Walnut Creek, California: Left Coast Press, Inc.

Marshall, J. P. 2016. 'Geo-engineering, imagining and the problem cycle: a cultural complex in action'. In: *Environmental change and the world's futures: ecologies, ontologies, mythologies*. Marshall, J. P. and Connor, L. H. (eds). London: Routledge.

McAndrew, W. 2014. 'OPINION: Mining only winners in Resources for Regions funding'. *Newcastle Herald*: Available at www.theherald.com.au/story/2317042/opinions-mining-only-winners-in-resources-for-regions-funding/?cs=308 archived by WebCite at www.webcitation.org/6QF04nlaU (acessed 11 June 2015).

McCarthy, J. 2015. 'Peabody to press for Wambo mine plan'. *Newcastle Herald*. Available at www.theherald.com.au/story/2795059/peabody-to-press-for-wambo-mine-plan/ archived by WebCite at www.webcitation.org/6Vi3Wdgz5 (accessed January 2015).

McManus, P. and Connor, L. 2013. 'What's Mine is Mine(d): Contests over marginalisation of rural life in the Upper Hunter, NSW'. *Rural Society* 22 (2): 166–183.

Milton, K. 1996. *Environmentalism and Cultural Theory: Exploring the role of anthropology in environmental discourse*. London: Routledge.

Newcastle Herald 2014a. 'EDITORIAL: Newcastle deserves better than this political trainwreck'. *Newcastle Herald*. Available at www.theherald.com.au/story/2474932/editorial-newcastle-deserves-better-than-this-political-trainwreck/?cs=313 archived by WebCite at www.webcitation.org/6Vgk0erSK (accessed August 2014).

Newcastle Herald 2014b. 'Native animals are bearly surviving drought'. *Newcastle Herald*, 7 February. Available at www.theherald.com.au/story/2075215/native-animals-are-bearly-surviving-drought/ archived by WebCite at www.webcitation.org/6W86VkA2r (accessed 29 January 2015).

Newcastle Herald 2014c. 'Wild weather lashes NSW'. *Newcastle Herald*, 7 December. Available at www.theherald.com.au/story/2747437/wild-weather-lashes-nsw-photos/?cs=2452 archived by WebCite at www.webcitation.org/6WCWJqIYA (accessed 9 February 2015).

news.com.au 2015. 'Emergency warning downgraded for Victoria fires as South Australia gets rain after 32 homes gone'. News.com.au. Available at www.news.com.au/national/emergency-warnings-downgraded-for-victoria-fires-as-south-australia-gets-rain-after-32-homes-gone/story-fncynjr2-1227175252546 archived by WebCite at www.webcitation.org/6Vi3j4gG9 (accessed January 2015).

Norgaard, K. 2011. *Living in Denial: Climate change, emotions and everyday life*. Cambridge & London: MIT Press.

NSW Department of Industry 2014. *Coal*. Available at www.resourcesandenergy.nsw.gov.au/investors/investment-opportunities/coal archived by WebCite at www.webcitation.org/6aWC1BZUZ (accessed 24 June 2015).

NSW Department of Planning 2012. *Newcastle Urban Renewal Strategy, Part Two: Methodology*. NSW Government, Planning and Infrastructure.

NSW Department of Primary Industries 2013. *Upper Hunter Region: Dairy profile*. Department of Trade and Investment, Regional Infrastructure and Services.

O'Neill, P. and Green, R. 2000. 'Global economy, local jobs'. In: *Journeys: The making of the Hunter region*. McManus, P., O'Neill, P. and Loughran, R. (eds). St Leonards: Allen & Unwin.

Parkinson, G. 2013. 'Tony Abbott says climate link to bush-fires is "complete hogwash"'. *RenewEconomy*. Available at http://reneweconomy.com.au/2013/tony-abbott-says-climate-link-to-bush-fires-is-complete-hogwash-99506 archived by WebCite at www.webcitation.org/6Vi45FyjX (accessed January 2015).

Peace, A., Connor, L. and Trigger, D. 2012. 'Environmentalism, Culture, Ethnography'. *Oceania* 82 (3): 217–227.

Pearse, G. 2007. *High and Dry: John Howard, climate change and the selling of Australia's future*. Camberwell, Victoria: Viking.

Peterson, N. and Broad, K. 2009. 'Climate and Weather Discourse in Anthropology: From Determinism to Uncertain Futures'. In: *Anthropology and Climate Change: From Encounters to Actions*. Crate, S. and Nuttall, M (eds). Walnut Creek, California: Left

Coast Press, Inc.

Pew Research Center 2013. Edited by Dimock, M., Doherty, C. and Christian, L. *Continuing Partisan Divide in Views of Global Warming: Keystone XL pipeline draws broad support*. Washington DC. Available at www.people-press.org/files/legacy-pdf/4-2-13%20Keystone%20Pipeline%20and%20Global%20Warming%20Release.pdf (accessed 25 June 2013).

Phillips, J. and Malone, U. 2014. 'Climate change forcing rethink on fire risk, RFS chief Shane Fitzsimmons says'. ABC News. Available at www.abc.net.au/news/2014-10-17/climate-change-forcing-rethink-on-fire-risk-bushfire-chief/5821386 archived by WebCite at www.webcitation.org/6Vi4EJsD3 (accessed January 2015).

Rayner, S. 2003. 'Domesticating Nature: Commentary on the Anthropological Study of Weather and Climate Discourse'. In: *Weather, Climate and Culture*. Strauss, S. and Orlove, B (eds). Oxford: Berg.

Reser, J., Bradley, G., Glendon, A. and Ellul, M. 2012. *Public risk perceptions, understandings, and responses to climate change and natural disasters in Australia and Great Britain*. Griffith University, School of Applied Psychology, Behavioural Basis of Health: Griffith Climate Change Response Program, National Climate Change Adaptation Research Facility.

Rintoul, S. 2009. 'Town of Beaufort changed Tony Abbott's view on climate change'. *The Australian*. Available at www.theaustralian.com.au/archive/politics/the-town-that-turned-up-the-temperature/story-e6frgczf-1225809567009 archived by WebCite at www.webcitation.org/6WoYnheYj (accessed 6 March 2015).

Rose, D. 2005. 'Rhythms, Patterns, Connectivities: Indigenous concepts of seasons and change'. In: *A Change in the Weather: Climate and culture in Australia*. Sherratt, T., Griffiths, T. and Robin, L. (eds). Canberra: National Museum of Australia.

Rosewarne, S., Goodman, J. and Pearse, R. 2014. *Climate Action Upsurge: The ethnography of climate movement politics*. London and New York: Routledge.

Sartore, G., Kelly, B., Stain, H., Albrecht, G. and Higginbotham, N. 2008. 'Control, Uncertainty, and Expectations for the Future: A qualitative study of the impact of drought on a rural Australian community'. *Rural and Remote Health* 8 (Article 950): 1–14.

Scully, A., Evans, P. and Fitzroy, L. 2007. 'Wild weather causes havoc in the Hunter'. *1233 ABC Newcastle*. 20 June. Available at www.abc.net.au/local/stories/2007/06/08/1945661.htm archived by WebCite at www.webcitation.org/6YX7qBqI2 (accessed 5 February 2015).

Sherratt, T. 2005. 'Human Elements'. In: *A Change in the Weather: Climate and culture in Australia*. Sherratt, T., Griffiths, T. and Robin, L. (eds) Canberra: National Museum of Australia.

Speight, J. 2012. 'SEND YOUR PICS: Hunter heatwave'. *Newcastle Herald*. 30 November. Available at www.theherald.com.au/story/1155195/send-your-pics-hunter-heatwave/#slide=1 archived by WebCite at www.webcitation.org/6WCgj1RBu (accessed 6 February 2015).

Spence, A., Poortinga, W., Butler, C. and Pidgeon, N. 2011. 'Perceptions of Climate Change and Willingness to Save Energy in Relation to Flood Experience'. *Nature Climate Change* 1: 46–49.

Stern N. 2006. *Stern Review on the Economics of Climate Change, 30 October 2006*. London: HM Treasury. Available at http://webarchive.nationalarchives.gov.uk/+/www.hm-treasury.gov.uk/independent_reviews/stern_review_economics_climate_change/sternreview_index.cfm (accessed 30 November 2006).

Strauss, S. and Orlove, B. 2003. 'Up in the Air: The anthropology of weather and climate'. In: *Weather, Climate and Culture*. Strauss, S. and Orlove, B (eds). Oxford: Berg.

Sydney Morning Herald 2014. 'Julie Bishop criticises Barack Obama over Great Barrier Reef comments'. *Sydney Morning Herald*: Available at www.smh.com.au/federal-poli-tics/political-news/julie-bishop-criticises-barack-obama-over-great-barrier-reef-comme nts-20141120-11qupd.html archived by WebCite at www.webcitation.org/6VsjzmcEC (accessed 27 January 2015).

The Climate Institute 2010. *Climate of the Nation: Australians' attitudes toward climate change and its solutions*. Canberra: The Climate Institute. Available at www.climateinstitute.org.au/verve/_resources/climateofthenation_august2010.pdf (accessed 18 September 2012).

van Dijk, A. I. J. M., Beck, H. E., Crosbie, R. S., de Jeu, R. A. M., Liu, Y. Y., Podger, G. M., Timbal, B. and Viney, N. R. 2013. 'The Millennium Drought in Southeast Australia (2001–2009): Natural and human causes and implications for water resources, ecosystems, economy, and society'. *Water Resources Research* 49 (2): 1040–1057.

Watson, M. 2015. 'Firefighters are getting pretty miffed with Tony Abbott over his lack of action on climate change'. *Junkee*. Available at http://junkee.com/firefighters-think-tony-is-not-great-hey/48296 archived by WebCite at www.webcitation.org/6Vi3tRqEn (accessed January 2015).

Weber, E. U. 2010. 'What Shapes Perceptions of Climate Change?'. *Wiley Interdisciplinary Reviews: Climate Change* 1 (3): 332–342.

Whitmarsh, L. 2011. 'Scepticism and Uncertainty about Climate Change: Dimensions, determinants and change over time'. *Global Environmental Change* 21: 690–700.

World Meteorological Organization 2015. *Meteoterm – Heatwave*. Available at http://wmo.multicorpora.net/MultiTransWeb/Web.mvc (accessed March 2015).

4 Living environmental change

Our surrounding environment shapes what we can and do perceive, and these perceptions are foundational elements of ways of being (or ontologies, as discussed in Chapter 3) that in turn constitute their participants' collective worlds through cultural practices, social organisation, economic activity and all other dimensions of human life. 'The dialectic of perception and place (and of both with meaning) is as intricate as it is profound, and it is never-ending', says Edward Casey, in a succinct statement of his place phenomenology (1997: 19). Environmental change is part of the 'senseful' lives (in Husserl's evocative phrase) of all humans' collective worlds. Changes to the places in which people dwell may be routine, expected and often welcomed. Buildings are constructed, gardens are made, glaciers advance and retreat, different crops are planted, new species are introduced or arrive. Weather-related events that cause damage, like storms and floods, while distressing, are not unexpected, and institutional arrangements are usually in place to assist victims and repair the after effects. Industrial development can change surrounding environments in damaging ways, often exacerbating inequalities – class, gender or race, for example. Unwelcome changes that degrade familiar and loved places can cause the forms of psychological and social distress that Glenn Albrecht has termed 'solastalgia' (2005; Albrecht et al. 2007). 'Natural disasters', no longer so 'natural' as awareness of anthropogenic climate change impacts grows, are by definition extreme events of calamitous magnitude, for which preparedness may be minimal. All communities live with a spectrum of environmental changes – welcomed, contested, ambiguous, worrying, terrifying. Growing awareness of global warming has made changing weather, seasonal cycles and patterns of climate an increasingly salient part of the environmental understanding of people living in the particular space-time conjunctures that places form.

In this chapter I begin with a discussion of perceptions of environmental change as reported in the householder surveys that colleagues and I conducted for the purpose of gaining a broad base of information about residents' views in two highly climate exposed subregions of the Hunter Valley. I then turn to the political ecology of coal mining and burning viewed from the Hunter Valley perspective. The gross transformation of landscape wrought by these forms of extractive capitalist accumulation creates its own emplaced politics of perception, embedded in institutional politics. I highlight the situation of Aboriginal traditional owners as a particular instance of the suppressed onto-logical reality of 'Others' who share the time-space of Western modernity but whose places are constituted by different modes of knowing, embodied experi-ence and ethical reasoning. The chapter then goes on to consider the experiences of environmental change in the rural district of Jerrys Plains. In interviews, farmers relate their ordeals with drought and mining impacts. Climate change by contrast is a distant or unacknowledged threat for most. In the next section, I discuss coal industry myths of co-existence, which suppress both the harms of coal mining on rural production and coal's contribution to climate change. I describe the recent history of Camberwell, distinguished by an intense politics of place in which the constellation of state and corporate extractive power has rendered residents' lives precarious, unhealthy and dishon-oured. Such conflicts marginalise the reality of climate change, requiring locals to take an urgent stand against the obliteration of life worlds in particular hotspots of extractive capitalism. I conclude with a discussion of the dialectic of perception and place as manifested in lived experiences of environmental change. Hunter Valley places and people provide a striking example of how this dialectic becomes a constitutive element of a wider political field in which quotidian worlds come into play.

Perceptions

Phenomenological analyses of place locate human perceptions in 'an entire teeming place-world', where 'sensations and spaces are themselves emplaced from the very first moment, and at every subsequent moment as well' (Casey 1997: 17–18). There is a dialectical relationship between cultural meanings and embodied perceptions: in Casey's words, 'the lived body is the material condition of possibility for the place-world while being itself a member of that same world' (1997: 24).

This embodied interdependence of people and places presented in the work of phenomenological theorists like Casey is a critique of the negation of place in Western modernity. Place, asserts Casey, is either premodern or postmodern; it has been obliterated in modern Western thought, 'where space and time have held such triumphant and exclusive sway' (1997: 20). However, the epochal determinism he attributes to Western thought does not necessarily extend to experiences of place in quotidian worlds. There is plenty of ethnographic evidence that Western modernity, and the naturalist ontologies that are part of its timescape, is not seamlessly dominant in every place (e.g. Feld and Basso, 1997). Casey's phrasing encompasses the ruling ideas of Western modernity – progress, developmentalism, hegemony of scientific knowledge, uniformly meas-ured and commodified time – but not necessarily the experience of people who live in this era. Ethnographic research is required to discern situational under-standings of people in specific places who are encountering, shaping and responding to environmental change in many different ways.

Places where people live call on the social researcher 'to see the *simultaneous and the successive as one*', as Goethe strove to do in his methodological approach to understanding natural phenomena (Nassar 2014: 305, emphasis in original). In the Hunter Valley surveys conducted by the author and colleagues, patterns of change and stability in responses over time foster 'an impression of the whole that does not destroy the particular' (Nassar 2014: 306), the whole in this case being the place worlds of selected Hunter Valley locales. In general, residents' reported observations of 12 climate-related environmental indicators declined between 2008 and 2011. In 2008, 30–60 per cent of respondents were observing a higher frequency of core climate change weather indicators like heat and drought. Upper Hunter residents were seeing significantly more prolonged dry spells but lower levels of intense fires, storms and flash flooding than their coastal cohort. In 2011, four weather indicators dropped significantly: prolonged drought observations decreased; perceptions of high-intensity bush fires and severe storms halved. In Lake Macquarie, reports of flash flooding halved to about 20 per cent. Only observations of hotter days increased, with half of all respondents reporting more 'hotter days', up from 35 per cent in 2008.[1]

The surveys also asked about seven climate related natural events including 'loss of native plants and animals', 'loss of fish and marine life', 'mature trees dying' and 'sea level rise'. In 2008, between 30 per cent and 70 per cent of respondents observed the seven climate-related natural events at baseline, but only three significant differences emerged. Lake Macquarie residents living near the water reported more loss of fish/marine life and sea level rise, while Upper Hunter residents saw more mature trees dying. In 2011, these area differences persisted. However, reports of all 'natural event' sightings significantly declined, particularly for loss of plants, animals and marine life. Much smaller declines were reported for mature trees dying and changes to rhythms of nature. Upper Hunter residents still reported considerable tree deaths (45 per cent) and changes to nature's rhythm (55 per cent), while a majority in all areas saw changing seasonal patterns (60–68 per cent). Significantly fewer Lake Macquarie residents reported noticing sea level rise.

Across most of the 12 climate change indicators, 60–70 per cent of respondents at both survey periods reported they would be 'very concerned' if these events occurred over the next 20 years. Rural and coastal dwellers' concerns differed. Significantly more Upper Hunter residents felt intense concern about events affecting agricultural productivity in their rural districts – hotter days, arrival of new plants/animals and changing seasonal patterns, while Lake Macquarie residents were concerned about marine life loss and flash floods. Lake Macquarie residents living near the water were the most concerned about sea level rise.

The dialectical relationship between cultural meanings and embodied perceptions is very apparent in these responses. The results can be contextualised in larger patterns of weather and environmental changes that residents experience, either directly or through historical and generational narratives. The effect of local weather conditions prior to our two surveys is unmistakable. In 2008 the Hunter region had just emerged from the Millennium Drought (see Chapter 3) that had wrought damaging environmental, economic, social and mental health consequences, especially for rural producers (Hart *et al.* 2011; Polain *et al.* 2011). In the previous year, a 'once in 100 years' East Coast cyclone (the 'Pasha Bulker storm' discussed in Chapter 3) had severely damaged the Lower Hunter with torrential rain, flooding, extensive power cuts and loss of life. Respondents' perceptions of more frequent droughts and mature trees dying in the Upper Hunter and storms and floods in Lake Macquarie are associated with these events.

Just before the 2011 follow-up interviews, an unprecedented number of extreme weather events struck Eastern Australia, with a highly destructive 'inland tsunami' in Queensland, followed by severe tropical Cyclone Yasi and a week-long extreme heatwave in the Hunter reaching temperatures (43°C) normally associated with arid inland areas of Australia. Respondents' perceptions of hotter days rose, with all other climate indicators dropping. Despite the ongoing flood trauma in Queensland, and its associated media coverage, coastal informants did not generalise these distant conditions to increased concerns for their local area.

Results also show that while weather-related observations are influenced by recent local events, observations of other natural events, such as changes in seasonal patterns (earlier spring/longer summer) and usual rhythms of nature (plants flowering), are stable and tied to long-term observations and beliefs about the environment and nature as exemplified in the natural cycles framework discussed in Chapter 3. While climate scientists and some anthropologists (see, for example, Ingold 2007; Kempton *et al.* 1996) suggest that lay people cannot detect climate change signals amid the background noise of weather fluctuations, it is evident that many think they do perceive such changes and do so differentially across indicators and time. Reser *et al.* (2012: 172) concur, saying: 'We must seriously ask ourselves how else would most individuals be able to make psychological and adaptive sense out of the complexity of climate change, but through such analogical thinking and personal and local experience'.

The embodied nature of these perceptions of environmental change is apparent in the open-ended optional comments made by respondents in each iteration of the survey:

> My husband and I discussed climate change seven years ago. My attitude has completely changed as I can see the changes happening. My block of units has already been built up to protect from floods.
>
> (Lake Macquarie resident 2011)

Long-term residents (median = 25 years residence) tend to report small changes in the frequency of climate-related weather and natural events in their area that contribute to their stance on climate change:

> When we first came here in the late 60s/early 70s there was frost on the sports playing fields but we haven't seen this for years.
>
> (Lake Macquarie resident 2008)

By the same token, verbatim comments frequently drew on past experiences as justification for current perceptions of indicators that are *not* changing:

> *I have lived here for 58 years right on the lake and the water level has not risen at all.*
>
> (Lake Macquarie resident 2008)

> *I haven't seen sea levels rise and I live across the road from the beach.*
>
> (Lake Macquarie resident 2008)

Farmland residents were seen, by themselves and others, to be more attuned to changing indicators of climate, by virtue of their physical proximity to 'the land':

> *A lot of farming people are already aware of the changing climate before climate change was mentioned. Not enough notice is being taken of people that live on the land who have had more experience with the changing climate, and have experience with irrigation and water saving.*
>
> (Upper Hunter resident 2008)

Some respondents observed that all sorts of pollution caused degradation, and such pollution was also responsible for climate change:

> *Where I live now in Belmont … the lagoon used to be four times bigger than it is now. That's why there is no prawns and fish – it doesn't filter. I reckon if they unblocked it and cleaned it up a bit there would be more wildlife. It is really polluted like with old cars. That is why we are getting climate change, everything is so polluted.*
>
> (Lake Macquarie resident 2011)

Other people, particularly in the Upper Hunter, saw pollution from coal mines as a cause of environmental damage, but did not link this to climate change:

> *Blue tongue lizards were not around this year. There was lots of frogs though. Nine of my gold fish died within two months of each other. There is too much pollution from the mines and the dust is not dampened down. It's bad on windy days. The government is not giving enough to the people in the valley for our health, such as asthma. We feel forgotten by the government.*
>
> (Upper Hunter resident 2011)

> *Fill the coal mines in and stop them from creating the havoc of gases and pollution.*
>
> (Upper Hunter resident 2008)

The implicit 'they' in these locutions is the authorities – government and powerful corporations who are not looking after citizens whose lives and places are becoming disordered by the planetary damage they observe all around them.

Environmental change, and for some, climate change, cannot be separated from other depredations of government, industry and modern life whose impacts are observed in the surrounding environment and in people's own bodies:

> *Mines and power stations are doing much more damage than farming. They are affecting people's health.*
>
> (Upper Hunter resident 2011)

The institutions that structure economy and society purport to maintain an ordered world but are experienced as creators of disorder in many forms of sentient life, from fish to frogs and lizards to people. There is a common if not universal language of political critique embedded in these embodied perceptions, which for those in close proximity, often turns on the mining and burning of coal.

Coal encroachment

'The history of capitalism is punctuated by intense phases of spatial reorganization' wrote David Harvey (1993: 7), remarking on the intensification of these changes in the era of highly mobile corporate capital since the 1970s. The Hunter region has a diversified economic and employment base, but coal-based developmentalism and the notion of limitless growth dominate industry and government discourse (Evans 2008). State and federal planning and regulatory frameworks, energy policies, tax and investment regimes favour fossil fuels above other forms of energy, and the mining sector benefits from extensive subsidies (Campbell 2014). On an international scale, growth coalitions dependent on capital accumulation through spatial reorganisation activate forms of cooptation and coercion (Harvey 1993: 9) that achieve a convergence of economy, ideology and politics to establish the hegemony of coal in cultural life. In Australia, Guy Pearse has referred to this syndrome as 'quarry vision' (2009). A recent survey of Hunter residents found that they 'had a heavily inflated impression of the coal industry's economic importance' (Campbell 2014: 2).

This view is cultivated by the industry, in academic forums, websites, events and publications. *Mining: The Foundation of Our Region* was the issue title of a Hunter business magazine in 2009, while the slogan for the 2015 Hunter Coal Festival sponsored by the Singleton Business Chamber was *Your Industry, Your Community, Your Festival: Industry and Community Together*. Major party politicians decry Greens parties, environmentalist organisations and other critics of the coal industry as 'eco-traitors' who 'are really about destruction, because they want to destroy our way of life and our biggest industry' as one federal government backbencher recently complained (Medhora 2015).

While never Australia's 'biggest industry', coal was integral to nineteenth-century colonisation, industrialisation and food production. Mining of Hunter coal began early and grew apace. Official statistics are imprecise and patchy over long periods of time, but they broadly depict the steady growth of a coal dependent energy economy from the late nineteenth century, aligned with most industrialised nations at that time (Mitchell 2009). By 1950, annual production nationally had reached 11 million tonnes (Mt) of saleable black coal, with most used for domestic electricity production and the manufacture of iron and steel (*Sydney Morning Herald* 1950). In the post-World War II years of economic reconstruction and assertion of new consumer appetites, energy demand was high but competition from another fossil fuel, oil, kept a brake on production rates. In 1960, Australian collieries produced 23 Mt, with 1.6 Mt exported (Huleatt 1981). More than 75 per cent of this coal was from New South Wales (NSW), and most of that from the rich seams of the Hunter region coalfields. In the Hunter Valley, coal mines were the centre of working communities from Lake Macquarie to Cessnock. Underground mines predominated, and by the mid-twentieth century, many of the Hunter mines were owned by Broken Hill Proprietary Company (BHP) and other steel producers, or by the NSW government, contracted to supply coal to government-owned power generators.

In the 1960s, the country embarked on the path of large-scale exports of coal and iron ore, responding to demand from the burgeoning industrial economies of East Asia. The rise of the Japanese steel-making industry created a flourishing market for coking coal exports, and by 1970 Australia was producing 45 Mt of saleable black coal, with 18 Mt exported, mostly to Japan (Huleatt 1981). Domestically, most coal was used for electricity generation, with iron and steel works consuming a lesser but still significant proportion (51 per cent and 32 per cent respectively in 1970). Increasing demand for coal was met by development of open-cut coal mining technology, part of a radical restructuring of rural spatial relations in the 1970s. Coal operations emerged from their underground world and manifested across increasing swathes of rural and bushland landscapes in new magnitudes of scale.

The massive mines and final voids that now dominate much of the Upper Hunter landscape are manifestations of what Stuart Kirsch has termed the 'colliding ecologies' of large-scale resource extraction projects (2014). The largest open-cut mines in the Hunter Valley are now each producing between 10 and 20 Mt per annum and extend over thousands of hectares.[2] Overall the 42 open-cut and 15 underground pits in the Hunter Valley have a current production capacity of over 200 Mt of coal and leases for coal mining and exploration extend over 64 per cent of the Upper Hunter Valley floor (Lock the Gate Alliance 2014; McManus and Connor 2013).

In boom times the mines have produced superprofits for corporations and healthy dividends for shareholders. Coal mining also provides revenue for the government. In NSW, royalties are calculated on an *ad valorem* basis: the more tonnes of saleable coal extracted, the higher the royalty revenue. In the favourable conditions that prevailed between 2003 and 2011, royalties from coal production more than tripled, reaching AUS$1.36 billion in 2011–12 with slight declines in subsequent years (NSW Trade & Investment 2014b). Revenue from exploration and mining leases can yield hundreds of millions of dollars for larger mines during boom conditions. In the regional context, coal is a relatively small

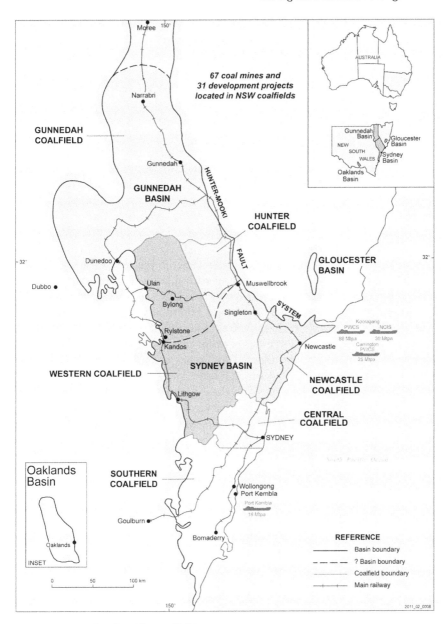

Figure 4.1 New South Wales coalfields
Source: NSW Trade & Investment, 2011

contributor to the economy compared to other sectors like construction, manufacturing, retail services, public administration, health and education. About 5 per cent of the Hunter workforce, or about 13,000 people, were directly employed in the industry in 2011 (Campbell 2014). At least 2,000 workers have lost their jobs in the coal industry's recent downturn.

The pitfalls of reliance on a small number of resource commodities have become all too evident in the boom and bust conditions of twenty-first century Australia, but these conditions also prevailed in earlier times. As early as the 1850s, Hunter coal mines and other industries experienced a labour shortage as workers joined the gold rushes in NSW and Victoria, just as workers in recent years have fled manufacturing and rural industries to enjoy high wage mining jobs. East Asian industrial economies have fuelled a hectic pace of minerals extraction since the 1960s, skewing investment capital into high-return mining, especially black coal and iron ore. State and federal governments have become reliant on economic growth, taxes and royalties from these industries, and have developed a generous suite of subsidies, planning legislation, greenhouse emissions concessions and benign regulatory frameworks to protect these extractive forms of capital accumulation.

Ownership of coalmines and exploration leases in the Newcastle and Hunter coalfields is mainly in the hands of multinational resource companies including BHP Billiton, Anglo American, Peabody, Rio Tinto and Glencore, and state-owned enterprises (SOEs) such as Yancoal (Yanzhou Coal Mining Company). East Asian corporations such as Mitsui, Mitsubishi, Posco and Idemitsu are prominent in the joint venture partnerships that increasingly characterise the ownership structure of mines. Bloomfield Group, which owns Rix's Creek mine (Figure 4.2) is one of the few Australian-owned private companies operating in the region. The primary business of all these companies is the export market. In 2014, about 75 per cent of the 201 Mt coal produced from the Hunter coal chain was exported (Campbell 2014).[3] NSW has participated in Australia's 'resources boom' through exploitation of coal resources, and this exploitation has become more intensive with increasing production to maintain profits in the current climate of falling prices. Until the resource economy decline over the last three years, coal exports contributed to an expansion of the economy, high government credit ratings and favourable terms of trade, along with high profits and dividends for companies and shareholders. The industry promotes its employment opportunities, but coal mining is no longer a labour intensive industry. In 2011 only 1.5 per cent of the NSW labour force was employed in coal mining (Campbell 2014). This amounted to 29,798 employees (Australian Bureau of Statistics 2012), but by 2015, 4,000 of these jobs had gone as a consequence of declining industry conditions (Lannin 2014).[4]

In the last decade, large-scale exploration and mining has extended to methane gas found in coal seams, one of the sources of 'unconventional gas'. Export demand for gas has increased and infrastructure developed as the Port of Gladstone in Queensland has opened up the previously protected Eastern Australia domestic market to higher prices in overseas markets. The centre of production is Queensland where 98 per cent of Australia's unconventional gas is produced, and where there are now more than 3,500 exploration and production wells in operation. The industry has been slower to develop in NSW, with about

Figure 4.2 Rix's Creek mine northwest of Singleton
Source: Allan Chawner, 2008

90 pilot and producing wells reported in early 2015 (NSW Trade & Investment 2015). In NSW, successive state governments have allocated petroleum explo- ration licenses (PELs) for coal seam gas, which together with pending applications and production licenses extended over about 50 per cent of the state's area including suburbs, towns, state forests, state conservation areas and productive agricultural lands (NSW Trade & Investment 2014a). Dozens of companies hold licenses including multinational corporation Santos and Australian subsidiaries of multinationals like Shell, Mitsui and PetroChina. Until July 2015, almost the entire Hunter Valley had been held under PELs allo- cated to AGL Upstream Investments Pty Ltd, which also holds the production licences for the wells at Camden, an outer suburb southwest of Sydney.

In both NSW and Queensland, there has been a vigorous mobilisation of resi- dents' groups against coal seam gas (CSG) extraction, much of it coordinated by the national organisation Lock the Gate Alliance. The active pilot and produc- tion wells in NSW at the time of writing are located in Camden and near the town of Gloucester. The electoral backlash against CSG amid fears about its hydraulic fracturing technology has been strong. While the industry invokes the spectre of a looming domestic gas 'shortage' (in fact precipitated by higher export prices), farmers and other residents demand caution in the face of hazards to health, water supply, biodiversity and productive land (Mercer *et al.* 2014). Not yet the juggernaut that the coal industry has become in NSW, CSG production appears more amenable to citizen resistance and regulatory restraint, and indeed anti-CSG electoral pressure prior to the 2015 NSW state election prompted both major parties to develop CSG policies to address the concerns of residents and rural industries, with the government extinguishing pending licence applications and freezing all new applications prior to the election.

Coal economy, coal politics and coal myths are a daily reality in media discourse. The coverage took a different turn in 2014, as thermal coal prices slid to about 43 per cent of the resource boom peak of US$142 per tonne in 2011 (McHugh 2015). Unemployment and mine closures are now the big stories of the day (Hagemann 2015). But even while industry analysts foretell long-term decline in demand (*Economist* 2015), mining lobbyists predict the next upswing in the commodity cycle:

> The Hunter has some of the best quality coal in the world, an experienced and highly accomplished mining workforce, and the world's largest coal export port. So, while the local industry is experiencing short-term challenges, the long-term prospects are good, provided we can continue to meet the future demand.
>
> (Galilee 2014)

The Panglossian prognoses of coal lobbyists are belied to some extent by evidence of declining coal production employment and mine closures in the Hunter. Stuart Rosewarne has suggested, however, that the vertical integration of mining with steel making and power generation through joint partnerships with East Asian energy and manufacturing corporations may protect the commodity from too quickly becoming the stranded asset that is the target of opponents' divestment campaigns. In capitalist hierarchies of accumulation, multi-stranded transnational links consolidate coal's place in the fossil fuel value chain: mining companies, industrial conglomerates, power generators and states (Rosewarne 2013).

A 'devastating place to be a traditional owner'

Aboriginal people have not willingly participated in the marginalisation of place worlds that David Harvey and Edward Casey analyse as diagnostic of Western modernity. The coal industry perpetuates the violent history of environmental change that has characterised the Aboriginal experience of their country since settlement, but refuses to engage in political dialogue with contemporary Aboriginal people whose country is appropriated. The cultural distinctiveness of the Hunter's Aboriginal people is acknowledged in very general terms in many coal company websites, under rubrics such as 'Society, Our Contribution' and 'Community Support and Development'. On its webpage, BHP Billiton declares:

> BHP Billiton's operations embrace respect, nurture mutually beneficial relationships and provide opportunities for inclusion and advancement of Indigenous peoples ... BHP Billiton also aims to identify who is connected

to and uses the land in order to establish an effective community consultation and engagement program.

(BHP Billiton 2015)

These are discourses of consultation and negotiation, not of rights or land ownership; they avoid the hard political questions about dispossession, dislocation and harm that mining inflicts. In this and other ways, the impact of the colonial past continues to reverberate in Hunter demographics and lives. The original inhabitants of the region now form a small fraction of its population, with residents of Anglo-Celtic origins in the majority.[5] Approximately 9,000 people or 3.4 per cent of residents self-identified as Aboriginal or Torres Strait Islander in the 2011 census.[6] It is not surprising, given their history of violent dispossession, that Aboriginal people form a socio-economically disadvantaged and politically fragmented minority in the Hunter, as in the rest of Southeast Australia.

After decades of segregation on missions followed by relocation into towns, and years of land rights demands, the NSW Aboriginal Land Rights Act was passed in 1983. The act mandates the development and preservation of land rights, which are bestowed by limited freehold or perpetual lease grants, and which now form the basis of 119 Local Aboriginal Land Councils. The Land Rights Act aimed to promote self-determination for communities and protection of 'culture, identity and heritage' but in many ways served to further control Aboriginal people through bureaucratic structures (Macdonald 1988). Gaynor Macdonald (1988: 38) argues that:

> The Aboriginal Land Rights Act is not about 'rights' except in so far as it changed the form of tenure of lands previously reserved for Aboriginal use to one of inalienable freehold title. Of over 12,000 hectares reserved in earlier years, only 2,300 hectares remained in Aboriginal hands anyway. Aborigines protested that the land, which had been illegally revoked by governments in previous years, had not been included or compensated for. Whilst the government conceded that the revocations had been illegal, it drew up legislation, passed the same night as the Land Rights Act, which retrospectively legalised all previous revocations.

By contrast, the Federal Government Native Title Act (1993) provides for 'the recognition, under Australian common law, of pre-existing Indigenous rights and interests according to traditional laws and customs' rather than rights granted by governments (Australian Government Attorney-General's Department 2014). The NSW government differentiates the two sets of rights as follows: 'Native title rights and interests held by traditional owners are inalienable. However, lands granted to local Aboriginal land councils are granted as freehold and can, subject to some restrictions, be alienated' (Law Handbook 2012: 50).

It has been challenging for Aboriginal people in NSW to obtain recognition of Native Title. The violent displacement and landscape alteration that took place from the beginnings of colonial settlement make it difficult to demonstrate 'traditional connection' to the land, which has become a requirement of case law since the Yorta Yorta Aboriginal community lost its native title claim against the State of Victoria in 1998. The court judged that 'the tide of history has washed away any real acknowledgment of traditional law and any real observance of traditional customs' resulting in 'the foundation of native title' to disappear, and 'once traditional native title expires, the Crown's radical title expands to a full beneficial title, for then there is no other proprietor than the Crown' (Federal Court of Australia 1998).

This is a pressing problem for Upper Hunter Aboriginal people who are heavily impacted by the 'tide of coal mining'. One Wanaruah man who is active in negotiations with mining companies described his people's situation thus:

> *We went as far-reaching as the Liverpool Ranges, down the Great Dividing Ranges to the McDonald River, across the Yango [Creek] and back up the Barrington Tops. It's well within the main economic hub of the State's major resources. So we're copping an absolute hammering from industry at the moment. Devastating place to be a traditional owner.*

(Judd interview 2014)[7]

The absence of native title in turn disadvantages Aboriginal groups whose rights as 'traditional owners' are weakly specified under NSW law. The NSW National Parks and Wildlife Act (1974) outlines the criteria for the identification of sites, objects and places of significance to Aboriginal people, and the measures in place for their protection. Proponents of development projects are required to consult with registered Aboriginal owners who have 'cultural association with particular land' (Department of Environment Climate Change and Water 2010: v). After the specified consultation requirements have been followed, the proponent can apply for an Aboriginal Heritage Impact Permit when 'harm cannot be avoided' (Department of Environment Climate Change and Water 2010: iii). This is in effect a licence to destroy Aboriginal heritage even where traditional owners object, as regulations permit the Department, tribunal and court system to assess the heritage as of insufficient significance.

Compensation for heritage destruction may be paid by the proponent, but this in turn can divide groups with different histories of relationship to country. The procedures for Aboriginal heritage evaluations create many tensions among rival groups and individuals claiming to have 'cultural associations' with mining-impacted lands. Judd commented:

> *And we get this influx of mobs coming in the country who are not from there, who are getting paid fee for service to say what they want. So we'll argue about something and say, 'no you can't touch this, this creek leads into a place of grinding or axe head sharpening stones or grinding groove sites, which represents a continued connection of coexistence of our people in this particular part of the Valley. The campsites where all the women were, the kids, and over there you've got circumcision sites and this site and that site and so on'. But you'll have mobs then turn*

*around who are not from there and say 'there's plenty of those grinding grooves'
because they don't understand the importance of why it was selected.*

(Judd interview 2014)

The situation of competition for short-term heritage consultation employment
and the compensation arrangements work against any unified Aboriginal voice
opposing mining in the Hunter region, and is compounded by the divisive relations intrinsic to state and federal land rights legislation. Any group making a
claim is likely to have it contested by another group. For example, the Awabakal
and Guringai native title claim to tracts of country from Hornsby to Maitland is
challenged by Wanaruah and Worimi groups (Kelly 2013a), and the Worimi
dispute the Awabakal right to their Land Council premises in Newcastle (Smee
2011), in both cases because of disputes about the boundaries of traditional lands.
These divisive legal and regulatory regimes compound entrenched problems for
Aboriginal people, which are acute for Hunter Valley groups who can only stand
by while the remaining material traces of their traditional occupation of their
land – allowable evidence under the Native Title Act – is obliterated by the
encroachment of open-cut mines and burgeoning CSG drilling. Like the settler
residents, any climate change worries of Wanaruah and other groups are overshadowed by the daily struggles against fossil fuel companies and strongly
pro-development governments in a legislative context that offers scant protection for affected groups and individuals.

Place-based perceptions: Jerrys Plains

Indigenous people dwelling on ancestral lands have countless generations of
embodied sense-making in long inhabited places, forming the paradigmatic case
of integrated, emplaced identities – an idealised case in the Hunter Valley
context. At the other end of the 'place-bound' spectrum, Harvey among others
has proposed that highly mobile postmodern subjects are disconnected from
'older material and territorial definitions of place', opening the way for new
place-making to occur, and new forms of place-based identity, perhaps territorial,
always metaphorical and psychological (1993: 4). Long-established communities
of rural dwellers, persisting over multiple generations, exist in apparently incon-
gruous conditions of postmodernity. These are conditions of rupture and violence
– familiar and valued place-based identities linked to economic production on
agricultural properties can be born from settler appropriations of Indigenous
lands in violent colonial pasts; and of mobility and change – producers can now
be hostage to the fickle fate of food and fibre demand in uber-globalised
commodity markets. The social relations of capitalism reorganise space with each
crisis and each new cycle of accumulation (Harvey 1993: 7).

Extractive capitalism brings a new cycle of accumulation and material practices that destroy agricultural communities. The research placed a high priority
on investigating the place-based perceptions of environmental change in
affected farming communities as the processes of extraction occur. In Upper

Hunter settlements, we find a settler consciousness of place worlds that is created from the people dwelling in land and waterscapes from season to season, practicing agriculture and the art of rural social life. One of the study areas for the research project was the farming district of Jerrys Plains, located to the west of the town of Singleton on Wanaruah country, in a fertile valley traversed by the Hunter River and its tributary, the Goulburn River. During on-farm visits by the researchers between 2008 and 2010, residents were asked about their family histories and perceptions of change in the local area, as well as indicators of climate change and possible impact on their enterprises. Although we were not asking specifically about conflicts with mines, an important context of the research was major disputes Jerrys Plains residents were having with the US-based multinational corporation, Peabody Energy, over plans to expand its Wambo Mine open-cut operations close to the Wollemi National Park, and its existing underground operation under the historic village and cemetery.

Jerrys Plains was explored in the early decades of European settlement, at a time when the Aboriginal people who lived there were still able to challenge intruders in their country. Even so, colonists were receiving land grants for farms by the 1820s, creating one of the earliest rural settlements in the Upper Hunter. By mid-nineteenth century, as disease, force and depopulation overcame Wanaruah resistance, the colonial government, responding to growing population pressure, had surveyed, gazetted and sold the land to settler farmers. Many

Figure 4.3 Coal mine near Jerrys Plains. Drill holes for blasting preparation in
foreground, farmland in background

Source: Allan Chawner, 2008

of the residents of Jerrys Plains have ties to the district going back several generations; marriage within the 'farming families' of the Upper Hunter and neighbouring districts is common and social networks are dense.

These days, the Aboriginal and settler inhabitants of Jerrys Plains face a different sort of intruder: the rapidly expanding coal and CSG mining operations of some of the world's largest resource corporations – Anglo American, Peabody, BHP Billiton, Rio Tinto and Glencore among others. The district is bordered by internationally renowned thoroughbred horse studs such as Coolmore and Darley (McManus *et al.* 2013). For almost a decade, these once conservative bastions of rural communities have formed a well-organised opposition to mine expansion into horse breeding districts with their campaign 'Protect Our Industries', under the auspices of the Hunter Thoroughbred Breeders Association (HTBA) (2015). They are joined by the district's winegrowers, organised in the Hunter Valley Protection Alliance (HVPA), whose slogan is 'Committed to safeguarding the Hunter Valley, Australia's oldest and most visited wine producing region – for future generations' (2015). The many beef cattle, dairy and mixed farming operations in the district have also been vocal in their opposition to

Figure 4.4 Breath-taking Upper Hunter
Source: Peter Lewis, *Newcastle Herald* 2009

mining on agricultural land, a position supported in principle by the NSW Farmers Association. In the lead-up to the NSW State election in 2015, the Hunter Valley Wine and Tourism Association and the HTBA called on both major parties to support 'a 10km buffer around the equine and viticulture critical industry clusters, with new open cut and underground coal mines and coal seam gas mining banned' (ABC News 2015).

The journey northwest along the Golden Highway, from south of Singleton to Jerrys Plains, is disorienting, travelling as one does through a rapid succession of verdant farming properties, horse studs and woodlands interrupted by giant road-side bunds with sparse vegetation that hide the workings of the open cut mines. Derelict farmhouses and outbuildings on run down properties acquired by mines dot the landscape. Villages like Warkworth and Mt Thorley no longer exist, sucked into the mining voids. However, the sense of disorder, of 'no place' engendered by the mines is belied by the roar of machinery and dust plumes coming from behind the bunds: these are places where people work and companies reap profits. The intensification and expansion of mining operations in the years since the research project started is palpable in the increased dust, noise, heavy traffic, loaded coal trains and night lights that impact on the highway. When we asked Rosalyn, a beef cattle farmer in Jerrys Plains, if people she knew were aware of the environmental changes wrought by the mines, she exclaimed, 'You'd have to be blind Freddy not to be aware of it around here'.

Despite the ongoing conflict over Peabody's Wambo Mine expansion and the intensity of mining operations in the area, 'a scar on society' according to Rosalyn, when we questioned farmers about the most important environmental changes affecting them, drought and lack of water were on everyone's mind. The first trips to Jerrys Plains took place in 2008, just a few months after the Millennium Drought had broken in the area. Producers' experiences had been harrowing. Craig, a viticulturist, had a 'disastrous season' in 2007. Cameron said, 'We've never had a drought like we just had'. He had planted crops of wheat each of the last five years – all had failed. Rosalyn reported only two good seasons in the last 19 years, seasons 'where it was lovely, we had good growth, we had ground moisture, we had run-off, the whole bit'. The drought had caused Blake to let his dairy farm run down, and he now worked off-farm in a nearby coal mine. He commented:

> [The drought has] driven farmers to go and get jobs off the farm. Farming becomes a second job … It takes the pressure off the land use in the sense that you are not trying to push more and more productivity out of your land every year.
>
> (Blake interview 2008)

Increasing numbers of hotter days were also a major concern, especially for grape growers who were already farming at the warmer end of ideal conditions in the industry. Deep-rooted grape vines are hardy in drier weather but hotter temperatures are a significant threat to yield and quality. Jared, a grower who produced his own label organic wines, explained that small incremental changes in day temperatures over 15°C, resulting in higher 'degree days', as well as rising night temperatures, affect the quality of wines and their regional distinctiveness. Grapes matured more quickly and lacked flavour. He commented: 'In my experience of 25 years, the average beginning of harvest date has come forward in the Hunter Valley by two to three weeks'.

Shaun, also a full-time grower and winemaker, had a similar story, reporting fewer winter frosts and earlier budburst. He said:

> *The most obvious thing that's emerging is the early ripening of the fruit. At the rate it's going it'll be ripening by Christmas time … From a quality perspective it's quite negative as the quicker the fruit ripens, the less chance it has to develop all the flavour precursors, all the complexity that you find in wine … Some varieties are just unsustainable in this situation.*
>
> (Shaun interview 2009)

Long-term crops like fruit trees and vines can be risky. The viticulturists, with substantial investments in slow-maturing vines, felt they had little scope to adapt to the changing growing conditions. Craig exclaimed, 'On a practical level, what do you do when you've got a very fixed crop situation like this?'.

Like the people living in direct dependence on land and waters discussed in Chapter 1, Jerrys Plains farmers had observed a new and worrying unpredictability of the weather. 'Incredible variability' in rainfall, 'no real pattern to it', was a threat to producers, for whom water is the critical factor of production. Cameron, who owns an agricultural supplies business as well as his farm, reflected on the recent years of drought:

> *People were talking about, you know, how things just aren't right anymore. The confidence in the seasons then started to wane, people weren't prepared to put their crop in. People weren't prepared to spend the money any more, and that impacted us greatly and still is today.*
>
> (Cameron interview 2008)

Climate change, whether anthropogenic or not, was not necessarily linked to producers' experiences of these challenging environmental changes. Despite the decline of his dairy due to drought, off-farm miner Blake was not sure that it was connected to climate change. The natural cycles thinking documented in the previous chapter provided an alternative and more reassuring explanation for many. Craig analysed it this way:

> *The drought was starting to force people to change, because you just couldn't go on doing what you were doing … But now the rain's come, everyone's been able to slip back, you know. Yeah, they kind of, they go, 'Oh right, it was just a cycle'.*
>
> (Craig interview 2008)

Like the respondents in the regional survey discussed in the previous chapter, climate change can be a 'touchy subject'. Craig went on:

It's not a subject that anyone really wants to discuss … Accepting that climate change is a reality, I mean there's a big resistance to that. A lot of people will just go, 'Ah, no, there's always been cycles, we've seen them'. The big drought of '37 or whatever.

(Craig interview 2008)

Among the nearby thoroughbred breeders studied by McManus and colleagues towards the end of the Millennium Drought period in 2008, climate change was a similarly divisive issue. One breeder remarked to the researchers, 'We are going through a dry spell and we have been through these dry spells before. It's not something unique to the twenty-first century' (quoted in McManus *et al.* 2013: 125). Others expressed concern about the impacts: 'It's an issue. With climate change if this ceases to become reasonably high value rainfall area with good access to water then all the other things decline as well, so those things snowball' (quoted in McManus *et al.* 2013: 126).

For producers like Craig, Shaun and Jared who are all involved in the climatically hypersensitive business of grape growing and who are not descended from farming families in the district, anthropogenic climate change is a reality they acknowledge they must deal with. Jared thought the Hunter growers had been given a reprieve by the shift in consumer preferences from more temperature sensitive red wines to more resilient white wine varieties. They all had an eye to a radically different future, and were all attempting to implement environmentally and economically sustainable cultivation practices to prepare for the droughts and hotter weather that lay ahead. Irrigating more efficiently, increasing soil carbon, planting new varieties and seeking south- rather than north-facing paddocks, were all part of their adaptation strategies. They were aware that the industry was under stress, in the Hunter and elsewhere, partly because of climate change but also because of a long-term glut of grapes that had driven prices down below a viable 'bottom line'. Industry peak bodies like the Australian Wine and Brandy Association were not addressing climate change issues, and viticulturists struggling to survive in the short term were uninterested in long-term projections and adaptive practices. Craig reflected:

The reality at the moment is that everybody is struggling for survival in the grape industry because prices are so low, below the cost of production … So the issues of changing varieties are just completely irrelevant, the choice at the moment of some people is, to carry on or bring in a bulldozer and get rid of them.

(Craig interview 2008)

In these circumstances, responding to climate change was irrelevant, in Craig's scenario:

At the moment, if [climate change projections] came up at a meeting, and somebody said, 'Well, you know, in fifteen years time, or twenty years time, it may be unviable to grow grapes here', there'd just be a kind of uneasy laughter and it would be like, 'Yeah, well you know, I might be unviable in two years' time'.

(Craig interview 2008)

There is a sense here that climate change is a 'greenie' issue, part of a radical urban politics that is culturally foreign to rural dwellers. 'There's a strong feeling of "The bloody greenies will get you"' if farmers were to give credence to climate change, according to Craig. His comments give a sense of the 'effortful cultural work' (Eliasoph 1997: 639) that maintains more conservative farmers' disengagement with climate change.

Coal mining is a problem for rural productivity: farmers link the mines in their immediate surroundings to water scarcity, pollution and other hardships they experience. They rarely, however, discuss the links between mining and climate change, or specifically, coal and greenhouse gases (GHGs). Dust, blasting, water shortages and the like are sharply perceived negative changes that demand immediate attention; climate change is not, or much less so. Robert, a long-established dairy farmer, deplored the scarcity of water, made worse by the heavy allocations to nearby coal mining operations and coal-fired power stations. Rosalyn noticed the hotter, drier, dustier climate near her place that she attributed to climate change but which was made worse by the removal of natural vegetation and machinery operation in mining areas. Saline discharge and runoff from mines polluted the rivers, which are 'full of crap and mud', complained Cameron. Shaun observed that 'Upper Hunter [viticulture] is decimated, absolutely, by the expansion of the mines'. These views are similar to those of the thoroughbred breeders in the district who perceived coal mining as a major threat to their industry and who mobilised against it in the early years of the recent boom (McManus *et al.* 2013: 103–4). Nonetheless, several of the farmers we interviewed made qualified comments in support of the mining industry, because of the employment it offered as well as welcome cash flow in small-town businesses, a 'fall-back' for a struggling rural sector. Hopes were expressed that clean coal technology may ameliorate environmental damage. Robert felt it was better to mine coal in Australia than China or other countries where workers' conditions were unsafe and production was more polluting. These themes of clean coal and ethical responsibility to produce resonate with prevalent discursive fields that were shaping national climate policy regimes at the time (Christoff 2013).

Myths of co-existence

Understandings of landscape change are threaded through with mythical themes – of decline and destruction on the one hand, of growth and a prosperous future on the other. New myths articulated as part of opposition to coal and CSG mining in NSW are particularly evident in rural communities where productive landscapes and settlements are being irreversibly destroyed by fossil fuel corporations. Mining-affected inhabitants start to reimagine their future as something unwelcome, disconnected with the present and out of their control – what Benson and Kirsch have referred to as a 'politics of resignation' (2010). Corporate interests, and the government agencies that support them, present paternalistic myths of co-existence founded on independent state regulatory processes, reliable scientific knowledge and environmental responsibility. On its website, the NSW Minerals Council (NSWMC) states: 'Mining is a temporary land use and when mining is complete, we restore the land to valuable post-mining uses that are determined by the government' (NSW Mining 2013a). Each set of myths conceals as much as it reveals – of lived experience, ruling values, ethical imperatives and material realities. Corporate myths reverberate through the commercial and civic circles of the towns that serve as hubs to extractive industries. The Business Chamber and local council of Singleton recently sponsored a 'Hunter Coal Festival', 'aimed at bringing our region together in celebration of coexistence and of recognising the mining industry's contribution to the Hunter Valley' (Hunter Coal Festival 2015).

But corporate myths do not go unchallenged; the micro-processes of these forms of governmentality enable tactical opposition. Co-existence is a myth that can be questioned. The lived reality of the colliding ecologies of mining and rural production is part of residents' quotidian worlds. A few years ago, an outraged mayor of Muswellbrook exploded some of the industry myths of co-existence when his council's proposal for a 750-lot housing development in the town of Denman received objections from the NSW Department of Planning (infamous in coal-affected communities for its pro-development stance on mining), which wanted to reserve the land for a possible future coal mine:

> 'The failure to address urban land use conflict with coalmining has meant the community has become a second class consideration in the process now proposed to manage coalmining land use considerations in the Upper Hunter ... It is inconceivable that a coalmine, whether open cut or under-ground, could ever be permitted to adjoin residences in Denman, and yet that is the basis for these objections,' Cr Rush said.
>
> (McCarthy 2012)

The mayor's dystopian imaginings are not without foundation. A study of 'disappearing coal towns' in the Hunter by the *Newcastle Herald* documented the annihilation of many villages:

> Upper Hunter communities have disappeared off the map over the past 30 years – the result of relentless urbanisation and the region's mining boom. Those that remain, such as Bulga and Camberwell, are surrounded by massive open-cut projects that are likely to swallow them within 10 years.
>
> (Kelly 2013b)

Even in the few years since the Jerrys Plains' interviews, the political ecology has changed significantly. The benchmark price of Hunter Valley thermal coal has

Figure 4.5 Rio Tinto mine expansion vs. village of Bulga
Source: Peter Lewis, *Newcastle Herald*, 2015

plummeted due to declining East Asian demand and global overproduction. Applications for new mines have all but ceased. Some mines with high production costs have closed while others have expanded in order to maintain returns in a period of decreased profitability. 'Take or pay' contracts with rail and port companies have eroded profits and contribute to overproduction that further lowers prices (Ker 2014). Jerrys Plains and other upper Hunter settlements, surrounded by large multinational mining operations, have been greatly affected by mine extensions, but opposition to further incursions has also become more intense in the last few years. Organised campaigns by peak rural producer bodies have gained force as the mines have crept closer and ever more CSG exploration licenses have been handed out by the successive state governments. The thoroughbred breeders and wine and tourism industry associations have challenged the slogan of 'co-existence' head on: 'Co-existence is a term used to conceal and avoid dealing with decades of bad planning and the real and growing land use conflict issues now in the Hunter Valley. It is a term used to avoid taking hard decisions' (Hunter Thoroughbred Breeders Association and Hunter Valley Wine and Tourism Association 2015: 15).

The national organisation Lock the Gate Alliance has successfully mobilised thousands of rural residents to 'lock their gates' literally and figuratively, against coal seam gas projects. Driving through Jerrys Plains now, many farm gates display the bright yellow 'Lock the Gate to Coal and Gas Companies' placards. The report, *Unfair Shares: How Coal Mines Bought the Hunter River* declares:

> Vast quantities of water are now owned by coal mines. Agricultural industries have not only been pushed out of rich farmland but are grappling with worsening salinity caused by mining and are struggling to compete for the water they rely on for their livelihoods.
>
> (Lock the Gate Alliance 2014)

The minerals industry counters by minimising the water problem using large area statistics, not impacts on local water users, while perpetuating myths of technological solutions:

> The mining sector in NSW understands there is an environmental impact on the relatively small areas of land where mining takes place. However, we are seeking to meet the challenge of mitigating environmental impacts as much as possible. Not only does mining use only 1.4 per cent of NSW water resources, but it recycles 80 per cent of the water it uses. There is more to be done. Mining in NSW must rise to the challenge of ensuring that our mining techniques are world-class to mitigate any environmental impacts.
>
> (Galilee 2012a: 11)

Benson and Kirsch (2010: 465–6) have characterised this tactic as 'phase 2 corporation response' (phase 1 being denial):

> Phase 2 corporate response to critique involves the acknowledgment that a problem exists, that something is defective or harmful, and that the basis of critique has some scientific or ethical validity. However, phase 2 responses are primarily limited to symbolic gestures of recompense or amelioration.

Farmers advocate the precautionary principle of environmental ethics that is antithetical to the logic of extractive capitalism. They challenge corporate myths with assertions of their own self-image as careful custodians of local ecologies whose practical knowledge trumps industry modelling. As one vigneron cautioned: 'Until we have some real knowledge about what is going to happen with the aquifers, particularly in this valley where the geological formation is so interconnected, we shouldn't be tampering with things' (quoted in Kelly 2011: 15).

The discursive strategies of opponents – 'Enough is enough'; 'Dining not mining'; 'Foals not coals' – are countered by corporate publicity campaigns that play on what Stuart Kirsch has called the 'corporate oxymoron'. These are 'figures of speech [that] seek to disable the critical facilities of the consumer or shareholder with claims that require one to simultaneously subscribe to two contradictory beliefs, as suggested by the Orwellian notion *doublethink*' (Kirsch 2010: 88–9, emphasis in original). The chief executive officer of the NSWMC, for example, maintains that there is a 'close working relationship between miners and landholders in the Hunter … with viticulture, agriculture and mining all developing alongside one another' (Galilee 2012b: 12). Industry websites and media releases are peppered with catch phrases like 'clean coal' and 'sustainable mining'. The latest public campaign of the NSWMC, titled 'Hurt mining. Hurt NSW' has a webpage featuring personal stories from 'real miners and workers' whose jobs are threatened by community challenges to mines (NSW Mining 2013b). The 'World Class Miners' website of the NSWMC features examples of 'sustainable community development' sponsored by mining companies, including articles about agricultural projects that are flourishing on mining land: 'Mines and vines working together'; 'Canola, wheat and barley grown on mining land'; 'Hunter Valley coal mine producing olive oil'; 'Cattleman and coal mine unearth the formula for shared success' (NSW Mining 2012b). The economics of these 'success stories' – the bottom line for every farmer – are not revealed. Rather, in a seeming miracle of transmogrification and oxymoronic excess, they extol the high-quality food that 'mines produce':

> Our NSW mines provide coal to keeps our lights on, and gold, copper and other minerals that help make our state a strong exporter. But some of our mines also produce top notch wines, Wagyu beef, gourmet olive oils and grains, showing that mining and farming can and do work together.
>
> (NSW Mining 2012a)

Miners whom we interviewed were more circumspect about the impact of their industry than the corporate hyperbole would imply. One mining union official, while generally positive about existing environmental regulations, reflected that ever-increasing production levels were linked to companies' greed for profits and could ultimately threaten workers' jobs:

> *We're supportive of the industry. We think it's important to have an industry that continues to grow and continues to rebuild itself. But the challenge for us ultimately is when is enough enough? So for example take a mine that produces somewhere between 20 and 30 million tonne of coal a year. If that mine only produces 10 tonne a year, then obviously it's going to last longer, which keeps us all employed longer.*
>
> (Ryan interview 2014)

Nelson, a miner with relatives working in nearby horse studs, was critical of companies that just want to make money regardless of community or environmental damage. He favoured the more temperate concept of 'balance' in weighing the relationship between mining and agriculture:

There's got to be a limit on the extent of development, they can't just go ahead and approve endless mines everywhere … there needs to be a balance too, you don't want to just go and rip the whole place up.

(Nelson interview 2013)

A fantasy elaboration of the myth of coexistence is found in one industry expert's vision of transforming the Hunter's huge mining voids into recreational lakes, as reported in the *Newcastle Herald*:

Disused Hunter mines could be transformed into picturesque lakes and used for aquatic activities such as boating, fishing and swimming. This is a practice carried out successfully in Europe and North America and is under investigation in Western Australia. Mine closure expert and senior research fellow at Edith Cowan University in Perth Dr Clint McCullough, said he could not see why the practice could not be evaluated for disused mines in the Hunter and urged mining regulators, companies and regional communities to consider the idea and start planning.

(Thompson 2013)

Others' imaginings of the future of the voids are not so sanguine. Mining businessman turned industry critic Ian Hedley recently posed the question to the *Newcastle Herald*, 'What's next after coal?':

While governments, mining companies and entrepreneurs have reaped untold profits from the valley's coal deposits, Mr Hedley asks who will be held responsible for the lasting environmental damage. 'There will be over 30 final voids left from mining activity in the Hunter, which will cost an estimated $500 million each to rehabilitate'.

(Kelly 2015a)

CSG companies also promote the myth of co-existence. Until July 2015, AGL (Australian Gas Light Company) held gas exploration licenses over most of the Hunter Valley, from Lake Macquarie to Murrurundi. Pilot wells remain in production very close to houses on its leases at Gloucester in the north of the Hunter Valley. Beneath an image of beef cattle in a lush pasture, the company's webpage, titled 'Agriculture and Coexistence', states:

AGL works side by side with landholders, communities and business to develop natural gas from coal seams for NSW. Our projects coexist with agriculture, viticulture and livestock production. Our priority is to be a good tenant, neighbour and community member, ensuring our operations peacefully and successfully coexist with the communities and landholders we work with.

(AGL 2015)

Claims of co-existence are belied by resident action groups affiliated with Lock the Gate Alliance that have sprung up in all the affected gas mining areas. Counter myths envision a future of renewable energy and a sustainable local economy without mining. Gloucester Groundswell, typical of many anti-gas and mining groups, states its manifesto on its website: 'The people of Gloucester and the region will not stand aside for mining companies to make a profit, while imposing long-term damage to our existing, sustainable agriculture and tourism industries' (Groundswell Gloucester 2015). 'Mining is like a sore, a festering sore, everywhere' says one woman in the group's YouTube clips that purvey starkly different messages to the companies 'co-existence' videos. For several months in 2015, AGL had all its Gloucester CSG operations suspended because of failure to report toxic BTEX chemicals in its flowback water, and it still does not have adequate plans for the disposal of toxic wastewater from hydraulic fracturing at its wells (Hannam 2015).

In the midst of residents' growing sense of risk, harm and environmental degradation, the mining/government alliance constructs a mythology of an authentic fossil fuel dependent future in which the destruction of living ecologies and social worlds is concealed, as is any acknowledgement of the planetary impact of these industries' heavy GHG emissions.

Contested sites of harm: Camberwell

If symbolic capital were the main asset in contests over coal, the increasingly defensive stance of proponents and mounting evidence of harm would see the industry on a downward slope that is as marked as the ongoing fall in prices. But government support of coal remains strong. Opposition to coal mine expansion has become more difficult as regulators attempt to close down every opportunity for opponents in an inexorable process of weakening landholders' and residents' rights as the industry has expanded its footprint in the state. These conditions came to national attention in findings of corruption by the NSW Independent Commission Against Corruption (ICAC) in 2012–1214 against several NSW ministers and other members of parliament, company directors and businessmen over the award of coal mining exploration leases in the Hunter Valley, including the Doyle's Creek Mine in Jerrys Plains (Notzon 2013).

The momentum of state-supported capital accumulation in mining has its counter-movement in a history of opposition to coal mine development in the Hunter Valley that goes back several decades. There is a pragmatic politics at work here, in which residents who must cope with the material realities of encroaching mines directly challenge their structural disadvantage and the symbolic violence of industry co-existence myths. Residents, like those in the settlement of Camberwell, have little choice but to deal with the specific circumstances of corporate exploitation at the actual site of the harm: the places where they live.

About 25 km to the east of Jerry's Plains, straddling the New England Highway, is Camberwell, settled in the early decades of the nineteenth century

Figure 4.6 Camberwell village and surrounding farmland, looking south and west, with
        Ashton Mine in foreground

Source: Allan Chawner, 2008

on Wanaruah land. Like Jerry's Plains, Camberwell is almost encircled by coal
mines. Ashton Coal's open-cut and underground mine complex is situated on the
northern boundary of the village, separated by Glennies Creek Road and
Glennies Creek. The open-cut mine was worked out and ceased production in
2011 while the underground operations produced a dwindling 1.5 Mt of coal in
2014. The company has been trying for several years to win approval for a new
open-cut mine to the southeast of the original mine. The mines are operated and
78 per cent owned by SOE Yancoal Australia, selling its product ('quality semi-
soft coking coal') to 'a number of Asian based steel mills' (Yancoal 2014).
Camberwell Mine, part of an underground and open-cut complex wholly owned
and operated by Brazilian multinational Vale Integra, occupies 1,900 hectares of
land about 1 km to the southeast of the village. This complex, which produced
2.5 Mt of semi-soft coking coal and thermal coal in 2013, was placed in 'care and
maintenance' in 2014, due, the company stated, to falling coal prices. Rix's
Creek Mine, wholly owned by the Australian Bloomfield Group, and currently
producing 2.4 Mt per year of coking and thermal coal, straddles the New England
Highway 2 km to the south of the village, sharing a boundary with Camberwell
Mine, forming a sort of 'superpit'. A few kilometres to the north on both the east
and west sides of the highway, is the Glencore complex of mines, producing 3.6
Mt per annum: the Ravensworth West superpit, next to the former village of

Ravensworth, and Mt Owen, Glendell and Ravensworth East operations. The Hunter River and Camberwell district farmlands separate the village and the huge Hunter Valley Operations mining complex further to the southwest. This mine complex, once the village and farming community of Lemington with fertile agricultural soils, produced 13 Mt in 2013 and is wholly owned and operated by Coal and Allied, a subsidiary of Rio Tinto.[8]

As coal mines have occupied increasing areas of land in the Camberwell district, population has fallen. The 2011 census recorded 181 residents, half the population recorded in the 2006 census (Australian Bureau of Statistics 2011). The majority of the population is employed in coal mining or agriculture, with farmers in the surrounding district growing beef cattle, mixed crops and dairy. By 2011, Ashton Coal, the closest mine, had purchased many of the farms in the district, as well as 49 of the 56 village houses, which are now rented properties – mostly to mineworkers, who 'do not complain or become part of the community' (Munro 2012: 12). As mines expanded, residents experienced increasingly untenable living conditions. Dust, noise, light, traffic and almost daily blasting from 24/7 mining operations dominate the landscape. 'A big blast went off the other day and it took six seconds before the house stopped shaking', one resident complained to a journalist (Lyons 2008: 21). Those who rent mine-owned properties are gagged by 'no complaint' clauses in their contracts, while the 'angry minority' of owner-occupiers has become a strong voice against the worst impact of the mines (Ray 2005a). Owner residents are offered a few thousand dollars a year for 'compensation' for the disturbances, for which they are reputedly required to 'sign an agreement not to make any complaints against the mine or contact any department or media about it or make a formal objection' (Munro 2012: 14–15).

Ashton Coal has been involved in successive disputes with residents, some of whom live within 500 metres of the pit, since its approval in 2002. Originally developed by White Mining Pty Ltd, a company owned by leading Upper Hunter horse breeder and racer, Geoff White, the mine has been majority owned and operated by Yancoal Australia, a subsidiary of the Chinese SOE Yankuang Group, since 2009. Incursions into the lives of residents began early, as the mine, then owned by White Mining, initiated variations to its initial conditions of approval in order to extract coal more quickly and profitably. Plans to divert a creek in 2003 were changed after residents expressed concerns about damage to water supplies (Maguire 2003). In 2004, the specifications for overburden dumps approved on the basis of the original environmental impact statement (EIS) were changed to accommodate a single higher dump, with 'high visual impact', blocking views of the horizon and generating more dust in the village (Thompson 2004). After a blast in October 2004, large boulders, 'some more than two feet in length' rained down on Camberwell Common, a 49 hectare stretch of grazing and recreational land between the mine and houses, held in a community trust since 1876. The company's general manager said the event was 'highly unusual' and 'we don't fully understand why it happened' (Singleton Argus 2004):

Mrs De Jong recounts the day when she heard an unusually loud blast, looked out the window and saw a big rock hurtle over the lip of the hill that separated the village from the mine. 'It came bouncing down the hill. We put it in a barrow and took it to the coal discussion day in Singleton, but I don't think they were too happy to see it,' she said ... No comment was available from the management of the Ashton mine but Singleton Mayor Fred Harvison said his council was proud of the consultation that had taken place between the council, the mine and the villagers before the mine began operating.

(Ray 2005b: 5)

The Department of Environment and Conservation fined the company AUS$1,500 for breaching its noise limit on the day, but it was not fined for the flying rocks. A spokesperson for the Department told the *Newcastle Herald* that 'These are very, very large-scale developments and it's very difficult to control their operations to where it's not noticeable at all' (McCarthy 2005: 8). Resident Deirdre Olofsson commented: 'It's like a sacrifice thing. They sacrifice a few for the many' (McCarthy 2005: 8).

By late 2005, residents initiated a concerted campaign, holding a public meeting to draw attention to the worsening environmental damage caused by Ashton mine, then acquired by Felix Resources. Their concerns included rising dust levels that were affecting their health, bright night lights, constant breaches of noise limits affecting sleep and outdoor activity, blasting vibrations and cracks, and ongoing damage to creeks and wildlife:

'They promised they'd never touch the creek but they threw in a big submersible pump with a four-inch line that kept blowing out and wrecking the creek bank. It took twenty calls to get them to fix it, but the damage was done by then. A tree fell into the creek and the family of platypus that lived there hasn't been seen since,' resident Chris Green told the *Newcastle Herald*.

(Ray 2005a: 4)

The disappearance of the platypus family was emblematic of the imminent annihilation that landholder residents both feared and resisted. People felt they were in 'an unequal fight for their community's survival', with their complaints ignored by the company, and little support from government officials (Ray 2005a). The company in turn dismissed these concerns from 'a couple of very vocal critics'. 'There's no point compensating somebody if they won't agree to stop complaining', said the manager. Resident Toby Olofsson expressed a cynical view of the compensation arrangements offered by the company for 'impact on lifestyle':

If we accept their offer they say we have to sign an agreement not to complain to the authorities about anything and not to speak to the media.

I'm not prepared to do a deal with them because I have seen how they have addressed their consent conditions and I don't trust them. The mine treats us with contempt. They have ruined our whole life.

(*Newcastle Herald* 2005: 5)

Imagined futures, building on the present and the past, were disappearing with the displaced residents. Wanaruah people, dispossessed of their country many generations before, still have important cultural sites at Camberwell and the waterways in the area, including songline sites of the Dreaming creator Baiame (Rickarby 2011). Some Wanaruah people have joined the fight to save Camberwell from Ashton's mine expansion, although others have supported the mine development. Scott Franks, a native title claimant and spokesman for the Plains Clans of the Wonnarua People, has requested the Federal Court of Australia to determine Indigenous title over 60 hectares near Camberwell to protect Aboriginal sites (Maguire 2012). The native title case is ongoing.

The village's future as a bucolic retirement haven with a productive rural hinterland started to wane after the mines proliferated in the early 2000s. Buyers had bought acreages when there was only one mine, Ashton, scheduled to close in 2010. But the boom in coal prices intervened. Residents who wished to sell properties at market prices were unable to do so, with 'buyers put off by the mines'. Mining companies offered low prices to those in designated affected zones, subject to approval of applications. Wendy Bowman, the president of Hunter Valley Minewatch organisation, founded to protect and advise property owners in transactions with mining companies, outlined the flaws in this system of compensation:

A mine had to assess the value as if that mine did not exist, but this did not make provisions for any other mines in the same area. 'It was fair years ago, but when there are so many mines close together now it doesn't apply,' Ms Bowman said. 'There is not market value. The cost of buying a similar property elsewhere, the replacement value, should instead be the guide,' she said.

(Harris 2008: 7)

The *Newcastle Herald* has consistently followed the plight of Camberwell residents since the first negative incidents occurred, and their assiduous coverage provides insights into environmental changes being experienced in many Upper Hunter communities close to mines, as well as the micro-strategies that companies and government officials deploy to neutralise criticism.[9] Opinion writers, less obliged to follow conventions of 'balance' in reporting, were outspoken: 'Pillaged Camberwell, village of the damned' wrote columnist Greg Ray, arguing that the NSW government should 'evacuate the shattered disaster victims who are the last residents of the dying Hunter Valley village of Camberwell' (Ray 2008: 24).

Residents' tactics evolved in the face of escalating disputes 'over everything from pollution to property', in the words of a *Newcastle Herald* editorial. Their lobbying for an independent cumulative impact study of mining on the community was agreed to by the Department of Planning at the end of 2008. Camberwell beef cattle farmer Wendy Bowman, whose husband's great grandfather was one of the first land grant holders in Jerrys Plains in the 1820s, emerged as a leader in the campaign to recognise and redress the deteriorating situation in Camberwell and surrounding communities. After a previous move due to mine developments, she farmed the Bowman family's heritage property near Rix's Creek until dust and saline water from the surrounding mines made the milk from her dairy cattle unsaleable. Having reluctantly negotiated a sale with the Rix's Creek Mine, she moved to a 190 hectare grazing property at Camberwell and started anew in her mid-70s when many farmers might think of retiring: 'It's the third time I've been kicked out', she said. 'It is why I am staying [in the area]. These companies need to be pulled into line' (Thompson 2005: 5). Wendy combines farming with the campaign for fairer treatment from mines and government, ecological preservation and healthier communities. A reserved demeanour belies her feisty words: 'Sometimes I think I'm too old and angry. Then you wake up the next day and say "Bugger it – they're not going to win"' (Jameson 2009).

While the cumulative impact study slowly progressed, Ashton Coal prepared an application for a major new open-cut pit to the south of the existing mine. Health problems among residents were proliferating, and concerns about contamination of drinking water were high. Wendy Bowman sought assistance from university scientists for a water study, which found dangerously high lead levels in village drinking water (NSW Government 2010). Then in April 2010 cracks opened in Camberwell Common and movements of houses were felt outside blasting times. In a development that shocked even the most cynical mining adversaries among residents, the Department of Lands revoked the community's access to the Common, with 'a licence for access and grazing ... passed on to Ashton Coal'. Another 10-hectare parcel of land was offered as compensation, but loss of the Common deprived residents of customary grazing land for their cattle (Kelly and Harris 2010).

There was a reaction of outrage at this gross violation of citizens' rights from many quarters. Even moderate critics were moved to strong words, with a *Newcastle Herald* editorial proclaiming:

> The more the coal industry spreads itself across new land – much of it rural, some of it forest – the more that Singleton, Muswellbrook and the surrounding townships are hemmed in by this immensely powerful industry. This death by a thousand cuts cannot go on forever. Perhaps, instead of a mining health study, the time is ripe for a more far-reaching official inquiry into the costs of coalmining across the Hunter Valley as a whole.
>
> (*Newcastle Herald* 2010: 8)

Despite the public support for inquiries, return of the Common and remediation, Ashton's plans for mine expansion proceeded apace. The cumulative impact study of surrounding mines, released by the Department of Planning in July 2010,

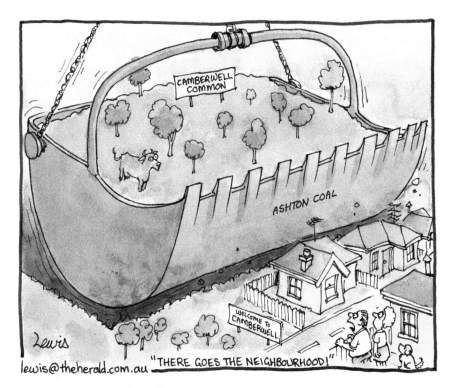

Figure 4.7 Loss of Camberwell Common

Source: Peter Lewis, *Newcastle Herald*, 2010

was a bland document finding no severe exceedances of dust or noise levels and providing the residents with little purchase for further action (NSW Government 2010). Seeking restitution of their Common, residents enlisted the aid of the NSW Environmental Defender's Office (EDO) and launched legal action in the NSW Land and Environment Court against the Lands Minister, Ashton Coal and White Mining, in April 2011. This appeal was successful in August 2013, and the Common plus the additional lands granted were 'returned' to the community (Nichols 2013) but under stronger state government control.

In a further boost to opponents' hopes of turning the tide of coal mining, Ashton Coal's application for the South East Open Cut pit received negative reports from the NSW Department of Health (health risks to residents from excessive exposure to mine dust and pollutants) and Office of Water (concerns about the impact on Glennies Creek). The Planning Assessment Commission (PAC), in an unusual negative decision, rejected Ashton Coal's application in December 2011, because of 'serious concerns about the potential impacts' on nearby Glennies Creek (Environmental Defenders Office NSW 2014: 18). The company quickly organised an appeal to the NSW Land and Environment

Figure 4.8 PAC approves Ashton's South East Open Cut pit

Source: Peter Lewis, *Newcastle Herald*, 2012

Court, which determined that a revised application should be submitted. With a more favourable report from the Office of Water (seen by critics to have capitulated to higher level pressure), the PAC approved the application in October 2012, despite a second negative report from the Department of Health.

The Hunter Environment Lobby (HEL) sought the assistance of the EDO to appeal the PAC approval. This appeal was rejected in August 2014 but the judge determined to set additional conditions on the approval, relating to air quality, water resources and the acquisition of properties (Davis 2014). The final ruling, handed down in December 2014, was seen by residents as a stunning and unexpected victory. The HEL applauded the Court's recognition of 'the rights of citizens and landholders. This decision has saved the future of the Camberwell community and many others in the region' (Nichols 2014). In her ruling, the judge imposed a number of conditions favourable to residents, including the right of acquisition upon the request of the property owner, and compensation at market value of an equivalent property in an area free from mining. The most striking condition was that Yancoal must first acquire Mrs Bowman's property before beginning development of the new open-cut pit. Wendy exclaimed: 'I felt numb when I heard Justice Paine's ruling' (Nichols 2014). She announced that she would endeavour to place a conservation covenant on her property, saying: 'The fight to save this farm is about our need as a society to protect valuable farm lands and our vital water ways from complete destruction by the mining industry' (quoted in Nichols 2014).

Like other Camberwell residents, Wendy Bowman is worried about the fate of the wildlife that is also impacted by mines. As I stood with her on her property recently discussing the outcome, we surveyed a large area of native woodland she had let grow on the ridgelands, 'I want to keep it for wildlife conservation', she told me. 'There is a wonderful abundance of species but they are getting trapped by mines, and there's so little habitat. They have nowhere else to go'.

In public responses to the ruling, Yancoal said little, but quickly lodged an appeal against the decision. This was announced as unsuccessful in April 2015, giving the Camberwell property owners reason to celebrate (Kelly 2015b). However, in May 2015 the company announced that it was lodging a further appeal in the NSW Supreme Court, and this appeal is pending at time of writing.

Figure 4.9 Camberwell cornered by coal

Source: Peter Lewis, *Newcastle Herald*, 2014

In a larger frame of reference, the fight to preserve what is left of Camberwell is of small consequence in the ongoing expansion of coal mining in the Upper Hunter. Companies expand production to compensate for lower prices, supported by governments locked in to fossil fuel based capitalism and majority voters for whom coal-affected communities and climate change are a minority issue. Meanwhile companies wait for the next upturn in the market cycle, making ever more unrealistic prognoses for the health of their industry. The chief executive officer of Yancoal recently stated that 'a price recovery in coal [is] unlikely until late 2016 at the earliest' (Williams 2015). Perhaps this stance can be construed as another instance where coal proponents are hostage to their own myths and impervious to the growing signs of climate crisis and significant international efforts to curb GHGs from burning coal.

Dialectic of perception and place

The groups of people considered in this chapter – suburban and rural survey respondents, Wanaruah traditional owners, farmers and other rural dwellers – are deeply concerned about processes of environmental change in their localities. Most people have multigenerational histories of residence in the Hunter Valley, an important attribute for exploring the dialectic of perception and place for the purposes of this research. Most of them are experiencing adverse changes that trigger discontinuities of past and present, fracture place worlds and jeopardise their imagined futures. These futures are not utopian visions of new worlds, made anywhere, in expendable environments, but an aspiration towards rootedness in sustaining place-worlds as the grounds of being.

Many people ponder whether the environmental changes they perceive are an indicator of climate change (usually in response to researcher questions), and some espouse anthropogenic causation with all its disquieting uncertainties. But these are minor concerns compared to the constant remarks people make to each other about their embodied perceptions of the state of the surrounding environment. These experiences variously constitute and reinforce ideas that can be discordant: natural cycles thinking at odds with climate science, for example. The biosphere brings its own agency to bear in endless feedback loops: people experience more very hot days, 'no frost anymore', 'the blue tongue lizards are gone'. The political economy, by definition out of locals' control, exerts another agency: 'the coal dust is on every stone and gully', [after the mine blast] 'it took six seconds before the house stopped shaking', 'my water tanks are one third full of coal dust', 'Scone is covered in a brown haze [from power stations]', 'the [coal] company wants to move the creek our [Dreaming] Creator has laid down'.

These environmental changes are, at the least, disturbing. Some of them are very harmful. People living in close proximity to mine operations and power stations experience a lot of the latter. Climate change is not the primary concern here. The fossil fuel economy overshadows other domains when it comes to the consequences of adverse environmental change: struggling for survival.

Residents become reluctant opponents of these developments because the immediate foundations of their existence are threatened: health, livelihood, community, heritage, sacred sites, security and well-being. The possibility of understanding emplaced lives as both successive and simultaneous is closed off. All around are the spectres of destroyed villages replaced by mining pits, or depopulated districts like Wybong, once the site of an unsuccessful residents' campaign against Glencore's Mangoola mine west of Muswellbrook (Connor *et al.* 2009). The residents of nearby Bulga have for several years been fighting Rio Tinto's extension of the Mt Thorley-Warkworth mine that would move the pit to within 500 metres of the town. People become locked into lengthy and exhausting conflicts with powerful corporations and pro-mining government departments on very unequal terms.

Residents, who typically eschew any association with 'activism', 'environmentalism' or 'greenies' or even 'politics' in the institutional sense, have their own appreciation of the long-term significance of their struggles. Wendy Bowman reflects that the Camberwell contest is about protecting irreplaceable land and water resources from destruction by mining. On Aboriginal heritage destruction, Wanaruah man Scott Franks states: 'I don't want my sons to have to walk into a museum to look at our artefacts, the artefacts of our people' (Rickarby 2011). These are momentous concerns, and these contests have decisive consequences for the fate of place worlds. The dialectic of locally experienced environmental change and modes of climate activation will be considered in the next chapter.

Notes

1   All changes are statistically significant. See Higginbotham *et al.* (2014) for further details.
2   The largest mine, Mt Arthur, owned by BHP Billiton, produced 18 Mt in 2012–2013 (BHP Billiton 2013).
3   In the 2013–2014 financial year, Australia exported a total of 201 Mt of thermal coal and 180 Mt of metallurgical coal (Department of Industry and Science 2015).
4   The 2011 figure is 329 more than at the 1954 census, with vastly greater productivity now due to technological innovation and increasing mechanisation.
5   In the 2011 census, 35.7 per cent of Hunter residents stated they were of Australian ancestry, followed by English (31.8 per cent), then Irish (7.7 per cent) and Scottish (7.6 per cent), all of which are above the national averages (Australian Bureau of Statistics 2012).
6   Ancestry is defined by the Australian Bureau of Statistics as the ethnic or cultural groups that a person identifies as being his or her ancestry (Australian Bureau of Statistics 2006).
7   Pseudonyms are used throughout for interviewees, unless otherwise specified.
8   These production statistics are derived from the most recent annual reports of companies and company websites.
9   As noted by Sharyn Munro, the Singleton Argus has also provided 'evenhanded coverage' and 'invaluable ongoing history' (2012: 13).

References

ABC News 2015. 'Baird offers more talk on protection for Hunter wine, horse and tourism zones'. *ABC News*. 25 March. Available at www.abc.net.au/news/2015-03-25/baird-offers-more-talk-on-protection-for-hunter-wine2c-horse-a/6345928 archived by WebCite at www.webcitation.org/6XKprJeYS (accessed 27 March 2015).

AGL (Australian Gas Light Company) 2015. 'Agriculture & Coexistence'. Available at www.agl.com.au/about-agl/how-we-source-energy/natural-gas/agriculture-and-coexistence (accessed 25 May 2015).

Albrecht, G. 2005. '"Solastalgia": A new concept in health and identity'. *PAN: Philosophy, Activism, Nature* 3: 41–55.

Albrecht, G., Sartore, G., Connor, L., Higginbotham, N., Freeman, S., Kelly, B., Stain, H., Tonna, A. and Pollard, G. 2007. 'Solastalgia: The distress caused by environmental change'. *Australasian Psychiatry* 15 (Supplement): S95–98.

Australian Bureau of Statistics 2006. *Census of Population and Housing: Media Releases and Fact Sheets, 2006*. Available at www.abs.gov.au/ausstats/abs@.nsf/7d12b0f6763 c78caca257061001cc588/6ef598989db79931ca257306000d52b4!OpenDocument (accessed March 2014).

Australian Bureau of Statistics 2011. *Census QuickStats: Camberwell (NSW)*. Available at www.censusdata.abs.gov.au/census_services/getproduct/census/2011/quickstat/ SSC10433?opendocument&navpos=220 (accessed June 2013).

Australian Bureau of Statistics 2012. *Census 2011: Census for a brighter future*. Available at www.abs.gov.au/census (accessed 1 January 2013).

Australian Government Attorney-General's Department. 2014. *Native Title*. Available at www.ag.gov.au/LegalSystem/NativeTitle/Pages/default.aspx (accessed 20 September 2014).

Benson, P. and Kirsch, S. 2010. 'Capitalism and the Politics of Resignation'. *Current Anthropology* 51 (4): 459–486.

BHP Billiton 2013. *Our shared values. Annual Report 2013*. Available at www.bhpbilliton.com/home/investors/reports/Documents/2013/BHPBillitonAnnualReport2013.pdf (accessed 2 September 2013).

BHP Billiton. 2015. *Indigenous communities*. Available at www.bhpbilliton.com/home/ society/ourcontribution/Pages/Indigenous-communities.aspx archived by WebCite at www.webcitation.org/6XtbiYEsQ (accessed 7 April 2015).

Campbell, R. 2014. *Seeing Through the Dust: Coal in the Hunter Valley economy*. The Australia Institute.

Casey, E. S. 1997. 'How to get from space to place in a fairly short stretch of time: Phenomenological prolegomena'. In: *Sense of Place*. Feld, S. and Basso K. H (eds). Santa Fe: School of American Research Press.

Christoff, P. 2013. 'Climate Discourse Complexes, National Climate Regimes and Australian Climate Policy'. *Australian Journal of Politics and History* 59 (3): 349–367.

Connor, L., Freeman, S. and Higginbotham, N. 2009. 'Not just a coalmine: Shifting grounds of community opposition to coal mining in Southeastern Australia'. *Ethnos* 74 (4): 490–513.

Davis, B.-J. 2014. 'Camberwell residents "vow to keep fighting"'. *Newcastle Herald*. August 27. Available at www.theherald.com.au/story/2519408/camberwell-residents-vow-to-keep-fighting/ archived by WebCite at www.webcitation.org/6SUkEftSq/ (accessed 11 September 2014).

Department of Environment Climate Change and Water 2010. *Aboriginal cultural heritage consultation requirements for proponents*. Part 6 National Parks and Wildlife Act 1974. Sydney: Department of Environment Climate Change and Water.

Department of Industry and Science 2015. *Resources and Energy Quarterly*. June Quarter 2015. Available at www.industry.gov.au/Office-of-the-Chief-Economist/Publications/ Documents/req/REQ-June15.pdf archived by WebCite at www.webcitation.org/ 6aij4xHiH (accessed 7 July 2015).

Economist 2015. 'Coal mining: In the depths'. *The Economist*. Available at www.econo-mist.com/news/business/21647287-more-countries-turn-against-coal-producers-face-p rolonged-weakness-prices-depths (accessed 25 May 2015).

Eliasoph, N. 1997. '"Close to Home": The work of avoiding politics'. *Theory and Society* 26 (5): 605–647.

Environmental Defenders Office NSW 2014. *Annual Report 2013/14*. Available at https://d3n8a8pro7vhmx.cloudfront.net/edonsw/pages/1674/attachments/original/ 1415573074/Annual_Report_Final_Web.pdf?1415573074 archived by WebCite at www.webcitation.org/6XyJmL6zz (accessed 22 April 2015).

Evans, G. 2008. 'Transformation from "Carbon Valley" to a "Post-Carbon Society" in a climate change hot spot: the coalfields of the Hunter Valley, New South Wales'. *Ecology and Society* 13(1): 39.

Federal Court of Australia 1998. *Members of the Yorta Yorta Aboriginal Community v Victoria & Ors* [1988] FCA 1606 (18 December 1998).

Feld, S. and Basso, K. H. 1997. *Sense of Place*. Santa Fe: School of American Research Press.

Galilee, S. 2012a. 'Ideological criticisms threaten livelihoods'. *Newcastle Herald*, p.11.

Galilee, S. 2012b. 'Mining's part in the Hunter Valley'. *Newcastle Herald*, p.12.

Galilee, S. 2014. 'OPINION: China's coal demand will continue to grow'. *Newcastle Herald*. July 30. Available at www.theherald.com.au/story/2453747/opinion-chinas-coal-demand-will-continue-to-grow/?cs=308 archived by WebCite at www.webcitation.org/6Rc4wSKyk (accessed 6 August 2014).

Groundswell Gloucester 2015. 'The beautiful Gloucester Valley is threatened by destruc-tive coal and gas mining'. Available at www.groundswellgloucester.com/index.html archived by WebCite at www.webcitation.org/6Xy0w6ry5 (accessed 22 April 2015).

Hagemann, B. 2015. 'Coal employment fallen in the Hunter'. *Australian Mining*. February 5. Available at www.miningaustralia.com.au/news/coal-employment-fallen-in-the-hunter archived by WebCite at www.webcitation.org/6Xtb9ILeL (accessed 7 April 2015).

Hannam, P. 2015. 'Coal seam gas: AGL cleared of adverse findings to resume operations in Gloucester'. *Sydney Morning Herald*. May 19. Available at www.smh.com.au/envi-ronment/coal-seam-gas-agl-cleared-of-adverse-findings-to-resume-operations-in-glouc ester-20150519-gh4nc3?stb=twt&skin=dumb-phone archived by WebCite at www.webcitation.org/6ZVpVq9I5 (accessed 2 June 2015).

Harris, M. 2008. 'Dreams undermined; owners unable to sell land'. *Newcastle Herald*. Januart 14, p.7.

Hart, C., Berry, H. and Tonna, A. 2011. 'Improving the mental health of drought-affected communities in New South Wales'. *Australian Journal of Rural Health* 19: 231–238.

Harvey, D. 1993. 'From Space to Place and Back Again: Reflections on the condition of postmodernity'. In: *Mapping the Futures*. J. Bird, B. Curtis, T. Putnam, G. Robertson and L. Tickner (eds). London: Routledge.

Higginbotham, N., Connor, L. H. and Baker, F. 2014. 'Subregional differences in Australian climate risk perceptions: coastal versus agricultural areas of the Hunter Valley, NSW'. *Regional Environmental Change* 14 (2): 699–712.

Huleatt, M. B. 1981. 'Year Book Australia 1982: Black coal in Australia'. Australian Bureau of Statistics. Available at www.abs.gov.au/AUSSTATS/abs@.nsf/Previousproducts/1301.0Feature%20Article1501982?opendocument&tabname=Summary&prodno=1301.0&issue=1982&num=&view (accessed 2 September 2013).

Hunter Coal Festival 2015. 'About'. Available at www.huntercoalfestival.com.au/sample-page/ archived by WebCite at www.webcitation.org/6XxzAlBCu (accessed 7 April 2015).

Hunter Thoroughbred Breeders Association 2015. 'Protect our industries'. Available at www.htba.com.au/#!protect-our-industries/c1agp archived by WebCite at www.webcitation.org/6Xu6xErzZ (accessed 7 April 2015).

Hunter Thoroughbred Breeders Association and the Hunter Valley Wine and Tourism Association 2015. 'Time to Protect the Hunter Valley's State Significant Agricultural Lands and Industries'. Available at www.huntervalleyprotectionalliance.com/pdf/HVPA_Time_To_Protect_HTBA_D_20150324.pdf. Scone NSW.

Hunter Valley Protection Alliance 2015. 'Hunter Valley Protection Alliance'. Available at http://huntervalleyprotectionalliance.com/ archived by WebCite at www.webcitation.org/6Xu7C80Lq (accessed 19 April 2015).

Ingold, T. 2007. 'Earth, sky, wind and weather'. *Journal of the Royal Anthropological Institute* (S19–S38): S25.

Jameson, N. 2009. 'To protect and defend'. *Herald Weekender*. 18 April. Available at http://newsstore.fairfax.com.au/apps/viewDocument.ac?sy=afr&pb=all_ffx&dt=selectRange&dr=1month&so=relevance&sf=text&sf=headline&rc=10&rm=200&sp=brs&cls=2717&clsPage=1&docID=NCH0904182H4H66DH5LF archived by WebCite at www.webcitation.org/6XeKiH0Co (acessed 9 April 2015).

Kelly, M. 2011. 'Tamper at our peril: Vigneron'. *Newcastle Herald*, p.15.

Kelly, M. 2013a. 'Awabakal land claim lodged'. *Newcastle Herald*. October 9. Available at www.theherald.com.au/story/1831422/awabakal-land-claim-lodged/ archived by WebCite at www.webcitation.org/6XtcZG0bt (accessed 5 November 2013).

Kelly, M. 2013b. 'Hunter coal towns disappear'. *Newcastle Herald*. May 31. Available at www.theherald.com.au/story/1541839/hunter-coal-towns-disappearing/?cs=305 archived by WebCite at www.webcitation.org/6H8WRMloL

Kelly, M. 2015a. 'Mining businessman asks what's next after coal'. *Newcastle Herald*. March 30. Available at www.theherald.com.au/story/2980227/life-after-coal-whats-next/?cs=305 archived by WebCite at www.webcitation.org/6XeKEPdhe (accessed 9 April 2015).

Kelly, M. 2015b. 'Yancoal appeal rejected; win for Camberwell's Wendy Bowman'. *Newcastle Herald*. May 1. Available at www.theherald.com.au/story/3051020/yancoal-appeal-rejected/ archived by WebCite at www.webcitation.org/6ZXIKOMMJ (accessed 25 May 2015).

Kelly, M. and Harris, M. 2010. 'Losing ground'. *Newcastle Herald*. April 16, pp.1–4.

Kempton, W., Boster, J. S. and Hartley, J. A. 1996. *Environmental Values in American Culture*. Cambridge and Massachusetts: MIT Press.

Ker, P. 2014. 'Yancoal suffering under "take or pay" contracts'. *The Sydney Morning Herald*. April 14. Available at www.smh.com.au/business/mining-and-resources/yancoal-suffering-under-take-or-pay-contracts-20140414-36ncx.html archived by WebCite at www.webcitation.org/6aifxFrIU (accessed 20 July 2015).

Kirsch, S. 2010. 'Sustainable Mining'. *Dialectical Anthropology* 34: 87–93.

Kirsch, S. 2014. *Mining Capitalism: The Relationship between Corporations and their Critics*. Oakland, CA: University of California Press.

Lannin, S. 2014. 'Coal communities in NSW's Hunter Valley trying to survive the mining slowdown'. *ABC News*. Dec 15. Available at www.abc.net.au/news/2014-12-14/coal-communities-trying-to-survive-the-mining-slowdown/5966418 archived by WebCite at www.webcitation.org/6bHdxEhVo (accessed 3 September 2015).

Law Handbook 2012. *Aboriginal People and the Law*. Twelfth Edition. Redfern Legal Centre Publishing. Pyrmont: Thomson Reuters.

Lock the Gate Alliance 2014. 'Unfair shares: how coal mines bought the Hunter River'. Available at www.lockthegate.org.au/unfairshares archived by WebCite at www.webcitation.org/6RJpxNste (accessed July 25 2015).

Lyons, M. 2008. 'Open cut and dried life'. *Newcastle Herald*. 13 September, p.21.

Macdonald, G. 1988. 'Self-determination or control: Aborigines and land rights legislation in New South Wales'. *Social Analysis: The International Journal of Social and Cultural Practice* 24 (Aborigines and the state in Australia), pp.34–49.

Maguire, P. 2003. 'Pit plan to save streams'. *Newcastle Herald*. January 1, p.6.

Maguire, P. 2012. 'Ashton heats up'. *The Singleton Argus*. June 1. Available at www.singletonargus.com.au/story/209480/ashton-heats-up/ archived by WebCite at www.webcitation.org/6ZMmwZHZ0 (accessed 20 May 2015).

McCarthy, J. 2005. 'Blast falls on deaf ears'. *Newcastle Herald*. February 9, p.8.

McCarthy, J. 2012. 'Muswellbrook ready to fight over housing'. *Newcastle Herald*. August 12. Available at www.theherald.com.au/news/local/news/general/muswellbrook-ready-to-fight-over-housing/2648058.aspx archived by Webcite at www.webcitation.org/69tyUfpwp (accessed 14 August 2015).

McHugh, B. 2015. 'Coal prices to pick up in second half of 2015 while cost cutting may continue'. *ABC Rural*. Available at www.abc.net.au/news/2015-01-07/coal-outlook-still-soft-most-2015/6002028 archived by WebCite at www.webcitation.org/6Vi2p3yKL (accessed 10 January 2015).

McManus, P., Albrecht, G. and Graham, G. 2013. *The Global Horseracing Industry: Social, Economic, Environmental and Ethical Perspectives*. Abingdon, UK: Routledge.

McManus, P. and Connor, L. 2013. 'What's mine is mine(d): contests over marginalisation of rural life in the Upper Hunter, NSW'. *Rural Society* 22 (2): 166–183.

Medhora, S. 2015. 'Great Barrier Reef: Nationals MP says environmentalists are guilty of treason'. *The Guardian*. 25 March. Available at www.theguardian.com/environment/2015/mar/25/great-barrier-reef-nationals-mp-says-environmentalists-are-guilty-of-treason archived by WebCite at www.webcitation.org/6XqqTFZ3Q (accessed 17 April 2015).

Mercer, A., de Rijke, K. and Dressler, W. 2014. 'Silences in the boom: coal seam gas, neoliberalizing discourse, and the future of regional Australia'. *Journal of Political Economy* 21: 279–302.

Mitchell, N. 2009. 'Climate Change and the Psyche'. The All in the Mind Blog, 21 November. ABC Radio National, Available at www.abc.net.au/rn/allinthemind/stories/2009/2746165.htm (accessed 26 May 2010).

Munro, S. 2012. *Rich Land, Wasteland: How Coal is Killing Australia*. Sydney: Macmillan.

Nassar, D. 2014. 'Romantic empiricism after the "End of Nature": Contributions to environmental philosophy. In: *The Relevance of Romanticism*. Nassar, D. (ed.). Oxford: Oxford University Press.

Newcastle Herald 2005. 'No apology as company shrugs off vocal minority'. *Newcastle Herald*. September 24, p.5.

Newcastle Herald. 2010. 'Camberwell common'. *Newcastle Herald*. April 19, p.8.

Nichols, L. 2013. 'Camberwell Common is back in community hands'. *The Singleton*

Argus. August 16. Available at www.singletonargus.com.au/story/1708165/camberwell-common-is-back-in-community-hands/ archived by WebCite at www.webcitation.org/6XeKa2E6w (accessed 9 April 2015).

Nichols, L. 2014. 'Court ruling protects Wendy Bowman's farm'. *The Singleton Argus*. December 23. Available at www.singletonargus.com.au/story/2782153/court-ruling-protects-wendy-bowmans-farm/ archived by WebCite at www.webcitation.org/6WxfVTTR0 (accessed 12 March 2015).

Notzon, N. 2013. 'Documentary special: farmers of the Hunter Valley'. *ABC News*. December 23. Available at www.abc.net.au/pm/content/2013/s3916715.htm archived by WebCite at www.webcitation.org/6ZVpq0tYJ (accessed 25 May 2015).

NSW Government 2010. *Independent Review of Cumulative Impacts on Camberwell*. Available at www.planning.nsw.gov.au/Portals/0/planningsystem/pdf/DoP%20overview1.pdf archived by WebCite at www.webcitation.org/6XyJ3y5M2 (accessed 7 April 2015).

NSW Mining 2012a. 'Mining and farming thriving together'. Available at www.worldclassminers.com.au/news/environment/mining-and-farming-thriving-together/ archived by WebCite at www.webcitation.org/6Xy0YNRgi (accessed 22 April 2015).

NSW Mining 2012b. 'World Class Miners'. Available at www.worldclassminers.com.au/news/environment/ archived by WebCite at www.webcitation.org/6Xy0PGlId (accessed 22 April 2015).

NSW Mining 2013a. 'Environment'. Available at www.nswmining.com.au/environment archived by WebCite at www.webcitation.org/6XxyzeZjZ (accessed 7 April 2015).

NSW Mining 2013b. 'Hurt mining. Hurt NSW'. Available at www.nswmining.com.au/people/hurt-mining-hurt-nsw archived by WebCite at www.webcitation.org/6Xy08YHq8 (accessed 22 April 2015).

NSW Trade & Investment 2014a. 'NSW Government's Gas Plan'. Division of Resources and Energy. Available at www.resourcesandenergy.nsw.gov.au/__data/assets/pdf_file/0009/535059/NSW-Gas-Plan-Flier-FINAL.pdf archived by WebCite at www.webcitation.org/6XtafrrvW (accessed 7 April 2015).

NSW Trade & Investment 2014b. 'Miners & explorers: Royalty'. Available at www.resourcesandenergy.nsw.gov.au/miners-and-explorers/enforcement/royalties (accessed 25 May 2015).

NSW Trade & Investment 2015. 'Coal Seam Gas: Informing the community'. Division of Resources and Energy. Available at http://cdn.digitalservicesnsw.com/csg/mapv2.1/index.html archived by WebCite at www.webcitation.org/6XtaPyVzx (accessed 7 April 2015).

Pearse, G. 2009. 'Quarry vision: Coal, climate change and the end of the resources boom'. *Quarterly Essay* (33): 1–122.

Polain, J., Berry, H. and Hoskin, J. 2011. 'Rapid change, climate adversity and the next "Big Dry": Considerations for older farmers' mental health'. *Australian Journal of Rural Health* 19: 239–243.

Ray, G. 2005a. 'It's the pits, say angry residents'. *Newcastle Herald*. September 24, p.4.

Ray, G. 2005b. 'Residents battle dust in hoes, gardens'. *Newcastle Herald*. February 7, p.5.

Ray, G. 2008. 'Pillaged Camberwell, village of the damned'. *Newcastle Herald*. March 15, p.24.

Reser, J., Bradley, G., Glendon, A. and Ellul, M. 2012. *Public Risk Perceptions, Understandings, and Responses to Climate Change and Natural Disasters in Australia and Great Britain*. Griffith University, School of Applied Psychology, Behavioural Basis of

Health: Griffith Climate Change Response Program, National Climate Change Adaptation Research Facility.

Rickarby, L. 2011. 'Coal versus Hunter native title claims'. *Newcastle Herald*. June 24. Available at www.theherald.com.au/story/471945/coal-versus-hunter-native-title-claims/ archived by WebCite at www.webcitation.org/6ZMn296kX (accessed 20 May 2015).

Rosewarne, S. 2013. 'Beyond the market: the transnationalisation of Indian coal economy and the Australian political economy'. Paper presented to Academy of Social Sciences in Australia symposium: The Coal Rush, and Beyond: Comparative Perspectives. University of Technology Sydney. 12 & 13 December.

Singleton Argus 2004. 'Village showered with mine rocks'. *Singleton Argus*. October 22, p.4.

Smee, B. 2011. 'Tribe proclaims Awabakal office "Worimi land"'. *Newcastle Herald*. June 29. Available at www.theherald.com.au/story/473618/tribe-proclaims-awabakal-office-worimi-land/ archived by WebCite at www.webcitation.org/6Xtcio8Mf (accessed 7 November 2013).

Sydney Morning Herald 1950. 'The nation faces another great coal deficit'. *Sydney Morning Herald*. September 26. Available at http://trove.nla.gov.au/ndp/del/article/18182509 (accessed 12 June 2013).

Thompson, F. 2004. 'Mine admits to ugly dump'. *Newcastle Herald*. September 17, p.29.

Thompson, F. 2005. 'Mine set to gobble last slice of history'. *Newcastle Herald*. May 13, p.5.

Thompson, F. 2013. 'Hunter open-cut mines for boating'. *Newcastle Herald*. January 13. Available at www.theherald.com.au/story/442083/hunter-open-cut-mines-for-boating/ archived by WebCite at www.webcitation.org/6JJuotib5 (accessed 22 April 2015).

Williams, P. 2015. 'Yancoal boss warns mine sellers over inflated prices'. *The Sydney Morning Herald*. May 18. Available at www.smh.com.au/national/yancoal-boss-warns-mine-sellers-over-inflated-prices-20150515-gh2tgo.html archived by WebCite at www.webcitation.org/6bJJneysr (accessed 4 September 2015).

Yancoal 2014. 'Ashton'. Available at www.yancoal.com.au/page/key-assets/mines/ashton/ archived by WebCite at www.webcitation.org/6Xy6CZAvt (accessed 22 April 2015).

Part III
Counterpoints

5 Climate activation

When surveying the regional sites that are part of the social field of the Hunter Valley study – farms, villages, suburbs, mines, coal chain infrastructure, local governments, different organisations – one is struck by the heterogeneity of what might be termed 'the experienced climate change reality', its activity and silences. Environmental changes happen all the time: they are made, imposed, unfolded; they are valued and interpreted in different ways; actions taken may be reactive and conflictual, disconnected, generative, convergent, consequential or evanescent. This chapter focuses on climate change action, or what I term 'activation', among a necessarily small but diverse selection of sites in the regional setting and the wider contexts of which they are part. I use the concept of activation to delineate practices directed in some way to climate change, including but not limited to behaviours measured through self-report surveys, policy-making, planning and political activism. Activation is linked to the concept of 'engagement': 'a state of personal connection that encompasses cognitive, affective and/or behavioural dimensions' (Wolf and Moser 2011). Engagement can be negative, as in the case of suppression, or inattention or inertia, all of which must be considered in the experienced climate change reality.

Climate change policy and politics is a well-documented aspect of climate activation (Christoff 2014; Dryzek *et al.* 2013; Giddens 2009). The period of the author's research project overlapped with the years from 2007–2010 that Stuart Rosewarne, James Goodman and Rebecca Pearse have identified as 'climate action upsurge', when 'a "climate justice" movement was surfacing and developing a strong critique of existing official climate policies and engaging in new forms of direct action to assert the need for reduced extraction and burning of fossil fuels' (2014: i). This period in Australia has also been well analysed in the work of Verity Burgmann and Hans Baer (2012). These authors document the rising political salience of climate change science since the 1980s through the United Nation's agencies, conferences and programmes, culminating in the establishment of the United Nations Framework Convention on Climate Change (UNFCCC) in 1992 (Burgmann and Baer 2012: 59–62; Rosewarne *et al.* 2014: 25–7). In Australia, Labor governments courted the increasingly influential Green vote (which as elsewhere in the world had its foundations in the environmental movement of the 1960s) and negotiated with the large environmental non-government organisations (ENGOs) on environmental policy issues, including the National Greenhouse Response Strategy formulated in 1992. The 'business as usual' approach that finally defined the Strategy, in which Australia would take no significant initiatives in emissions reduction unless other developed economies did so, exposed the ineffectiveness of the pragmatic political approach taken by environmental organisations in the face of a corporate backlash. This was reinforced in the subsequent conservative government's failure to ratify the Kyoto Protocol (Burgmann and Baer 2012: 61–4; Rosewarne *et al.* 2014: 32–5).

The multilateral consultation process for the Kyoto Protocol brought climate change more forcefully to the attention of the Australian public, even if the national debates were focused on minimising obligations, maximising fossil fuel dependent growth and generally affirming Australia's stance as a reluctant follower, not a world leader, in emissions reduction policies. Polls during the 1990s and early 2000s show that public concern was growing, but in the absence of proactive political leadership there was no significant policy response. A convergence of circumstances in the mid-2000s (discussed in Chapter 3) created a peak of climate change concern, and gave Labor opposition leader Kevin Rudd the opportunity to mobilise voter support on 'the greatest moral challenge of our time', contributing to his 2007 election win. While negotiations by ENGOs with the new government continued (fortified by the balance of power held by the Australian Greens Party in the upper house), climate change had become an issue for mass rallies in the cities, well attended 'Walks Against Warming', new grassroots groups in some parts of the country, and intensive activist networking – all promising 'something different in environmental politics, a new radicalism and new visions for transformation' (Rosewarne *et al.* 2014: 50).

The Hunter Valley research continued through the years 2011–2013 when the radical upsurge had dissipated in the wake of the failed UN Climate Change Conference in December 2009, the enduring impact of the global financial crisis, the failure of the Australian Labor government's Carbon Pollution Reduction Scheme legislation, the internal leadership coup against its chief proponent, Prime Minister Kevin Rudd, and the election of the conservative government in September 2013. In 2012 prices for coal and iron ore exports started to fall in response to changing East Asian economic conditions and shifts in energy policies. In the Hunter Valley, this intensified the pace of coal extraction, with increased production compensating for lower prices, and coal mine extensions exerting more pressure on communities living in proximity to mines, railways and port. The specific practices of resource extractive capitalist accumulation under pressure of falling prices in the Asia Pacific seaborne coal trade continued to have major effects on lives and ecologies in the Hunter Valley.

This chapter explores the shifting reality of climate change in different contexts of social life, where activation, its decline and its absence are simultaneously significant constituents of the social field. The processes of climate change – the science, the physics, the politics and so on – create connections and conflicts, but also erasures and absences, zones of disengagement as well as 'zones of awkward engagement' (Tsing 2004). The fragmentation of experience and activity is challenging for the social researcher to represent. I begin with a discussion of the householder survey of climate change introduced in Chapter 3, to explore the dimensions of self-reported action among a population sample of Upper Hunter and Lake Macquarie residents. I then move to the activation of local planning authorities and property owners in highly climate-exposed lake and coastal suburbs. In the domain of local government planning we can observe a steady preoccupation with climate change threat as an encroaching reality coming hard up against the proprietorial instincts of ratepayers and property developers, in conflicts over sea-level rise and inundation guidelines.

I then consider a less ambiguous zone of climate activation in the groups formed in the Hunter as a political force to address climate change mitigation and adaptation. A spectrum of groups – manifesting the 'communitarian', 'market' and 'radical' trends of action delineated by Rosewarne *et al.* (2014) – were active in the period of climate action upsurge. The transformation of climate change politics is then examined through local strategies after 2010. The campaign against a fourth coal export terminal at Port of Newcastle – the 'T4 campaign' – provides a context of transmuted climate change activism, where climate justice issues are folded into environmental justice, social justice and specifically health justice, raising new questions about the political intelligibility of climate change activation in the region and beyond.

Householders

Climate change policy instruments formulated by governments, such as pricing carbon, have been notoriously difficult to legislate or implement effectively as the Australian experience shows. John Dryzek and colleagues (2013: 73) catalogue some of the reasons for this:

> powerful interests that bend seemingly attractive instruments to their own material advantage; … unproven technologies, some with major side effects; … options that are feasible and attractive because they promise little pain, but also in the end may not make enough of a difference; … complex schemes that create perverse incentives.

Government policies in countries like Australia and the USA do not aim for dramatic social transformation as part of the solution for climate change. Their policies are framed within neoliberal discourses of ecological modernisation that endeavour to ensure electoral survival and maintain economic growth with a range of mitigation and adaptation policies. 'Mitigation' policies aim to ameliorate climate change by decreasing the creation of greenhouse gases (GHGs) in the atmosphere through emissions trading or carbon taxes, or by removing GHGs from the atmosphere through bio-sequestration or geo-sequestration. 'Adaptation' policies, whether anticipatory or reactive, aim to cope with the effects of climate change – extreme heat and storms, drought, sea-level rise, water and food shortages, new disease patterns and the like (Dryzek *et al.* 2013: 56–74). Mitigation and adaptation are in fact interdependent, not alternatives, as climate policy analyst Ross Garnaut (2014: 141) has pointed out: 'Mitigation is the first and most important element of an adaptation strategy. The cost of adaptation and whether a planned adaptive response has any chance of working depend on the effectiveness of mitigation and therefore the extent of climate change'.

While the headline climate change policies are developed by national governments, state and local authorities have a critical role in policy development and implementation by virtue of legislated responsibilities for matters such as land use, water sources, transport, infrastructure, planning approvals and environmental regulation. Emission reduction programmes targeting individual and household consumption (generally estimated as accounting for about one-third of GHG emissions in developed countries) are seen as an important element of policy initiatives (Wolf and Moser 2011). Householders and local communities – neighbourhoods, villages, rural districts, suburbs and towns – engage with mitigation and adaptation policies as they impact on routines of consumption, work and leisure. 'Engagement' is multi-faceted. In their review of qualitative small-scale studies of climate change understanding from around the world, Johanna Wolf and Susanne Moser concluded that the various dimensions of engagement are not necessarily aligned (2011), a finding also evident in developed country surveys. Small-scale studies show that public understanding of climate change is limited, but also that neither well-informed knowledge of the science nor concern about climate change are necessarily linked to taking action to reduce emissions. Moreover, actions taken may not be efficacious, which Whitmarsh terms the 'asymmetry of intentions and impacts' (2009).

Social psychologists often include activities directed towards climate change amelioration in the wider category of 'pro-environmental behaviour' – actions that people undertake to protect the natural environment. People who are not engaged with climate change may be concerned about conservation and other environmental issues and take pro-environmental actions for different reasons (such as 'looking after the planet'), as can be observed with the natural cycles adherents in Chapter 3 and Jerrys Plains farmers in Chapter 4. Survey research with general population samples suggests that pro-environmental behaviours (like recycling) are popular and widespread despite evidence that they have little impact on reducing GHGs. Mark Graham concludes from his ethnographic research that recycling is a practice central to most Swedes' environmental self-image, even though it does not challenge consumption patterns of the affluent and has negligible impact on emissions (2016). Other studies find that behaviours that are categorised as relevant to climate change, such as reducing energy use, may be undertaken for other reasons, like reducing household bills.[1]

People may experience difficulties in making more impactful changes, such as shifting from private car travel to public transport, car pooling, walking or cycling, and such actions are relatively uncommon in both UK and Australian samples (Reser *et al.* 2012: 111; Whitmarsh 2011). For 'climate change engaged' individuals, these difficulties can be associated with a sense of frustration and cynicism about weak leadership on climate change. Wolf and Moser (2011: 563) suggest that people 'feel paralyzed' not just by the threat of climate change itself,

> but by not being able to do much about the ossified structures that constrain their actions (election systems, energy systems, transportation infrastructure, markets, etc.) … In other words, they may disengage because of their negative (but not at all irrational) appraisal of capacity and efficacy.

Pro-environmental and emissions reduction actions reported in the Upper Hunter and Lake Macquarie climate change survey introduced in Chapter 3 asked similar questions to other surveys, but supplemented these with items relevant to regional conditions: drought, flooding, sea-level rise and plant/crop selection. The most common actions that respondents reported clustered around daily conservation and money-saving routines under personal or household control. Reducing water and energy use were the highest scoring, and improved over time (65–85 per cent), with the latter reflecting a widespread trend in Australia for decreases in household electricity usage as prices have increased. Drought-prone Upper Hunter residents, many with long experience of water scarcity, reported the most water conservation.

UK and Australian surveys (Reser *et al.* 2012) have found that age is positively correlated with daily conservation and money-saving routines, and these also appealed to our older sample. Some personal efforts (modifying travel habits, drought proof plants/crops, and individual actions such as educating children about climate change or contacting authorities) scored moderately (40–50 per cent). There was increased resistance over time to undertaking more expensive and disruptive life changes, notably moving to avoid sea-level rise (2 per cent in 2011) and changing jobs (2.5 per cent in 2011). Taking part in climate action protests, letter writing etc. (4–7 per cent) was uncommon. It should be noted, as Whitmarsh also found for her UK sample (Whitmarsh 2011: 62), that direct political protest (apart from voting) on any issue is uncommon, and possibly more so in this older suburban/rural sample.

The open-ended comments made by 50 per cent of respondents in both iterations of the survey provide further insights into the nature of householders' engagement with climate change as indicated by reported behaviour. Approximately 20 per cent or 100 people in each iteration of the survey made comments on their own and others' actions. Respondents tended to make comments on issues related to the questions that they felt strongly about but hadn't had the chance to expand on in the structured questions. Many comments endorsed routines of energy and water conservation and recycling – 'doing our bit' – as desirable and achievable, especially if widely practised:

> *We are doing what we can. If everybody does their bit we should be on the way to helping.*
>
> (Upper Hunter resident 2008)

> *I can just do my bit but it's one step at a time.*
>
> (Lake Macquarie resident 2011)

Some respondents who were sceptical or uncertain about climate change still endorsed the precautionary principle:

> *Regardless of whether climate change is happening or not we should pollute the air less and do our best individually to help the planet.*
>
> (Lake Macquarie resident 2011)

The limits of 'doing their bit' were also clearly evident to some respondents, who pointed to government inadequacies in addressing the problem:

> *I try and do my little bit, governments need to do more.*
>
> (Upper Hunter resident 2008)

> *There is a lot of hypocrisy in government circles. At one scale we are being told to restrict our greenhouse gasmaking activities and then they are actively promoting Grand Prix racing.*
>
> (Lake Macquarie resident 2011)

Lack of trust in government and media presentation of 'the facts' was a further theme, especially among those who held more sceptical views about climate change:

> *I perceive climate change as cyclic. I would like a definition of climate change. I think climate change is media driven.*
>
> (Upper Hunter resident 2008)

> *I think the government is using scare tactics in regard to climate change. You can't trust any of them.*
>
> (Lake Macquarie resident 2008)

> *I just feel that they are pulling the wool over our eyes a bit, the government.*
>
> (Upper Hunter resident 2008)

Some of this mistrust was related to the federal Labor government's unsuccessful carbon emission trading scheme, aborted in 2009, followed by the implementation of a carbon tax policy in 2011 that the conservative opposition vigorously opposed as 'a big new tax on everything':

> *Federal and local governments are using it as an excuse to charge people unnecessarily and to travel overseas at taxpayers' expense.*
>
> (Lake Macquarie resident 2008)

I think a lot of the government talk is really to raise money by taxing us.
(Upper Hunter resident 2011)

Among those concerned about climate change, mistrust of government was also related to the view that the government lacked the political will to make hard policy decisions:

Our government and governments of the world put it in the too hard basket. Little people putting in our light globes and solar panels is not going to make any difference.
(Lake Macquarie resident 2011)

The government doesn't seem to want to do anything about climate change because of the jobs involved and putting industries out of action.
(Upper Hunter resident 2011)

By contrast, many respondents expressed the importance of dealing with climate change as an international or global problem:

Climate change should be addressed on a global scale. Australia cannot make an impact on its own.
(Lake Macquarie resident 2008)

It is a world problem. Everyone should be pitching in, not just a few countries.
(Lake Macquarie resident 2011)

Another strongly expressed view, echoing much of the conservative political rhetoric of this period, is that Australia should not have to make sacrifices unless other countries do so:

I think the countries in the northern hemisphere should be addressing these issues before us as they are the main polluters.
(Lake Macquarie resident 2008)

I think that this little country is not going to solve the problems as other bigger countries have a lot more industries and nothing is done there. It really has to be a worldwide effort to make a difference but we still need to do our bit here in Australia.
(Upper Hunter resident 2011)

The survey interviewers' invitation to make further comments led many respondents to talk about actions and policies at more inclusive levels, and the ethical values that should inform these. The links they made between actions at a small scale and wider politics suggest that household and individual practices are a meaningful domain of activity that bears on deeper values and concerns for the future. This conclusion is in accord with the summation of Reser and colleagues (2012: 116) whose survey of climate change related behaviours in Australia in 2010 suggested that:

> respondents are, on the whole, not only very actively engaged in some pro-environmental and carbon footprint-reducing behaviours, but that this engagement appears to be both mindful and quite 'psychologically significant' or meaningful for many. This in turn would suggest that climate change is an important and salient concern and issue for most survey respondents.

The values of collective responsibility and fairness are prominent in many of these comments as a positive force in dealing with climate change. They also underpin a critique of other parties – governments, business, media, other countries – that are seen to lack these values. This is not a call for fundamental changes to respond to climate change, but rather an affirmation of values that respondents view as important in the resolution of any threat to ordered social life.

Local government predicaments

National governments in Australia have been defensive and often-reluctant contributors to the multilateral agreements negotiated under the auspices of the UNFCCC. Mitigation targets of successive governments have been modest, and discourses of ecological modernisation exist in marked contradiction with energy and industry policies that reinforce the role of fossil fuel burning and export in the prosperity of the nation (Eckersley 2013: 390–1). These tensions are also marked in the policies of New South Wales (NSW) governments, where the major parties have been indistinguishable in their promotion of fossil fuel-based economic growth. Critics see Hunter Valley communities as the state's sacrifice zone, where mining and coal seam gas (CSG) extraction continue to expand along with royalties and associated revenue to state treasury.

Local governments, which have responsibility for local land-use planning, must deal with the downstream effects of state-supported fossil fuel profligacy. Throughout Australia local governments have front-line responsibility for adaptation planning on climate change risks that affect land use, notably bushfires, extreme heat and coastal hazards including sea-level rise. Almost 90 per cent of the Australian population lives in cities and major towns, and most of these are within 50 km of the coast (McDonald 2014: 173). It is not surprising then that the most rigorous adaptation planning to date has been for coastal hazards and sea-level rise, on which Jan McDonald (2014: 174) reports:

> Most jurisdictions have now adopted a planning benchmark for sea level rise (SLR) that guides building heights and set-backs from erosion and inundation lines, and require decision-makers to consider the effects of king tides and storm surge on higher sea levels in calculating such set-backs.

SLR benchmarks across the country based on the Intergovernmental Panel on Climate Change's (IPCC) Fourth Assessment Report projections (IPCC 2007) vary between 0.8 and 1 metre above 1990 levels by 2100, with lower benchmarks (2040 and 2050) for developments with a shorter asset life. In most cases, SLR guidelines were established after the publication of an Australian government assessment, *Climate Change Risks to Australia's Coast* (Department of Climate Change) in 2009. This report was based on the SLR projections of the IPCC's climate science and was produced by a Labor government striving for proactive policies in the optimistic atmosphere leading up to the Copenhagen climate change conference. It paints a stark picture of the SLR risk to coastal populations, built environment, industries and natural ecosystems, aiming to present 'a plausible "worst case" scenario over the longer term' and to provide a case for early action, including strategies of 'protect, accommodate or retreat' for at-risk areas (Department of Climate Change 2009: 6–7). The report is liberally illustrated with images of severe storm and inundation disasters: flooded settlements, eroded beaches, collapsed houses and simulation graphics of inundations over heavily populated areas. The period of proactive coastal risk assessment and policy development based on the IPCC's science was short lived, as conservative governments that denied or minimised climate change risks came to power in several of the states between 2010 and 2012. Federal Labor's policies were faltering as the government both fell into internal disarray and underwent a fierce opposition campaign against its carbon tax.

The backlash against SLR guidelines informed by climate scientists' projections cut a wide swathe in many communities among householders whose property values and property improvement plans were threatened as well as developers who saw the asset life of lucrative coastal sites shrinking under the new regulations. In response, some state governments have wound back their benchmarks. The Queensland Coastal Plan was suspended after only eight months in 2011, and the NSW government repealed its planning benchmark in 2012, soon after the Liberal National Party coalition was returned to power (McDonald 2014).

Lake Macquarie

These political conflicts and policy dilemmas were activated intensely in the City of Lake Macquarie, led by an environmentally proactive mayor between 2004 and 2012. The council developed progressive policies on adaptation for climate change impacts, as well as mitigation targets for GHGs. In 2004, the Lake Macquarie Community Greenhouse Action Plan was passed by Council, proposing 'actions that businesses and the community could adopt in order to reduce the amount of greenhouse gases they produce' (Lake Macquarie City Council 2004). Reduction of emissions, water and waste was the main focus of the Council's *Sustainable Living Guide*, a 44-page booklet published in 2007. Council guidelines built on NSW government mitigation schemes at that time, including the NSW Climate Change Fund established in 2007, which included the Residential Rebate Scheme 'to help householders make their homes more energy and water efficient'. Adaptation priorities became more prominent after the publication of the fourth IPCC Assessment Report in 2007. The council's own research, reported in its 2008 *State of the Environment Report*, had found that 'Lake Macquarie residents are becoming aware of climate change issues and the underlying causes', and the Council was set on 'taking a lead role in planning for sea-level rise due to climate change' (Lake Macquarie City Council 2008). A well-resourced Department of Sustainability was established in 2008, which one officer interviewed by the researchers described as 'cutting-edge':

> *We take an environmental risk analysis approach on all issues, and then operationalize strategies to address the issues. We operationally work in three sections, one is environmental security, and that includes climate change adaptations. There's sustainable living, which includes climate change mitigation, and the third is ecosystem enhancement, which relates to local Lake Macquarie ecosystems, but also takes on board climate change impacts on the Lake Macquarie ecosystems.*
>
> (Mitchell interview 2009)

The Council released the *Lake Macquarie Sea Level Rise Preparedness Adaptation Policy* in September 2008, using NSW government benchmarks. The 2009 Australian government report, *Climate Change Risks to Australia's Coast: A First Pass National Assessment*, identified Lake Macquarie City Council (LMCC) as the highest risk local government area in NSW for inundation of residential buildings 'from a sea-level rise of 1.1 metres and a 1-in-100 year storm tide' (Department of Climate Change 2009: 80). A total of 6,880 buildings were predicted to be affected. LMCC was lauded in the report for its 'proactive adaptation approach to planning for sea-level rise', which would allow 'Councillors, Council staff and the community to … make planning and development decisions that are suitable for the predicted change in conditions' (Department of Climate Change 2009: 82–3). In 2009, the state government published its *NSW Sea Level Rise Policy Statement*, specifying SLR planning benchmarks of 'a rise relative to 1990 mean sea levels of 40cm by 2050 and 90cm by 2100' and warned that the IPCC 'in 2007 also acknowledged that higher rates of sea level rise are possible' (Department of Environment and Climate Change and Water NSW 2009).

LMCC enthusiastically embraced the challenge. The mayor judged that there was sufficient ratepayer support:

> *There are groups that are attuned [to climate change risks]. We've got one of the largest Land Care networks in the country with over 200 groups, thousands of people involved. We've got a very strong demographic that is quite attuned and educated.*
>
> (Mayor interview 2009)

A ten-year 'Neighbourhood Empowerment' strategy was developed, by which identified localities could be supported to develop their own plans for sustainable

Figure 5.1 LMCC floodplan

Source: Peter Lewis, *Newcastle Herald*, 2008

living, environmental security and ecosystem enhancement. In March 2010, about 10,000 LMCC properties had 'sea level rise' notations inserted in their section 149 certificates, without informing owners[2] (Cronshaw 2010a). The terms in which this change was first reported in the *Newcastle Herald*, 'Sea rise may drop values', presaged the conflicts that ensued. The National Sea Change Task Force, representing 68 coastal councils, immediately picked up on the issues. 'Councils are in a major dilemma over the legal issues', commented the Task Force's executive director, Alan Stokes; 'It's going to be an area of litigation from one end of the country to the other' (quoted in Cronshaw 2010b). Stokes pointed to the horns of the dilemma: legal action now (from rejection of development applications) would ensue from aggrieved residents and developers, and legal action would occur in the future when risky approved developments suffered the impact of SLR.

Attuned to the risks of proactive policy rather than climate change itself, the NSW government began to change policy direction. In August 2010, the government approved the *NSW Coastal Planning Guideline: Adapting to Sea Level Rise*. While the SLR benchmarks remained the same, the aims and scope of the documents had shifted: the 2009 *Policy Statement* outlined the government's objective and commitments to SLR adaptation, and attested to 'the support that the Government will provide to coastal communities and local councils to prepare and adapt to rising sea levels' (NSW Department of Planning 2010). By the following year, all mention of support to communities had been expunged and the stated purpose of the *Coastal Planning Guideline* was 'to provide guidance on how sea level rise is to be considered in land use planning and development assessment in coastal NSW'. The contentious burden of responsibility for community adaptation and support was discarded by the state government and left in the lap of local councils.

The plight of local residents and developers, united in their opposition to 'unfair' and 'extreme' Council policies, was an ongoing source of stories for local media. Early in 2008 a controversy arose over NSW Department of Planning maps, withheld from the public, showing large areas of future inundation of Lake Macquarie suburbs (Cronshaw 2008a). The report was finally released in May 2008, with a front-page report titled, 'We're going under' and dramatic colour modelling of inundated coast and lake perimeter (Cronshaw 2008b). Headlines like 'Waters keep rising, and so does worry' highlighted the situation of retirees and other homeowners facing the prospect of stranded assets (Hawkins 2009). In response, the Sustainability Department promulgated its adaptation policies, with a 'climate change taskforce' and a '37-step plan to address the 91-centimetre sea level rise forecast for 2100' (Hawkins 2009). 'Drowning in opinions: property project thrown in limbo' headlined a story about a resident with a development proposal who had bought his $1.45 million lake waterfront property in 2008, just before LMCC published its first climate change and SLR statement (Cronshaw 2011a). Waterfront property values in the area had reputedly fallen by 30 per cent, and the aggrieved owner commented: 'I'm not a climate change sceptic, but I think man is smart enough to do something in the next 100 years to figure this out ... The Dutch live below the sea level and they sorted it out' (quoted in Cronshaw 2011a).

One of the largest property developers in the area, Jeff McCloy, threatened the Council with a class action over the devaluation of waterfront properties because of the climate change policy. 'I'll put them on notice and ask what evidence they have to make these ridiculous claims', he said. 'We have the right to know the scientific basis for their claims and whether they are using theoretical models that have no definitive way of determining the future'. The mayor was conciliatory but firm: 'Jeff, in my view, is being silly on this one. I have a lot of time for Jeff, but that doesn't mean he's right on everything'. He emphasised that the council had to 'apply the precautionary principle on what we're told is the best science' (Cronshaw 2011b). As early as 2008, the mayor had indicated that 'retreat from some areas' may be necessary, in addition to a range of adaptation options including 'seawalls, offshore breakwaters, raised floor levels, relocatable buildings, building setbacks, and dune reconstruction and protection' (Piper 2008: 13).

The progressive approach of LMCC came into increasing conflict with the pragmatic realities of electoral politics, the material interests of ratepayers and the momentum of climate change negativity that was developing in institutional politics and public discourse. Climate change realism was not a vote-winner, and the messages of fear about SLR that underpinned policy documents in early years were proving counterproductive. Back-pedalling occurred at all levels, with repeal or softening of some policies. Lake Macquarie remained committed to its adaptation and mitigation approaches, but councillors approved a medium-density development in a lakeside suburb, despite technical staff recommending against it because of SLR concerns (Cronshaw 2012a). At the same time, the Council considered reducing the benchmark for the unpopular SLR property notations to 1 metre rather than 3, effectively halving the number (Cronshaw 2012b). Residents in vulnerable zones have become increasingly strident in demanding government action to protect their properties:

> Marks Point and Belmont South residents will demand that state and federal governments provide the money to defend their properties against sea-level rise risk. Residents want authorities to build a levee and flood gates and raise land and infrastructure to protect their houses. They will defend against any move to let their properties go to the elements. Resident Frank Mieszala said, 'retreat is not an option.' 'We'll have an adaptation plan that says we're going to defend these properties,' he said.
>
> (Cronshaw 2014a)

In 2014, the Council passed a number of guidelines to 'give people multiple options' to adapt to increased flooding, including 'floating houses', raising floor levels, relocating homes, and portable housing (Cronshaw 2014b). Equitable solutions are sought, so as not to increase the burden on already disadvantaged or vulnerable residents. Communication strategies have been reviewed, and terms like 'sea level rise' have been largely replaced by 'current and future flooding'. As one officer commented to the author, SLR has the threatening connotation of permanent inundation, while for most residents the change will be an increase in flooding that already occurs and is temporary. Likewise, the term 'climate change' is used less often than 'being sustainable', 'reducing our carbon footprint' and 'reducing our waste'.

Council planning and environmental officers have been placed in a predicament, with lack of federal and state government leadership on climate change policy on the one hand, and intensifying predictions of risk and the need for adaptation and mitigation on the other. A dedicated risk manager on staff helps officers embed climate change impacts in all planning initiatives. Funding from federal and state agencies continues to flow to the Council's climate change initiatives, despite political failure to acknowledge the problems at this level. In the thinking of Council staff, they are the front line of skirmishes with disgruntled electorates, while other departments and agencies benefit without political pain. We see here a case of a high level of local government activation around climate change problems, supported initially by residents' environmental commitment and proactive state and federal government policies. In a situation

Figure 5.2 Hundred-year flood now frequent
Source: Peter Lewis, *Newcastle Herald*, 2015

of declining government support for climate change policy, associated with some residents' heightened appreciation of the negative impacts of adaptation initiatives on their property values, public engagement now includes more extreme tendencies towards denial or unrealistic demands on government protection. Online comments on SLR policies are often vituperous. A comment on a *Newcastle Herald* article on the implementation of SLR guidelines illustrates the tone: 'The BS meter is off the chart on this one. The LMCC are like a bunch of gypsies gazing into a doomsday crystal ball. The seas will rise and taketh away all that is good. UOOGAAA BOOGA BOOGGA!!' (online comment, 8 March 2015). In the words of one council officer, 'some people in the community are uncomfortable about the fact that the goalposts are now moving ... We all love to have a bit of certainty' (Alex interview 2014).

Climate Ready Dora Creek

While some highly exposed Lake Macquarie residents ignore or deny the risk of climate change impacts on their properties (all of which the Council has classified as 'increasing' in its State of the Environment reports), others are cognisant of the future scenarios. They make collective efforts at mitigation and adaptation, driven by their perceptions of the need to protect properties, local environments, health and livelihoods (and sometimes, the planet). The first group to form under the auspices of the Council's Sustainable Neighbourhoods Program was Climate Ready Dora Creek (CRDC) in 2009. The settlement of Dora Creek (population 1,671 (Australian Bureau of Statistics 2011)) is located on Awabakal country, on a flood plain that takes the form of a sandy peninsular divided by the mouth of Dora Creek on the south-western side of Lake Macquarie (see Figure 5.3). Most of the residences are located less than 1 metre above sea level, some only a few centimetres above the high tide level mark, and the village is one of the most flood-prone areas on the lake during storm inundations that will become much worse as sea levels rise. The settlement started as a colonial land grant in the 1830s, with economic activities focused on timber-cutting, fishing and horticulture, the last limited by the frequent flooding that is documented from the earliest years of settlement. With a railway station and good road access south to Sydney and north to other parts of the Hunter, Dora Creek has been a desirable lakeside suburb for many years, however, property values have started to fall, due, real estate agents claim, to LMCC's 'sea level rise rules' (Cronshaw 2014c).

Figure 5.3 Mouth of Dora Creek at Lake Macquarie looking east

Source: Lake Aerial Photo, 2015

A small group of residents formed the Dora Creek Catchment Group (DCCG) in 1998 with the aims of community education, water quality assessment and flood monitoring for the creek system. They were approached by LMCC in 2008 to form a pilot group in the Council's Sustainable Neighbourhoods scheme. Catchment Group members had a long-term focus on flood mitigation, and the group's secretary acknowledged the new difficulties the community faced in managing SLR. The initial public meeting organised by LMCC and DCCG to discuss the project was well attended and provided some important 'groundwork education' on climate change, although not uncontested by more sceptical residents, as one DCCG member recalls:

> *It was quite obvious at that time that there were people in the audience that were what I would call 'climate change sceptics.' They tended to middle aged or older, and they had the attitude, 'Well, back in '57, we saw this happen, it's nothing new to us,' that kind of thing.*

> (Barry interview 2009)

Another resident who became active in CRDC commented on the different stances of older and younger residents at the first public meeting and subsequently:

> *We had, in actual fact, a lot of sceptics. [Concerning] the long-term implications of a metre or thereabouts sea level rise, they'll all be gone, and they didn't care. The younger ones, some of them wanted to blame Council for even letting them build in that area.*

> (Anna interview 2009)

Young people who are new arrivals to the area are hard to engage, commented Anna. They are busy with young families, and 'they haven't experienced a flood before'. Many, while happy to own a coveted property near the water, seemed ignorant of the risks they faced, according to Barry:

> *It was interesting that people who've built on the Dora Creek delta mostly didn't even realise that they were building on a river constructed landform that could be changed dramatically by natural process. I guess they regard one bit of land as much like another bit of land, and don't see it in the context of physical processes that are going on in the environment.*

> (Barry interview 2009)

Despite some reservations about obtaining wider community involvement, a group of residents who volunteered as neighbourhood coordinators proceeded to work with the Council, which provided resources for venue hire, printing and publicity, as well as expertise coordinated by the Council's Sustainability Project Coordinator. The CRDC group was formed in September 2008, with the purpose of drafting a Climate Change Adaptation Plan. A glossy newsletter published in

July 2009 announced Dora Creek as 'the first community in Lake Macquarie, and possibly the first in Australia, to develop a draft local plan for adapting to climate change' (CRDC 2009). The Draft Climate Change Adaptation Plan was launched by the mayor in August 2009 at an 'Emergency Ready Dora Creek' workshop. The Saturday afternoon workshop, which was attended by the author and colleagues, was billed as 'an interactive workshop on preparing for, coping with, and recovering from natural disasters such as floods and storms'.

The workshop was a well-attended event, by both emergency services person-nel and (mostly older) residents. Interactive groups were arranged by street address, so that the flood and storm scenarios presented by experts could be worked through (preparation, response, recovery phases) in a fine-grained way. As one participant commented, 'even in the same suburb, one street is very different to another'. This fine-grained approach was reiterated in discussions of care for vulnerable neighbours (frail, elderly, children), reinforcing values of responsible community citizenship. Participants were also keen to highlight poor infrastructure, especially drainage and road construction, that required attention and repair from the Council. The mayor's laudatory speech to launch the Draft Plan was followed by some hard questions: 'Why were we allowed to build in this area?'; 'Well, a lot of these places were built before the Council knew anything about climate change', replied the mayor, fending off the spec-tre of responsibility and liability that was becoming a dominant theme at most public forums. 'What do we do about rising sea level?'. Barry recalls a tone of levity in the group:

> Apart from [the suggestion of] jacking the house up, if it's not already on stilts, I think the only other suggestion was to sell your property to a climate change scep-tic. Because you're not going to sell it to somebody who thinks it's going to happen! [laughs]
>
> (Barry interview 2009)

Declining house values were a chronic source of concern, as elsewhere in Lake Macquarie. 'Some people complain that the value of their houses is going down, but we've known for years that Dora Creek goes under in a flood', commented Elaine, a neighbourhood coordinator for CRDC. For those who were active in the group, the partnership with the Council was perceived as a source of assis-tance with a persistent problem that could only become worse. In this view, the adverse externality is climate change, and people need to have a realist position about it and be proactive in whatever ways they can in their local environment. Elaine put it this way:

> Climate change, whatever term they put on it, climate always does make an impact on us, whether it's no rain, too much rain, fires, huge storms – and we're experi-encing more and more of that. So we just have to be ready for whatever it throws at us, and putting your head in the sand is not going to help. And in cases of emer-gency everything runs on a priority, so if you've lost your roof and someone else is

in a worse way then you've just got to hang around and wait. So look after your own patch so you can minimise the damage. I just think it all starts at the bottom.
(Elaine interview 2013)

The emphasis on local knowledge and responsibility that informed the conduct of the Emergency Ready workshop was pervasive in residents' understandings of appropriate responses to the hazards they faced. In reflecting on the relationship of Council officers and residents, Elaine thought that the local knowledge of the latter, especially long-term and elderly residents, made an important contribution to Council's capacity to manage climate hazards:

At the grassroots level, the history of the area and the knowledge of the old people who have been here for a long time is of great value. Especially here in relation to floods, and where the water goes, and how it flows and things like that. We sort of shake our heads sometimes and think, 'if only [Council] would listen,' but you know, they can only do what they can do.
(Elaine interview 2013)

This valued knowledge at a micro-local scale provided a way of connecting with a wider group of residents, even if not active in CRDC. As for almost all action groups encountered in our Hunter Valley study, the core group was about six to eight people most of whom occupied the neighbourhood/street coordinators' positions. These people were typically involved in other groups as well. In interviews just a few months after the launch of the Draft Climate Adaptation Plan, several of them expressed doubts about the sustainability of CRDC, due to the small number of active members, the withdrawal of support by LMCC, which planned on starting up a large number of similar local groups, and the lack of enthusiasm of residents with 'busy lives' who preferred to live in the present with a 'wait and see' attitude and avoid thinking about a 50-year timeframe. As Anna commented on her efforts to expand the membership:

It's the same old; people tag you a Greenie, see you coming to talk to them about something, and they don't want to know. Even friends, yeah, they're so sceptical, they'll deal with things when they happen and if they happen. They're not going to sit on a committee, and go to meetings, and plan to avoid or all that sort of stuff. It's just, it's quite amazing! [laughs]
(Anna interview 2009)

She compared the high level of activation that had occurred several years previously when lakeside communities had been threatened with a coal mine development in close proximity to suburbs:

An open-cut coal mine behind your house is a motive. It's sudden, it's short-lived, in that it's going to last 20 years … And although both would depreciate land value, or have the potential to, climate change has too many sceptics, and it's too far away. And although there are climate change health issues – malaria, all sorts of things, heatwaves – people aren't experiencing them, as they would the threat of an open-cut coal mine.

(Anna interview)

Barry expressed similar reservations about the long-term prospects for CRDC when we asked him about the level of interest from residents:

I think the difficulty is going to be maintaining that interest for a longer term. I think that a few extreme happenings might keep the interest going, but if we just drift along with typical weather, then people are going to say, 'Oh yeah, yeah.' Interest just slowly ebbs away.

(Barry interview 2009)

CRDC was a beneficiary of the first wave of resources and enthusiasm for climate change adaptation in LMCC. Barry and other participants were worried that the Council would eventually transfer its support to emerging groups elsewhere, causing the group's decline. Over the next few years, the Council withdrew ongoing support to an increasing number of participating neighbourhoods, and new governance arrangements were put in place. The Sustainable Neighbourhoods Alliance (Inc.), to which Council provides some assistance, is a not-for-profit independent body with the aim of mutual support for member groups and advocacy for sustainable neighbourhood issues.

The Dora Creek group persists, with a small number of active participants, who comment that the suburb has benefited over time from the close relationships forged with Council officers in the early years. Council is seen as responsive to local incidents like blocked drains or traffic obstructions. Climate change seems to have faded from view. Asked in 2013 if climate change ever came under discussion at meetings, Elaine commented, 'No it doesn't because, we're probably a bit fatalistic in a way. If it happens it happens and we're doing the best we can for our environment and our ecology'. The 'Climate Ready' title of the group, formed in the first wave of Council enthusiasm for promoting climate change adaptation initiatives in the suburbs, sets it apart from later groups that adopted the 'Sustainable Neighbourhood' designation. The council's webpages for the programme no longer mention the term 'climate change'; the sample of group projects listed includes community gardens, trash and treasure sales, bulk purchase of water tanks and local energy audits. The threat of global climate change has been sidelined from civic concerns, while the less controversial rubric of sustainability activates residents' quests for better lives and localities, often through transient moments of environmental disruption.

Climate activism

Modes of activation in the quotidian worlds of householders and neighbourhoods and in local government reveal a linkage of pro-environmental and communitarian values embedded in daily routines and in bureaucratic processes. But these values come up against intractable challenges when peoples' perceptions of economic well-being are threatened by initiatives to reduce emissions and adapt to climate change impacts. The previous examples point to the contradictions that are experienced in many contexts of everyday life, where collective environmental responsibility is felt to be at odds with economic orthodoxy and consumer satisfactions. The individualising nature of capitalist societies, combined with divisive national narratives and citizens' aspirations for increased prosperity can undermine precautionary and adaptive environmental initiatives.

Different, sometimes radical, social imaginaries are expressed in the realm of activist politics that protagonists oppose to the corrosive forces of corporate capitalism and consumerism. In the Hunter region, struggles against coal-mine developments gain their impetus from directly impacted communities, while climate activist groups draw their membership from the Hunter's urban and suburban localities. During the period that Rosewarne *et al.* (2014) have identified as 'climate action upsurge' between 2007 and 2010, there were five groups that designated themselves as climate change focused: Transition Towns (Coal Point and Newcastle), Climate Action (Newcastle and Lake Macquarie) and Rising Tide Australia. All groups supported or were part of wider networks and alliances, including Climate Action Network Australia, the international Transition Network and Rising Tide International.

The membership, aims and values of the climate action groups are diverse, reflecting the diversity of climate action groups in Australia more generally (Burgmann and Baer 2012). They share similar aims of awareness raising and spearheading wider public support to achieve a sustainable low-carbon or zero-emissions society. Their structure, membership and means of achieving their aims are varied, as are their visions for the type of future society to be achieved.

Transition Newcastle (TN) is part of a global network of geographically localised TT (Transition Towns) groups that comprise the Transition Movement or Transition Network. The Network has as its core drivers the twin challenges of climate change and peak oil, with corresponding responses of building community resilience while reducing the community carbon footprint (Brangwyn and Hopkins 2008). TN officially joined the Network in 2008. This is a large group, with a diverse range of ages, backgrounds and occupations, reflecting the urban residential makeup of the city of Newcastle. TN sponsors workshops, lectures and activities in areas such as transport alternatives and sustainable food. The peak of activity of TN appears to have been the period from 2008–2010, but a current website, Twitter and Facebook site (with posts like 'Next week is International Composting Awareness Week!') are still evidenced in 2015.[3]

The two Climate Action groups (CAGs) in the Hunter were formed as part of the international Climate Action Network and its offshoot Climate Action Network Australia (CANA), which declares its vision as 'A strong, united and sustainable civil society working collaboratively for climate action in Australia'

(Climate Action Network Australia 2015). Climate Action Newcastle (CAN) was established in 2006 as 'a committed group of local residents from all backgrounds' focused on behaviour change and influencing government policy in relation to carbon emission reduction and a clean energy future. The membership is younger, well educated and oriented to market-based solutions to climate change. Lake Macquarie Climate Action (LMCA) was formed in 2007 in suburban Lake Macquarie 'by a group of local residents concerned about the threat and lack of action to mitigate climate change'. Both groups were in a peak of activity during the 2007–2010 period.

Neither the CAGs nor the TTs have articulated radical political visions. They strive for expanded public commitment to their cause, in different ways. CAN embraces market thinking in its quest to expand renewable energy through Smart Energy Expos, solar panel bulk purchase programmes, school education and publicity campaigns, and also endorses a moderate programme of activism that will appeal to the mainstream:

> not the lowest common denominator, but we do want to engage as many people as we can, and engage with them positively. And as I said before, start to try and influence their mindset and push boundaries a bit, just to show how serious this issue is, and the old rules don't apply any more.
>
> (April, CAN, interview 2009)

TTs have a communitarian ideal, focused on awareness raising, sharing and neighbourly cooperation to achieve more sustainable lifestyles:

> The biggest thing that probably we're doing is slowly awareness raising.
>
> (Jack, TN, interview 2010)

> Yeah, it would be good to see people sharing transport, sharing gardens, connecting with each other as well, using the hall.
>
> (Lydia, Transition Town Coal Point, interview 2010)

Rising Tide Newcastle (RT) represents the radical end of the climate action spectrum in the Hunter, and was affiliated with a network of groups in the UK and USA that were formed in the 'upsurge' period. It had a membership of students and young adults with a strong anti-capitalist and anti-consumerist ethic, for whom environmental activism is a large part of their self-identity and daily life. RT places less emphasis on geographically defined communities and incremental change. Its stated purpose is 'taking action against the causes of anthropogenic climate change and [campaigning] for equitable, just, effective, and sustainable solutions to the crisis'. Much of RT's activity focused on the coal industry in the Hunter Region. In 2004–2005, they joined a broad coalition of ENGOs and community groups that successfully blocked the state government plan to build another coal-fired power station in NSW. RT was the only group that had a selective process for membership. Humphrey, one of the founding members of RT in Newcastle, a veteran of forest activism since his early 20s and recently employed by a large ENGO, remarked:

> A lot of the climate action groups that are around in suburbs and towns all over Australia are basically just open door groups ... We do a lot of non-violent direct action, and we have to have some element of security ... We're not as open as a lot of other groups.

> (Humphrey, RT, interview 2010)

In 2010, RT had a small core membership and met weekly to plan campaigns and direct actions. They remained an active if diminishing group through to 2012.

Alignments and events

During their years of high activity, local climate action groups were part of a large political field in the Hunter Valley where many residents organised against coal industry threats to local environments, livelihood and health. This locally based opposition has been a persistent feature of the regional response to the accelerating coal-mine expansion associated with Australia's 'resource boom', as coal prices started to climb from 2003. Some resident-sponsored organisations, such as Anvil Hill Action Group, Bickham Coal Action Group and Southlakes Communities against Mining have had a limited lifespan and membership, until their battles with industry and government were won or lost. Others, such as Minewatch, Singleton Shire Healthy Environment Group and Correct Planning and Consultation for Mayfield Group, endure for many years as they take up new challenges and recruit new members and leaders. While their issues are 'live', groups have the capacity to garner other groups' support, through rallies, submissions, social media and website publicity (Connor *et al.* 2008, 2009). ENGOs like Greenpeace and the Wilderness Society intermittently join forces with local groups, usually on occasions where there is a high-profile issue like threats to a species or a habitat, or a particularly striking environmental case against a development.

Since 2012, a major regional campaign is being fought under the banner of the Coal Terminal Action Group (CTAG), a broad alliance of ENGOs and diverse environmental groups opposed to the building of a fourth coal export terminal by Port Waratah Coal Services (PWCS) at Port of Newcastle. The 'T4' will enable a massive increase in coal exports, and will increase mining, train movements, port activity and pollution, affecting people and environment along the whole Hunter Valley Coal Chain. The campaign is being facilitated by the Hunter Community Environment Centre (HCEC), 'a resource-hub for groups and individuals working towards environmental and social justice'. Another non-government organisation, the NSW Environmental Defender's Office, is regularly involved in assisting residents' groups fighting the coal industry and has coordinated key submissions to the Planning Assessment Commission review that is part of the fourth coal terminal application process. The NSW Greens party has been a visible presence in many campaigns and is currently supporting the CTAG campaign.

From 2007–2010, the convergence of interest in arresting destructive mining, burning and export of coal brought diverse groups together. This created a wider base of support for both local climate activists and mine opponents. Popular concern about the threat of climate change was high during the upsurge period, for the reasons discussed in Chapter 3. The annual Walks Against Warming, organised around the country by partnerships of environmental and development aid NGOs like Greenpeace, Australian Conservation Foundation, Oxfam and World Vision brought tens of thousands of 'ordinary voters' on to the streets 'to pressure federal political leaders to get serious about climate change' and similar consensual messages (Environment Victoria 2010). This was a period when hopes for an enduring, broad-based climate movement were high. The Hunter region was targeted as a strategic site by national climate campaigns because of its coal industry, and was the site of the first nationally organised Camp for Climate Action ('Climate Camp') in 2008, on the model of Camps organised in the UK from 2006–2010. Rosewarne *et al.* (2014: 109–30) provide a detailed account of the organisation of Climate Camps in Australia, which they see as a critical phase of non-violent direct action 'premised on building larger communities of activists and injecting more momentum into climate politics' (Rosewarne *et al.* 2014: 110).

Members of all the Hunter climate action groups often cite the Climate Camp in Newcastle in 2008 as the most significant collective achievement of the movement in the Hunter region. More than a thousand people, including interstate participants, gathered over six days in July for an 'information sharing and direct action camp' in a large inner-suburban park near Newcastle's coal port. Activities included lectures, film-screenings, music, kids' activities, rallies and marches, street theatre and numerous workshops, many focusing on skills and planning for non-violent direct action.

The culmination of the Camp was the 'Day of Mass Action' on Sunday 13 July (preceded by a 'Mass Action Simulation' the day prior), when about a thousand participants marched to Carrington Coal Terminal (Cubby 2008). Participants, previously organised in 'action teams', had designated 'arrestable and non-arrestable roles', the former involving walking onto the rail line to 'stop coal exports in their tracks'. The police presence was heavy, including 160 officers, riot squad, dog squad, mounted officers and water police. There were 37 people arrested after climbing on to the trains and chaining themselves to the carriages, and the delivery of coal to the Carrington Terminal was halted for about six hours (Cubby 2008). It was this aspect of the Climate Camp that received the most media attention, with graphic pictures of mounted police and leather jacket clad officers corralling and dragging protestors. The following day, in an incident that made national news, five protesters chained themselves to the Kooragang Island coal loader conveyer belt, stopping work for about two hours (*Sydney Morning Herald* 2008).

While the 2008 Camp for Climate Action and subsequent Camps in 2009 and

2010 were impressively large gatherings of people concerned about climate change, the involvement of the 'mainstream' seems slight. In our interviews, climate group members tended to recall the expressive moments of solidarity and *communitas*, especially at the first camp, and perceive this as 'a highlight' and 'a boost to the movement'. However, the media focused on the more dramatic incidents that received coverage in the predictable news genre of 'protestors versus police': 'Port strike force: Strong arm of the law on alert for climate protest'; 'Protestors again disrupt coal loading'. Public comments in newspaper letters and blogs ranged from the congratulatory to the censorious.

All the climate groups aspired to connect themselves ('the grassroots') to a large population ('the mainstream'). This alignment of ideals and feelings, which de Rijke (2012) has termed the 'symbolic construction of similarity', is difficult to achieve among a conservative regional population that views the direct action protests that distinguished the Climate Camps as radical fringe politics. A more successful initiative in creating fellow travellers was the annual protest day of small craft flotilla on Newcastle harbour, billed as 'The People's Blockade of the World's Biggest Coal Port'. RT took the lead in organising this event, in partnership with many other Hunter region environmental and social justice organisations. The blockades, which ran from 2006–2012, attracted hundreds of supporters in kayaks, rafts, canoes and sailing boats, or just spectating from the beach (see Figure 5.4). The Port of Newcastle authority suspended coal-shipping movements for the duration of each blockade. This event, with its picnic day atmosphere, beach volleyball, speakers and stalls, most fully realised activists' ideals of a 'family-centred' non-violent direct action to engage the mainstream. The 2012 flyer for the final iteration of the event invited: 'Join hundreds of people in a fun, effective and peaceful protest against the tripling of coal exports from Newcastle Harbour', a reference to the planned fourth coal terminal. Speakers at this event were drawn from RT, the HCEC, the NSW Greens, local government Greens councillors and trade union representatives.

Newcastle harbour was again the site of a well-attended flotilla protest when the international climate action organisation 350.org sponsored the Pacific Climate Warriors' trip to Australia in October 2014. The Warriors, young people from 13 Pacific nations bringing five traditional canoes, explicitly linked the proposed expansion of Newcastle's coal port to the threat of rising seas. According to Milan Loeak from Marshall Islands:

> The coal port is the largest in the world and there are plans for it to expand and we want to bring the message that the expansion is definitely going to have an effect on the islands, not just in the Marshalls but all over the Pacific.
>
> (Garrett 2014)

The event attracted hundreds of participants and local small craft, and succeeded in preventing the passage of 8 of the 12 coal ships scheduled for that day. The *Newcastle Herald* reported:

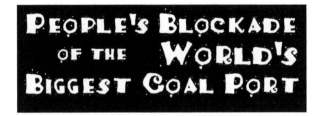

Figure 5.4 Flyer for blockade of Newcastle harbour

Source: Rising Tide Australia, 2010

the Pacific Warriors [took] to the water in their hand-carved boats … With the support of about 100 kayak riders, the warriors stared down the massive 226-metre bulk carrier Rhine as it attempted to leave the world's largest coal export port.

(Kelly 2014)

This story stimulated 146 online comments, many critical of the tactics and the message: 'Stunts like this achieve nothing. Just a waste of taxpayer funds as the police have to stop these idiots from getting killed'; 'Coral atolls eventually sink. Nothing to do with climate change! They have been sinking for years'. Expressions of esteem and support were also common: 'Go brave Warriors. Coal must be phased out, and our politicians are not listening'.

The Pacific Climate Warriors' harbour blockade is part of a spectrum of possibilities from direct action to organised protests like rallies and street marches through to collective support of practices like permaculture, cycling and farmers' markets. These activities have in common the attempt to create what Graeber has called 'small situations of dual power' in which a different social reality is prefigured (2009: 433). Some climate activists, like CAN, position themselves firmly at the moderate end:

> *We occupy a different part of the climate action spectrum, to more 'extreme', in inverted commas, groups like Rising Tide, who engage in direct action. I think that's beneficial in terms of being favoured, or being seen in a positive light by ordinary Novocastrians, who are fairly conservative, just like most people are, you know.*
> (April, CAN, interview 2009)

Some actions, however, seek to prefigure radically different social realities. RT distinguished itself by its commitment to non-violent direct action (NVDA), making a specialty of dramatic disruptions to the coal export chain, with occupation of train lines and carriages, and climbing loaders. RT members and others saw their group as having the most radical tactics for change, while also participating in the larger 'grassroots climate movement'. Caitlin was in her late 20s at the time of interview, recently graduated with a social science degree. She was an active member of the Australian Youth Climate Coalition when a student. She described herself as having 'a longstanding interest in environmental protection', including extensive experience of forest blockades, reflected in her comments on activism:

> *Because of the scale of the crisis that we face and the intractability of it and the power of the opposition we face, I think that large-scale civil disobedience campaigns are going to be essential, and so I really wish that other groups would get on board more in advocating and participating and direct action. Because that's the sort of radical action we need to shift the debate along. Not that I would want to call it radical. [Why not?] It's not radical; it's just rational.*
> (Caitlin, RT, interview 2010)

Caitlin described the 'ultimate objective' of the organisation as 'changing the structure of our society, our economic system, and people's value systems ...'. According to Edward:

> *The grassroots climate movement needs to be radicalising the population, radicalising themselves I think. Because at the moment they're still stuck in lobbying, in letter writing, in petitions, in marches, things like that, and I really think that the climate movement needs to get a lot more serious in campaigns of civil disobedience and just much more gung-ho kind of action ... Really pushing the boundaries of what's allowed, to really force the government's hand on the issue.*
> (Edward, RT, interview 2010)

Humphrey articulated the same impatience with 'soft' activism:

> *We're sick of talking and sick of research, and all this sort of stuff, and we just want to make stuff happen.*
>
> (Humphrey, RT, interview 2010)

In all these statements of impatience with more gradualist and moderate forms of activism, RT members expressed their sense of urgency about climate change and their hopes for a more radical mobilisation of the population that will achieve significant change – 'more elaborate, and more permanent, forms of dual power' (Graeber 2009: 434) where the crisis of the planet begins to take priority over established political and economic interests.

New activist directions

Like the other climate groups, RT was on the wane after 2010. Looking back, former members mention the usual personal circumstances that contribute to the demise of highly active but small, voluntary groups: burnout (especially after the failure in Copenhagen) and the need to earn an income. There was no formal structure holding the group together. The death in 2011 of Peter Gray, a core member of national renown, was devastating. Over and above these circum-stances, there is a perception that climate change lost political traction nationally and with the public. To be effective, the climate crisis needed to be tackled 'from different angles'. The campaign against the fourth coal export terminal under the auspices of the Hunter Community Environment Centre – an incorporated organisation – became a rallying point. The Coal Terminal Action Group made a strategic decision that their campaign would prioritise the health threats from T4 – air pollution not carbon pollution – that would impact resi-dents in the inner suburbs near the port as well as communities along the entire Hunter Valley Coal Chain, from Carrington to Narrabri (see Figure 5.5). Clare, a former RT member, reflected on the shift in tactical focus from increased GHGs linked with coal exports, to health impacts on nearby residents, especially children:

> *It's difficult to get traction amongst the public – wider than a small group of activists – when you talk about climate change. So I think [the focus on health impacts] is a strategic thing really. I mean we're all genuine in that we think T4 is a big health threat. But we feel like local people agree with us that it's a health threat and people are more likely to care about it [than about climate change]. It has political lever-age here.*
>
> (Clare interview 2013)

Both CTAG and HCEC have attracted grants and donations for office premises and paid coordinators, enabling a more sustained campaign of lobbying, submis-sions and rallies, and concerted opposition in the review and decision-making

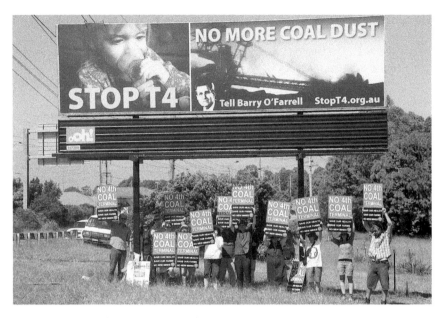

Figure 5.5 Stop T4 billboard, Newcastle
Source: Coal Terminal Action Group, 2012

processes of the NSW Department of Planning. Clare commented on the differences between this form of activism and RT's approach:

> *Rising Tide operated in a very different way compared to the way the Coal Terminal Action Group is running. Like we were always not so much about stopping things, even though that might have been what it appeared to others. For me, it was more just about mind bombs and just getting people to think about things …* *We were much more tactics focused. Shock value was important. Also I think because we were all volunteers that was just the biggest bang for our buck for the effort we could put in for the kind of outcome we could achieve.*
>
> (Clare interview 2013)

In Clare's view, the achievements of RT's shock tactics, especially getting the wider public to start thinking about the connections between climate change and coal exports, are an enduring legacy of the group as is the commitment to NVDA. Former members are now active – some as paid coordinators – in campaigns with local residents against coal and CSG developments, under the auspices of Lock the Gate Alliance (LtG). Clare thinks 'a little bit of RT has gone into LtG', a nationally based organisation where 'mainstream people and farmers' are taking direct action to protect their properties.

The fleeting period of a grassroots climate movement that Rosewarne *et al.*

(2014) have identified as a national phenomenon between 2007 and 2010 can be discerned in the Hunter region. During 2010 to 2012, the disappearance or devolution of these groups to a social media presence that maintains large but shallow networks of information sharing on a broad range of environmental issues, could be seen as symptomatic of the 'loss of political bearings' of the grassroots climate movement. This withering of the grassroots, however, cannot be separated from the poor policy, weak leadership and divisive party politics that beset the national effort (Eckersley 2013).

The Hunter research suggests that the former participants in these groups do not view their efforts as a failure. Commitment to environmentalist ideals is a stable life project for many who have been drawn into new modes of action where values of environmental and social justice are brought together. Their campaigns engage wider publics that are adversely impacted by the upstream end of fossil fuel dependence, like coal mines, export infrastructure and hydraulic fracturing, even if the downstream consequences in the form of climate change seem remote. These 'communities of concern' (de Rijke 2012) do not wait on more accessible translations of climate science or policy arguments; they are urgently engaged in grassroots mobilisations that challenge state and corporate destruction of peoples' communities, well-being and livelihoods. The fact that these campaigns are made on local issues and in local terms does not belie their relevance to climate activism more broadly.

Activating values

The analysis in this chapter confirms others' observations that climate change activism as a political movement has been on the wane in Australia since 2010 (Rosewarne *et al.* 2014). Ethnographic methods of inquiry into contexts of social life suggest, however, that there are numerous crosscurrents of activation related to the reality of climate change. Householders and neighbourhood groups may organise their thinking about energy use, care for local surroundings and reducing waste around the blandly generic idea of 'sustainability' but pro-environmental values are apparent even among the climate change 'negativists' of one orientation or another who responded to our survey. The ethic of individual responsibility evidenced in frequent statements about 'doing my bit' or 'looking after your own patch', may reflect the excessive individualism of neoliberal thinking, but can also be seen as an expression of self-reliance and fairness, values that are part and parcel of environmental justice and the 'grassroots' organising strategies of climate activist groups. The rise of conservative political ideology and the shifts in policy debates over the years since the first 'climate emergency' have created discursive spaces for virulent forms of climate change negativity, for example, in the destructive 'fair share' stance on the Kyoto Protocol negotiations by the conservative government of the time, in the repudiation of ethics of intergenerational and intragenerational equity, and the disavowal of the precautionary principle. In quotidian worlds, climate change negativity in its various manifestations – denial, modes of scepticism, suppression and apathy – is an unstable terrain where feelings, practices and beliefs are often unaligned. You can be sad or angry about pollution damage and biodiversity loss in familiar places, an opponent of council SLR policies, a supporter of the coal industry for jobs and growth, a passionate recycler, an agnostic on the topic of climate change, and confident that a solution will be found. These realities seem to be inconsistent from an environmentalist perspective, but they may not be contradictory from the standpoint of the people who hold them and in the contexts in which they are expressed.

Across the spectrum of groups and organisations considered in this chapter, climate change engagement exists in transmuted forms – sustainable living, energy efficiency, social justice, to name a few – below the radar of climate politics and forms of mobilisation that will be essential for future change. For protagonists, this is a tactic while awaiting another opportunity for renewal that will 'get traction amongst the public'. For others, it may be a way of slowly coming to terms with the 'moving goalposts'.

Notes

1   Reser *et al* (2012) found the most common reason (17.3 per cent of 500 Australian survey respondents) for 'reducing carbon footprint' was 'associated financial benefit, necessity, save money, reduce costs'.
2   These certificates are issued under the NSW Environmental Planning and Assessment Act, and state any planning or development restrictions that apply to the land (Lake Macquarie City Council 2010).
3   Transition Town Coal Point folded in 2010 due to lack of support.

References

Australian Bureau of Statistics 2011. 'Census QuickStats: Dora Creek (NSW)'. Available at www.censusdata.abs.gov.au/census_services/getproduct/census/2011/quickstat/SSC10724?opendocument&navpos=220 (accessed 20 July 2013).
Brangwyn, B. and Hopkins, B. 2008. 'Transition Initiatives Primer'. Available at http://TransitionNetwork.org (accessed 30 July 2014).
Burgmann, V. and Baer, H. 2012. *Climate Politics and the Climate Movement in Australia.* Melbourne: Melbourne University Press.
Christoff, P. 2014. *Four Degrees of Global Warming: Australia in a Hot World.* London: Routledge Earthscan.
Climate Action Network Australia 2015. 'Climate Action Network Australia'. Available at www.climatenetwork.org/profile/member/climate-action-network-australia-0 (accessed 14 July 2014).
Connor, L., Higginbotham, N., Freeman, S. and Albrecht, G. 2008. 'Watercourses and Discourses: Coalmining in the Upper Hunter Valley, New South Wales'. *Oceania* 78 (1): 76–90.
Connor, L., Freeman, S. and Higginbotham, N. 2009. 'Not Just a Coalmine: Shifting grounds of community opposition to coal mining in Southeastern Australia'. *Ethnos* 74 (4): 490–513.
CRDC (Climate Ready Dora Creek) 2009. *Climate Ready Dora Creek: A community update – July 2009.* Lake Macquarie: Climate Ready Dora Creek.

Cronshaw, D. 2008a. 'Homes sitting on hidden bay view'. *Newcastle Herald*. 13 March, p. 3.

Cronshaw, D. 2008b. 'We're going under: Lake Council acts on rising sea level threat.' *Newcastle Herald*. 3 March, p. 1.

Cronshaw, D. 2010a. 'Sea rise may drop values'. *Newcastle Herald*. 18 March, p. 5.

Cronshaw, D. 2010b. 'Sea change concern'. *Newcastle Herald*. 22 March, p. 13.

Cronshaw, D. 2011a. 'Drowning in opinions: property project thrown in limbo'. *Newcastle Herald*. 14 October, p. 7.

Cronshaw, D. 2011b. 'McCloy to mount climate class action against council'. *Newcastle Herald*. 27 October. Available at www.theherald.com.au/story/477818/mccloy-to-mount-climate-class-action-against-council/ archived by WebCite at www.webcitation.org/6bKRJUt4X (accessed 20 August 2014).

Cronshaw, D. 2012a. 'Sea level concerns overruled'. *Newcastle Herald*. 28 February, p. 14.

Cronshaw, D. 2012b. 'Rate rise fight goes to voters'. *Newcastle Herald*. 13 February, p. 3.

Cronshaw, D. 2014a. 'Marks Point and Belmont South residents act over sea-level rise threat'. *Newcastle Herald*. 7 September. Available at www.theherald.com.au/story/2542312/residents-act-over-sea-level-rise-threat/ archived by WebCite at www.webcitation.org/6TBoIuWrG (accessed 9 October 2014).

Cronshaw, D. 2014b. 'Lake council approves floating houses'. *Newcastle Herald*. 10 February. Available at www.theherald.com.au/story/2079398/lake-council-approves-floating-houses/ archived by WebCite at www.webcitation.org/6Nc60wiJb (accessed 24 February 2014).

Cronshaw, D. 2014c. 'Sea level rise rules push down Lake Macquarie land values'. *Newcastle Herald*. 4 April. Available at www.theherald.com.au/story/2198713/sea-level-rise-rules-push-down-lake-macquarie-land-values/ archived by WebCite at www.webcitation.org/6YegIz0Qw (accessed 20 May 2015).

Cubby, B. 2008. 'Protest halts coal train for six hours'. *Sydney Morning Herald*. 14 July, p. 2.

Department of Climate Change 2009. *Climate Change Risks to Australia's Coast: A First Pass National Assessment, November 2009*. Available at http://climatechange.gov.au/en/publications/coastline/climate-change-risks-to-australias-coasts.aspx (accessed 16 November 2009).

Department of Environment and Climate Change and Water NSW 2009. *NSW Sea Level Rise Policy Statement*. Sydney South.

Dryzek, J., Norgaard, R. and Schlosberg, D. 2013. *Climate-Challenged Society*. Oxford: Oxford University Press.

de Rijke, K. 2012. 'The Symbolic Politics of Belonging and Community in Peri-urban Environmental Disputes: The Traveston Crossing Dam in Queensland, Australia'. *Oceania* 82 (3): 278–293.

Eckersley, R. 2013. 'Poles Apart?: The social construction of responsibility for climate change in Australia and Norway'. *Australian Journal of Politics and History* 59 (3): 382–396.

Environment Victoria 2010. *Walk against warming*. Available at http://environmentvictoria.org.au/media/walk-against-warming-marches-backwards-protest-federal-climate-inaction (accessed 1 June 2015).

Garnaut, R. 2014. 'Compounding social and economic impacts: The limits to adaptation'. In: *Four Degrees of Global Warming: Australia in a Hot World*. Christoff, P. (ed.), pp. 141–154. London: Routledge Earthscan.

Garrett, J. 2014. 'Pacific climate warriors in Australia to protest coal industry'. *ABC News*. 14 October. Available at www.abc.net.au/news/2014-10-13/pacific-climate-warriors-to-protest-newcastle-coal-port/5809392 (accessed 1 June 2015).

Giddens, A. 2009. *The Politics of Climate Change*. Cambridge: Polity.

Graeber, D. 2009. *Direct Action: An ethnography*. Oakland, CA: AK Press.

Graham, M. 2016. 'Official optimism in the face of an uncertain future: Swedish reactions to climate change threats'. In: *Environmental Change and the World's Futures: Ecologies, ontologies, mythologies*. Marshall, J. P. and Connor, L. H. (eds). London: Routledge.

Hawkins, P. 2009. 'Waters keep rising, and so does worry'. *Sydney Morning Herald*. 14–15 November, p. 7.

IPCC (Intergovernmental Panel on Climate Change) 2007. *Fourth Assessment Report: Climate Change 2007*. Available at www.ipcc.ch/activity/ar.htm (accessed 5 February 2006).

Kelly, M. 2014. 'Pacific Climate Warriors block ships in Newcastle harbour protest'. *Newcastle Herald*. Available at www.theherald.com.au/story/2631698/newcastle-harbour-blockade-delays-ship-photos-video/?cs=310 archived by WebCite at www.webcitation.org/6TnKA6aQU (accessed 3 November 2014).

Lake Macquarie City Council 2004. *Lake Macquarie Community Greenhouse Action Plan*. Speers Point NSW.

Lake Macquarie City Council 2008. *2008 State of the Environment Report*. Boolaroo, Lake Macquarie City Council.

Lake Macquarie City Council 2010. '149 Planning Certificates'. Available at www.lakemac.com.au/page.aspx?pid=102&vid=1&kcid=26&kpt=Browse (accessed July 2014).

McDonald, J. 2014. 'Hot in the City: Planning for climate change impacts in urban Australia'. In: *Four Degrees of Global Warming: Australia in a Hot World*. Christoff, P. (ed.). London: Routledge Earthscan.

NSW Department of Planning 2010. *NSW Coastal Planning Guideline: Adapting to sea level rise*. NSW.

Piper, G. 2008. 'Rising sea levels a major challenge'. *The Post*. Newcastle, 28 May, p. 13.

Reser, J., Bradley, G., Glendon, A. and Ellul, M. 2012. *Public Risk Perceptions, Understandings, and Responses to Climate Change and Natural Disasters in Australia and Great Britain*. Griffith University, School of Applied Psychology, Behavioural Basis of Health: Griffith Climate Change Response Program, National Climate Change Adaptation Research Facility.

Rosewarne, S., Goodman, J. and Pearse, R. 2014. *Climate Action Upsurge: The ethnography of climate movement politics*. London and New York: Routledge.

Sydney Morning Herald 2008. 'Protesters again disrupt coal loading'. *Sydney Morning Herald*. July 14. Available at www.smh.com.au/news/global-warming/protesters-again-disrupt-coal-loading/2008/07/14/1215887510770.html archived by WebCite at www.webcitation.org/6bKS2v6Qg (accessed 20 June 2013).

Tsing, A. 2004. *Friction: An ethnography of global connection*. Princeton: Princeton University Press.

Whitmarsh, L. 2009. 'Behavioural Responses to Climate Change: Asymmetry of intentions and impacts'. *Journal of Environmental Psychology* 29 (1): 13–23.

Whitmarsh, L. 2011. 'Scepticism and Uncertainty about Climate Change: Dimensions, determinants and change over time'. *Global Environmental Change* 21: 690–700.

Wolf, J. and Moser, S. C. 2011. 'Individual Understandings, Perceptions, and Engagement with Climate Change: Insights from in-depth studies across the world'. *Wiley Interdisciplinary Reviews: Climate Change* 2: 547–569.

6   Fragile futurity

This final chapter explores the shifts in self–world relationships that come with increasing public awareness of environmental damage and of the prospect of irreversible climate change. Practices, ideas and emotions linked to climate change are indicative of imagined future worlds – worlds that may be the same, better or worse than now, but about which we cannot be certain. I discuss some of the insights of depth psychology that have informed analysis of death, immortality and the future in cross-cultural perspective. I draw on material from interviews with spirituality adherents undertaken over several years as part of the Hunter Valley study, exploring residents' thoughts and feelings about their future in relation to environmental change. These discussions provide insights into concepts of ecological deterioration, the collective nature of anxiety defences and hopes for survival. Spirituality adherents' realism about climate change is then contrasted with the heroic myths of consumer cultures that promise immortality through capitalist accumulation, not beyond it. The 'new worlds' of the Christian Apocalypse and of science utopias are then explored as parallel edifices of mortality denial – the former through God's salvation of the faithful, and the latter through the harnessing of technological innovation in the service of capitalism's endless growth and renewal. Different and more adaptive imaginings come into view when people talk about intimations of dystopian futures in relation to their hopes for their children and grandchildren. The last section of the chapter explores the strivings for generational immortality as a counteractant in the trajectory of planetary collapse.

Ecocosmic concerns

While the simultaneous growth of scientific evidence for anthropogenic climate change and various modes of denial appear to be contradictory trends, they are interdependent in some important respects. Climate science carries a message of human finitude, engendering powerful psychological resistance that resonates in collective immortality ideologies. This process can be illuminated by reference to the thought of Otto Rank and Ernest Becker. In *Psychology and the Soul* (1998 [1930]), Rank challenged Sigmund Freud's scientific materialism and reintroduced spirituality and metaphysics into psychoanalysis, while also rejecting

Freud's father-centred and sexuality-based theory of human personality in favour of group morality and collective ideals. He wrote:

> Psychoanalysis is less a psychological body of knowledge than an interpretation of animistic soul-values in terms of sexual-era science. Psychologized in sexual ideology, these values comfort us (they are 'therapeutic'), just as the naïve belief in immortality comforted primitives. Here as elsewhere, Freud denies this deep esoteric content of psychoanalysis in favour of scientific ideology, which understands the individual as coming into and going out of existence, not as a lasting, self-creating phenomenon.
>
> (Rank 1998 [1930]: 60)

In Rank's thought, there is always a conflict between the individual and the community, but collective soul-belief 'resists individual striving for immortality – whether through personal achievement, or in sexual pleasure stripped of generativity' (1998 [1930]: 62). Cultural anthropologist Ernest Becker developed these ideas about terror of death as the fundamental ontological anxiety of humans, and the denial of death as the primary work of culture in conscious and unconscious domains. Becker's stark analysis of the psychocultural underpinnings of human life worlds and the implications for human affairs was outlined in his last two books, *Denial of Death* (1973) and *Escape from Evil* (1975). He drew on evolutionary theory for the insight that: 'This absolute dedication to Eros, to perseverance, is universal among organisms, and is the essence of life on this earth' (1975: 2). The consciousness of death, however, is the 'unique paradox of the human condition' (Becker 1975: 3).

At the organismic level, there is a conscious quest for endurance; culture provides the 'alter-organism' that allows the symbolic transcendence of the individual life, and its endowment with meaning beyond death. Culture is, among other things, a collective means of repressing awareness of mortality and provides the framework of symbols and behaviours that counter ontological anxiety about death. 'Culture gives man [sic] an alter-organism which is more durable and powerful than the one nature endowed him with' (Becker 1975: 3). Messages or events that bring thoughts about death into consciousness, in many forms, may stimulate a range of conscious and unconscious defences from denial and postponement to marginalisation of outsiders, as well as an increase in actions that enhance self-esteem by strengthening feelings of immortality.

Defence mechanisms grounded in immortality thinking sustain myths that conceal the consequences of environmental destruction. In a later work, written in the darkening shadow of the emergence of German National Socialism, Rank commented on these 'immortalization tendenc[ies]': 'In religion this is of course obvious, but in the social ideologies too, with their political form and their national content, the tendency towards a collective conception of immortality is easily recognizable' (1932: xxvii).

Becker brought anthropological insights to these theories of the human condition with his linking of religion and the secular immortality ideologies of

Figure 6.1 Melting sceptic
Source: Peter Lewis, *Newcastle Herald*, 2015

modernity. His theory built on the fundamental secularism of psychoanalysis as well as the cultural relativism of anthropology. He drew the parallels between profane and religious forms of immortality ideologies both historically and cross-culturally. Like Otto Rank, he saw religion as the age-old cultural defence of humans against the terror of mortality. In pre-modern societies, many of the heroic projects that constituted the immortality of the social group were based in religious systems that depended on the 'practical technics' of generative ritual such as shamanism and totemic increase rites.

In the modern era, Becker focused on the Christian societies of the Western world. He argued that there was effectively a transformation of religion as the dominant immortality ideology in the Western world after the Enlightenment. Christianity became repositioned in a more anthropocentric (humanist) world view, and became the foundation of a new kind of secular-humanist value system that emphasised individuals rather than collectivities, and worldly human activities rather than direct agency of the divine (Becker 1975: 69–70). Sociologist Max Weber's thesis on *The Protestant Ethic and the Spirit of Capitalism* is perhaps the best-known articulation of this thesis, applied to post-Reformation societies of Northern Europe (Weber 1930).

In the era of anthropogenic climate change, Becker's work encourages us to interpret the flood of information about climate threats to all forms of life as a stark harbinger of mortality. A contemporary psychoanalyst phrased it thus: '[It] becomes intensely anxiety-provoking when we are faced with a picture of a damaged Mother Earth or her 'babies', even in far-away places' (Brenman Pick 2013: 136). This view suggests that the evidence of climate change impacts is bound to trigger a gamut of defence mechanisms. These range from the consciously articulated expressions of disavowal of human causes to unconsciously driven behaviours such as conspicuous consumption or the embrace of ideologies and leaders who deny the science and the catastrophic consequences of climate change.[1]

The spectrum of defences is evident in the preceding chapters as is the 'spirit of realism' – the conscious recognition of ecological deterioration, its human causes and the need for ameliorative action. In quotidian worlds, however, we have seen that environmental concern, pro-environmental actions and sustainability politics are not necessarily dependent on the acceptance of human-caused climate change.

At this juncture I want to consider the reflections on climate change that spirituality adherents shared with the researchers. As part of the Hunter Valley project, the author and research assistants interviewed 32 religious and spirituality adherents between 2008 and 2013. We explored participants' views about the causes of climate change, its seriousness and their feelings about it; their ideas about the relationship between religion/spirituality and nature/environment; the contribution of religion to their understanding and interpretation of climate change; and possible actions that should be taken.[2] Some of these people identified with organised religions, others preferred to characterise themselves as 'spiritual' rather than religious. Some were long-term members of religious denominations; others had changed their affiliations over their lives, often multiple times and often because of a perceived lack of priority given to environmental issues in the doctrines.

Causality and spirituality

In contrast to many of the random survey respondents discussed in earlier chapters, almost all these religious adherents linked climate change to human agency, and also to some form of moral decline. Moral critiques of contemporary society and culture are present in every case. Only one person, a Pentecostal Church minister, cited a divine (Biblically ordained) cause of climate change, identifying it with an apocalypse in the Christian sense, which I discuss in a later section of this chapter. Many of the interviewees subscribed to a prophetic discourse: an indictment of moral degeneration in humans' relationship to nature/the Earth, while rejecting that climate change was divinely caused. They apportioned blame variously to the systems of capitalism, consumerism and a wasteful society;

poor stewardship of nature; and population increase. Margaret, a middle-aged woman who had been a Uniting Church member since childhood, brought all these causes together in the idea of industrialisation:

A lot of it, I think, is industrialisation. It's higher population, more consumerism, so there are more cars on the road, there are more people wanting more things, so there is more industry, there's more people travelling a lot more, so there's a lot of planes in the air, there are more buildings being built, a lot more waste being produced, there's more food needed, so more fertilizers.

(Margaret interview 2008)

She was concerned about climate change, and based her commitment to environmental issues on biblical teachings: 'God has dominion over the Earth, man has been given the stewardship of the Earth'. Care for ourselves, care for others and care for the environment are interrelated: 'it's a matter of social justice and of common sense too'.

These concerns were also evident in our interview with Janice, who had been a Quaker for several years. She had been raised a Catholic and then moved into her husband's fundamentalist church community. In reaction to the rigid doctrines of that Church, she joined a Quaker group, reflecting: 'I think inside I was always a Quaker, because when I started attending, I just felt I'd come home spiritually'. She sees God as 'deeply involved with humanity' and the Holy Spirit as a 'light within' that guides her life, including environmental and social justice commitments.

Janice felt she was experiencing small local signs of climate change – unseasonal weather over long periods, lack of success with her veggie patch ('things don't go the way they used to'). She followed the popular science reports and was concerned about escalating greenhouse gases (GHGs). She disagreed with the fundamentalist Christian view prevalent in her former church, that climate change was God's punishment of human damage to the Earth. She commented that the Earth's decline may be inevitable and had to be 'coped with':

I certainly have no sense that this is God bringing a punishment on us because of what we do to the Earth. We're doing it to the Earth and this is happening, and I have a sense of inevitability about it, that we have to manage it, we have to cope with it, as much as trying to slow it down and halt it.

(Janice interview 2008)

While others indicted overpopulation, Janice said:

There are things we have to live with, because we do have these six billion people on the planet, and to me they're not a plague on the Earth, they're precious.

(Janice interview 2008)

She believed in 'people power and grass roots activism' as part of the solution to climate change, and was sceptical about the 'politically expedient' responses of government. She felt people could do more to resist the temptations of consumerism and carbon-intensive lifestyles, modelled this for her children, and didn't hesitate to speak out about her views: 'I hope I do it gently and nicely'. Working to achieve social justice was a major priority for Janice. She thought education for women and children around the world 'would go a long way to resolving the population pressure the world is under'. She was active in human rights organisations like Amnesty International. 'If there was justice, then we've made a big step towards dealing with the problem'.

Themes of social justice and personal responsibility to act also characterised the thinking of Western Buddhists. Callum, a young man who had been following Tibetan teaching for five years, saw Buddhism as 'like a science of the mind … I wouldn't call it a religion, but it's like a way of life'. He found environmental relevance of Buddhist teachings in the doctrine of interdependence and compassion for all life forms. He rejected the premise of Christianity 'that mankind becomes the centre of everything'. Desires and attachments – consumerism, easeful living, endless economic growth – were the root causes of climate change. Acting to reduce one's own harmful behaviours is an important first step in addressing climate change:

> From a Buddhist's point of view of enlightened self interest, if you recognise that other people will be harmed and therefore you will be harmed by your own actions, you will take responsibility for changing your actions.
>
> (Callum interview 2008)

The majority of the Christians interviewed loosely aligned with a sacramental theology (whereby nature can be understood as a sacramental disclosure of God). Among these adherents, there is a personal responsibility for one's actions, as individual persons are situated as part of the environment. This sacramental element develops the more 'immanent' (as opposed to transcendental) aspects of Christian religion, and overlaps to a considerable degree with the Buddhist ontology of interconnectedness and impermanence of all things, reincarnation and the ethic of compassion and non-harm, which also provides a framework for personal conservationist action.

In general, these were well-informed and concerned people who affirmed the human causes of climate change, and took a moderate and humanistic approach to strategies of amelioration and prevention. Their visions for change, while inspired by spiritual values, converge in many respects with other ecological framings of human/nature relationships found in many forms of environmentalist thought. In discussing the future, interviewees did not envisage fundamental changes in power structures but rather focused on 'true democracy' where change took place from the grassroots up. Some of the actions included 'localised living', strengthening the sustainability of community lifestyles and reducing carbon footprints.

Their ideals evoke Becker's interpretation of early Christianity's promise of 'universal democratic equality' (1975: 70), which also echoes in much environmental discourse on sustainable neighbourhoods and social justice, as discussed in the previous chapter. However, most of these people also felt that their spiritual values gave them a deeper and more 'holistic' understanding of climate change than could be found in environmentalist thought or secular scientific models. Bridget, a former Catholic and now a Quaker said:

> *I guess that's where my Quaker belief meshes for me in that if adverse things happen, my spiritual belief isn't that it's God's punishment or anything like that, it's just that there is an obligation for us to see things as holistically as possible. I think that one of the problems is that even in environmental groups they see a little bit of the picture and research that, and that's it.*
>
> (Bridget interview 2013)

A different sort of holism that included dissatisfaction with the limitations of science-based climate change discourses was expressed by the four Aboriginal people we interviewed. Jade said: 'With Aboriginal people, we don't compartmentalise things, we try and look at things as they evolve together'. Reg commented about former life on country: 'Your spirits moved on, and your spirits came back, and there was always a reason why things happened'. They all expressed a sense of threat from climate change, acknowledged human causes and reported their own perceptions of environmental change: ancient middens that had been inundated, unpredictable seasons, loss of flora and fauna. But these feelings were placed in the context of a recent history of death and destruction. Reg said of life now:

> *We don't have as close an attachment to the land, because we were pushed off our land. And then our land was abused, it was raped, it was virtually murdered. You know, mining and all these things, and not only pollution. I mean you go out and you look at some of these areas where they do the mines, the open-cut mines, and they're taking out thousands and thousands of various trees, trees that they don't need to take out.*
>
> (Reg interview 2010)

They all saw climate change not as the ultimate cataclysm, but rather from the perspective of the deep time of Aboriginal relationship to country, and the many hardships and tragedies experienced since European settlement. Continuity despite adversity, rather than world ending, was emphasised. Jade said: 'Our spirituality, our concept of the world is that we come from the land, we give back to the land. I don't think we view the world [as ending]'. Jeremy reflected: 'I think we'll always be here, in the spiritual sense'.

There is a melancholy to be found in the feelings expressed in the spirituality interviews, a feeling of deep loss that runs through much environmental concern, both Aboriginal and non-Aboriginal. When asked about her feelings, Bridget said:

Well that's quite interesting because I've got grandchildren and I'm obviously particularly close to them but I feel that any child that comes into the world has a right to expect to have a good future. And so I get on the one hand, quite sad thinking that not only do most children now not have the quality of life that one would like to think of, but that who knows what things are going to be like for my great grandchildren? So there's a sadness but yet there's a tremendous optimism I feel because I know that the human species is very resilient and I believe there's a lot can be done to mitigate the effect of climate change. I believe that can happen, and I feel this period of extreme individualism that we're in might just be a blip.

(Bridget interview 2013)

Political theorist and psychoanalyst Paul Hoggett has written, 'Once we lose our hope in each other, then there is no hope for nature' (2013b: 85). Active religious affiliations and spiritual beliefs of various types appear to facilitate a constructive and hopeful response to climate change threat. Rosemary Randall, a psychoanalyst who explored the idea of 'ecological debt' in interviews with participants in Carbon Conversations groups (Surefoot Effect 2015) in the UK, found her subjects were frequently 'overwhelmed with sadness, frightened or disorientated'. Only some managed to reduce their guilt about Western affluence and disproportionate use of resources, and to 'put some boundaries around their responsibility' (Randall 2013). Climate activists often expressed guilt and despair. One Transition Newcastle member we interviewed commented: 'My frustrations have been that we, we're not moving fast enough with anything ... Everyone's already as busy as' (Jack interview 2010). Edward, a climate activist with Rising Tide, expressed a strong view on the subsuming of public life by private concerns:

The whole culture has got everybody separated, looking after themselves, worried about their own futures, their own little patch ... The whole society is angled against working together, and working for common purpose, and certainly with ecological goals in mind.

(Edward interview 2010)

Spirituality adherents appeared better equipped to manage these depressive feelings. Bridget, for example, highlighted the recuperative aspect of her faith:

One thing about the message of Jesus is treating others with respect, and lots of other faiths do that too. It's just core that it's not right that we can just do stuff and then use resources that we know most people can't use. And that's the spiritual part of my faith and I think Quakers really support that too.

(Bridget interview 2013)

Other constructive ways of dealing with sadness, fear and guilt about climate change can be found in the psychotherapeutic group experience. Over a 12-month period, Sally Gillespie worked with a small group of participants in

Sydney, Australia, who shared feelings and ideas about climate change and the future through conversations about dreams and fantasies. She found that this process helped to: 'deepen an ecological understanding of the world and self which bears witness to the destructive and creative possibilities of life ahead, galvanizing engagements which forge new ways of being and acting in the world' (Gillespie 2016: 193).

In outlining the feelings associated with ecological debt, Randall goes on to propose that the self necessarily experiences depression in any realistic mode of dealing with climate change – the unexpected 'no' of nature (2013: 98). She writes that people need to be enabled 'to embrace the reality of limits in a world that has denied that such limits should exist' (2013: 98). Bridget made the pithy comment: 'Part of climate change is that we can't all keep wanting to live on endlessly'. Others are not so accepting of this reality. The anxiety defences of rejecting it are of a quite different kind, linked to fantasies of immortality, endless consumption and virtual realities.

Figure 6.2 Coal loader aground in Newcastle, 2007 storm

Source: Peter Lewis, *Newcastle Herald*, 2007

Consuming culture

While Becker did not live to see the late twentieth-century development of corporate capitalism and its cultural forms, he made some prescient comments about the destructive impact of secular-humanist immortality projects, the failure of science and democratic systems to eliminate economic inequality, and the risk of planetary environmental collapse driven by unfettered materialism (1975: 69–70). Lee, one of our interviewees who had recently become a member of a Quaker community, saw 'capitalism' as a widespread secular faith:

> *Yeah I think the difficulty is that the idea of dominion over the world has taken on its secular counterpart in capitalism, so a faith all of its own, if I can refer to it that way. But people who don't say they are religious in any way have a blind faith in capitalism. They are completely unaware of it I think. And that faith has dominion over the earth in a dangerous way.*
>
> (Lee interview 2008)

Central to this analysis is the understanding of the capitalism–consumerism nexus that prompted sociologist Zygmunt Bauman to observe that the post-industrial era is characterised by a profound cultural shift from the production-oriented work ethic analysed by Max Weber, to the 'aesthetic of consumption' that indicates 'differences so deep and ubiquitous that they fully justify speaking of our society as a society of a separate and distinct kind – a consumer society' (Bauman 2005: 24). Bauman, echoing Becker, asserted 'To consume also means to destroy' (2005: 23). For Becker, this destruction is understood as an immortality project of global scale, spreading wherever the relations of commodity capitalism permeate and reconstruct social identities, in societies both secularised and religious. The secular-humanist identity project of modernity – 'the task of "self-construction": building one's own social identity if not fully from scratch, at least from its foundation up' (Bauman 2005: 27) is further harnessed to the protean desires of the consumer citizen.

Consumer societies are also cultural systems that sustain the myths of happiness and immortality through values and practices of acquisition, affluence, endless exploitation of nature, novelty and perpetual renewal. While paid work may be drudgery for many, wages allow workers to exercise expanded consumer choices that are increasingly defined and experienced as freedoms, self-actualisation and ethical imperatives. Bauman (2005: 321) has aptly encapsulated the heroic projects of consumer societies, which revolve around:

> Seduction, display of untested wonders, promise of sensations yet untried but dwarfing and overshadowing everything tried before ... Consumption, ever more varied and rich consumption, must appear to the consumers as a right to enjoy, not a duty to suffer. The consumers must be guided by aesthetic interests, not ethical norms.

An important dimension of life in affluent societies of the global North is the growth of the 'virtual world' that Hoggett has linked to a 'perverse culture' based on 'ambiguity, illusion, evasiveness, trickery, collusion and guile' (2013a: 60). This is a world where neoliberal economics has become the ruling political ideology, where deregulation and instrumentality overtake civil society relationships, and where narcissistic pursuit of individual desires becomes the most esteemed heroic life project. The paradigmatic economic form is finance capitalism, which parasitically 'feeds off the wealth created by more productive forms of capital' (Hoggett 2013a: 61). Growth of consumer credit has expanded individuals' access to immediate gratifications divorced from the experience of ecological destruction. There is an incessant flow of information and images of crisis, misery and death that cannot be ignored but that is managed by 'perverse stances' of scepticism, 'turning a blind eye' and self-deception (Hoggett 2013a).

This virtual world differs from earlier times in that denial is 'a more pervasive aspect of institutional life' (Hoggett 2013b: 84), sustaining everyday practices of self-deception that we all collude in to some extent. This 'unhappy consciousness', writes Hoggett, is 'the lot of all of us who live in late-modern Western societies', engendered he suggests by failure to face up to the reality of human destructiveness (2013b: 85). These attributes of human experience were described in a different idiom by William James. More than a century ago, in his lectures on 'The Sick Soul' in *The Varieties of Religious Experience* (1902: 119), James articulated the phenomenological essence of secularist anomie and its fragility as an immortality system:

> This sadness lies at the heart of every merely positivistic, agnostic, or naturalistic scheme of philosophy. Let sanguine healthy-mindedness do its best with its strange power of living in the moment and ignoring and forgetting, still the evil background is really there to be thought of, and the skull will grin in at the banquet.

But in the twenty-first century, late modern-era life celebrates short-term pleasures, ignoring and forgetting; the sadness 'at the heart' goes unacknowledged. The virtual world images of affluent citizens are smiling and laughing; only the abject Other presents a miserable face. This extends to the surrounding world of nature. Awareness of damage is anxiety provoking. 'We do not want to be reminded of the dark side of our pleasures', writes Renee Aron Lertzman (2013: 120). In researching the ways residents responded to environmental threats in the Great Lakes region of the USA, Lertzman's in-depth interviews with non-activist residents revealed that stances that might be construed as apathy concealed 'complicated expressions of difficult and conflicting affective states' (2013: 130). He explains: 'I was struck by narratives of loss and what I sensed as an "arrested mourning" with regard to the places and ways of life, and earlier selves, that environmental issues seemed to evoke' (Lertzman 2013: 130).

Concepts of capitalist modernity take little account of the psychic costs of the exploitation of nature as well as its pleasures. Both are germane to the

Figure 6.3 Newcastle 2107

Source: Peter Lewis, *Newcastle Herald*, 2007

understanding of climate change as a cultural crisis in the contemporary world. Elaborate consumerist practices in the global North and affluent classes of the South (acquiring the newest, discarding the old, improving and renewing the body as a major life project, and associated rituals and beliefs) are ultimately at odds with negative messages about the future, including the spectre of a world destroyed by global warming of humanity's own making. Bauman's work on consumption suggests the incompatibility of climate change messages with the aestheticised self-identity of contemporary consumer citizens. Hoggett's argument, drawing on Freud's theory of sexual perversion and the post-structural semiotics of Baudrillard and his successors, outlines the negative force of disavowal of mortality and other unpleasant realities of the human condition in contemporary perverse cultures. Lertzman alerts us to the fact that the losses – of nature and loved surroundings – are recorded deep in the human psyche; the apparent lack of concern may be a defence mechanism for anticipatory mourning and a protective withdrawal of affect (2013: 124).

In his short essay, *On Transience*, Freud (2005 [1916]) introduced the concept of anticipatory mourning in his analysis of the ego's defense mechanisms against loss of loved objects. Hunter Valley residents sometimes articulated such feelings of mourning in relation to the degraded future world their children and grand-children would inherit. One mother said:

> My children are beginning school. I see them laughing and playing and wonder what the world is going to be like when they grow up. I remember the channel at Swansea when I was a child. I hope that it doesn't change too much in the future.
>
> (Lake Macquarie resident 2011)

This is an expression of a widespread 'structure of feeling' that the researchers in the Hunter Valley study conceptualised as 'solastalgia' (Albrecht *et al.* 2007). In the mother's statement above, it is the children's future loss that is mourned. Freud saw the process of mourning as having 'a spontaneous end', from which the ego attaches to new love objects. Climate change, however, if perceived as inex-orable, may overwhelm the ego's restorative capacities, leading to melancholia or depressive states. But Freud (2005 [1916]) also recognised the capacity for denial, rehearsing it thus:

> No! it is impossible that all this loveliness of Nature and Art, of the world of our sensations and of the world outside, will really fade away into noth-ing. It would be too senseless and too presumptuous to believe it. Somehow or other this loveliness must be able to persist and to escape all the powers of destruction.

This 'rebellion against the fact asserted' to avoid its painful impact is elaborated in a different way by Rank and Becker in their analyses of immortality ideologies and the heroic myths embedded in them.

Immortality in present and future worlds

In the conclusion to *Psychology and the Soul*, Rank declared, 'the psychological creed of mankind is immortality' (1998 [1930]: 128). Immortality ideologies create heroes, but heroes take many forms. In his posthumous work, *Escape from Evil* (1975), Becker argues that many 'heroic' meaning systems, by defini-tion focused on myths of immortality, contain their own undoing in the production of evil. In pre-modern societies, not just religion but many destruc-tive activities, such as warfare and other forms of institutionalised violence, were significant forms of heroic culture. Contemporary correlates, such as industrialised warfare, terrorism, genocide and environmental exploitation, boost self-esteem of proponents while accelerating mortality and finitude of all life forms.

Becker also explored the possibility of 'non-destructive myths' that acknowl-edge objective conditions of suffering without marginalising and dehumanising other humans, and without the annihilation of other life forms and nature itself. In essence, Becker's ideas and Rank before him foreshadow the many kinds of immortality ideology and heroic myths, each with a different genealogy and societal resonance, that the knowledge of world-ending climate change has stimulated or revived. Some examples of immortality ideologies are discussed in the next sections, each with its own nuances of denial and recuperation in relation to climate change futures.

Christian Apocalypse

In colloquial English, 'apocalypse' can refer to any catastrophic event, especially those that feature large-scale death and destruction reminiscent of Biblical imagery. Climate change, holding the seeds of such annihilation, is often expressed as an imminent apocalypse. In fact, in Christian doctrines, the idea of Apocalypse carries within it the prospect of salvation. The term derives from the Greek *apokalupsis* ('to uncover' or 'to unveil') and there is a literary genre of early Jewish and Christian writing called 'apocalypse' that speaks of God's revelations to humans (*New Oxford Annotated Bible* 2007). In the Bible, the Book of Revelation (also known as Apocalypse) specifically prophesies the end of the world associated with God's judgment and salvation of the faithful. Related ideas found in other books of the Bible, and currently embraced in many fundamentalist churches in the USA, concern the 'Rapture', or achievement of immortality by believers, during or before the Second Coming of Jesus Christ to Earth (Baker 2011).

The Christian faiths most closely associated with Apocalypse belief are Pentecostalism and its variants in fundamentalist and charismatic churches. Pentecostalism is growing in many parts of the world, and comprises the second largest grouping of Christian faiths internationally, with about 279 million followers in 2011 (Pew Research Center 2011). In Australia since 1996, the fastest-growing Australian Christian denomination is Pentecostal, increasing by 26 per cent (to around 220,000) by the 2006 census, and gaining about another 38,000 followers by 2011 (Hughes *et al.* 2012) The key features of Pentecostalism are its experientially God-centred world view, with the Holy Spirit connecting all worldly phenomena; literal Biblicism (like other fundamentalist groups); a view of the Bible as a living book in which 'the Holy Spirit is always active'; experiential knowledge through direct encounter with God; an anti-bureaucratic church structure; and end time beliefs (Poloma 2000).

We interviewed several Pentecostal Christians, and their views are summarised briefly. Ray, a Pentecostal minister, viewed climate change as due to the will of God, scripturally preordained as an end time precursor:

> *I believe we're facing climate change around the world, which is prefacing the end time events of the scriptures. We're seeing an increase in floods, we're seeing an increase in mudslides, we're seeing an increase in earthquakes, we're seeing an increase in famine and fires. Every aspect of climate is set in the records.*
>
> (Ray interview 2009)

For Ray, climate change goes hand in hand with the moral decline of society. He stressed that God was allowing the decline, not forcing it; hence the responsibility was with people to choose Christ:

> So God is simply allowing him [Satan] to degenerate the world, in the basis that, in the end, I mean, our time on earth is [he clicks his fingers] is but a vapour to eternity. Eternity is a long time. Now the Bible says there are only two places in eternity, that's heaven and hell. So if we haven't chosen Christ, if we haven't chosen heaven through Christ, then in actual fact, we've chosen hell. They are pretty serious consequences. Now you can reason hell any way you like, but if you read the Word, it's a hell of a place. It is exactly as the Bible describes it. How do I know? We are so close to end time, that God is allowing people to go to hell, and check it out.
>
> (Ray interview 2009)

Others, who also preached the scripturally ordained end time, did not necessarily see climate change as part of it. Vince (a Seventh Day Adventist) stated that as a Creationist he believed creation had some purpose, but that was in God's hands. He did not know whether climate change had anything to do with end time events, and that did not stop him from trying to do something about it. He favoured a science-based discourse of the 'tipping point' over a religious explanation:

> They talk about that tipping point where, if we go beyond that, that it's going to be difficult if not impossible to then try and reverse that trend toward global warming. So, but, yeah I don't believe that the end of the world is nigh. But at the same time I think that the governments around the world should have begun acting some time ago, and if they haven't they need to get on with it pronto.
>
> (Vince interview 2009)

Denial of climate change is also compatible with Pentecostal beliefs, as articulated by Will, another adherent interviewed in 2009. Will was keen to discuss in detail the 2009 University of East Anglia email hacking (dubbed 'Climategate' in the media) and fourth Intergovernmental Panel on Climate Change (IPCC) report errors. He said that he '[didn't] believe the science was there', 'the earth has been on a normal warming cycle' and 'most ... of the world's scientists don't believe in global warming'. He stated that 'there's a fair bit of arrogance in man to think he can fix the future of the world', and 'God will decide when the world ends'. He didn't think Christians were particularly protected from disasters in this world.

Will gave expression to another important strand of Christian fundamentalist thinking: the use of climate change as a pretext for forming World Government. 'The Bible talks about one World Government, it talks about the rise of the anti-Christ. I believe we're on the threshold of something like that'. For Will, evidence included the fact that the 2009 Copenhagen summit had produced a draft agreement prior to the event with 'the appointment of this committee, to oversee, and indeed bring down punishments, upon companies and countries that they don't rule over, and taxing them, and even imprisonment on people who aren't complying with their message'. In this understanding, climate change is not just a negative message about the entropy of the planet, but a challenge to the community of believers and their democratic rights. It is an instrument of the anti-Christ, and therefore a threat to the prospect of a post-Apocalypse afterlife for the born-again faithful.

The challenge of climate change for fundamentalist Christians relates to their belief that redemption is based on faith not works. The role of pastors is to minister to increasing numbers of people in order to provide them with the opportunity of salvation, whether or not climate change is implicated in end of world events.

It appears paradoxical that the portents of climate change meet with strong resistance from the Christian faiths of the Apocalypse. But not all Apocalypses are the same. Unlike the climate change scenario, the Pentecostalist Apocalypse is only a prelude to another life – the end of 'first things', and the path for a 'new heaven and new earth'. It is *not* a final ending for the faithful, who will be born again. In this, it shares many features with other immortality systems including earlier forms of Christianity, wherein Becker noted 'the individual could fashion his own salvation, independent of any earthly authority' (1975: 69), and with mythologised science.

The immortality ideologies of certain forms of science entrepreneurship prophesise a new life that transcends the perils of a warmed Earth – apocalypse repulsed or deferred. These are not utopias ('no places'), which by definition are unattainable imaginings of perfection. These new worlds perpetuate existing societal arrangements, and build on the political economy of 'contemporary capitalist technoscience' (Thorpe 2013: 3). They attempt to overcome or deny the metabolic rift that Marx identified as 'the material estrangement of human beings in capitalist society from the natural conditions of their existence' (Foster 1999: 383), now evident in the manifestations of anthropogenic climate change.

Ecological modernisation

Science utopias have become mainstream thinking in some of the ecological modernisation doctrines that infuse global climate change governance. In brief, proponents of ecological modernisation (in its various 'weaker' and 'stronger' forms) assert that economic growth on a capitalist model accompanied by increasing levels of consumption can be sustained without worsening global warming and other environmental harms, with GHG emissions reductions achieved through technical solutions provided by ever-advancing scientific knowledge. In this framework, states play a significant role in supporting the development and application of 'green science', reflected in suites of environmental policies and public communication. Ecological modernisation obscures the metabolic rift and avoids the political disruption of challenging the capitalist imperative of accumulation (Davidson 2012).

Northern European polities have been forerunners of ecological modernisation while at the same time exposing its contradictions. In Germany, for example, the parliament passed a package of laws in 2011, known as the 'Energy Transformation' (Energiewende), providing for a phase-out of all nuclear power plants by 2022 and setting ambitious targets of 35 per cent of total energy use from renewables by 2020, and 80 per cent by 2050 (German Federal Ministry of Economics and Technology 2012). Germany, however, is the world's largest producer of emissions-intensive soft brown coal (lignite), and in a post-nuclear 'dash for coal', in the context of rising energy costs, economic pressure is increasing for expanded brown coal production. In a paradox of ecological modernisation, the dirtiest form of energy production is being touted as a 'transition fuel' in the Energy Transformation (Pahle 2010).

Sweden is another country that shares some of these paradoxical parameters. Often ranked highly on ecological innovation and sustainability performance (OECD 2014), Sweden is the home of Vattenfall, one of Europe's most polluting energy companies, dependent on the expansion of lignite mines in eastern Germany for much of its power generation (Curry 2014). These displaced emissions never appear in Sweden's national carbon emissions accounting. Mark Graham undertook an anthropological analysis of Sweden's climate and environmental policies that are underpinned by ideologies of ecological modernisation (Graham 2016). He points to the utopian terms of industry and official claims about environmental management, including: reversibility of time (damage can be rectified); removal of GHGs from the atmosphere within ten years; decoupling of economic growth and increasing GHG emissions; 'an ontology of object thinking preoccupied with bounded units like "urban district" "city", "region" or "country" that are cordoned off from their "external" effects, CO2 emissions among them'; and, atoning for consumption by appropriation of nature through carbon offsetting (Graham 2016: 236–8).

In this model, various discursive practices mask the externalised costs of the consumerism that sustains capitalism, not least the production of waste. In his work on waste-making in global cities, David Boarder Giles has observed that waste is 'definitive within the cultural logic of capitalist production; it is an ontological and material substrate of value itself' (2016: 81). In the urban eco-district (Sjöstan) that Graham studied, the waste that is produced by residents is managed by elaborate disposal systems in which waste 'becomes a reified object that conceals its origins along with its possibly harmful environmental effects' (2016: 239).

Swedes perceive household recycling and appropriate waste disposal behaviours as having an exaggerated pro-environmental significance that somehow compensates for high levels of consumption. Waste disposal system malfunctions that periodically occur turn invisible waste into 'recalcitrant matter' bringing the hidden costs of consumption to unwelcome awareness (Graham 2016: 238–9). The habitual practice of recycling does not necessarily generalise into a wider concern to reduce consumption.

Harry, a well-paid Hunter Valley coal miner, explained his thinking about recycling in response to an interview question about the future:

> Interviewer: *So have your thoughts about the future changed in the last few years?*
> Harry: *Yes. We're getting older and we're getting wiser ... Since they brought out recycling I've always been a recycler. I can't understand why we throw so many aluminium cans in the ground when you can just throw them into a recycling bin, and yeah, plastic. As I'm getting older I'm getting more into recycling. Fifteen years ago I probably would've thrown it out because recycling wasn't around then.*
> Interviewer: *And what about actual consumption? Have your consumption patterns changed at all?*
> Harry: *No not really. I wouldn't think so, not a great deal. I think the recycling side of it has, but not the consumption side of it. Like I don't throw TVs out now, I make sure they go to the right place. And the electrical goods, they go to the right place. Yeah I'm more of a recyclist [sic] these days.*

(Harry interview 2013)

Harry's account of recycling, like Graham's account of Sjöstan residents, highlights one aspect of the contradictory experiences of participating in the consumer culture of capitalism. The substrate of waste is 'not there' and requires emotional work to return to consciousness. Bauman's statement: 'To consume also means to destroy' (2005: 311) can be restated in the mythical terms of ecological modernisation: 'To consume also means to recycle'. Recycling makes waste disappear and is a paradigmatic case where the mythologies of science and technological innovation are part of the social organisation of knowledge, fortifying the work of the unconscious in concealing the impact of high levels of climate-warming consumption.

Mythical ecologies of science

The magic of science is even more prominent in the striving to discover new habitable worlds outside the Earth's solar system where the cycle of exploitation can begin anew in a business-led wave of exoplanet colonisation. The Washington DC-based National Space Society has as its Vision Statement 'People living and working in thriving communities beyond the Earth, and the use of the vast resources of space for the dramatic betterment of humanity' (2010). The World Economic Forum, an organisation dedicated to 'improving the state of the world through public-private cooperation' (World Economic Forum 2015), highlights pioneering contributors to 'pressing global public good challenges', couched in the neoliberal lexicon of growth, emergence, innovation, development and investment. The annual meeting in January 2010 included a panel on 'Life on other planets' with speakers exploring the possibilities of finding new habitable worlds to support business in outer space (Copetas 2010). The featured speaker was Dimitar Sasselov, director of Harvard University's Origins of Life Initiative Project. Sasselov discovered the exosolar world OGLE-TR-56b (that he unofficially named after his wife, Sheila). He said:

> It's feasible that we'll meet other sentient life forms and conduct commerce with them … We don't now have the technology to physically travel outside our solar system for such an exchange to take place, but we are like Columbus centuries ago, learning fast how to get somewhere few think possible.
>
> (quoted in Copetas 2010)

Sasselov stated that he hopes to stir realisation that research about other planets can 'redefine life as we know it' and eventually create a market in the Milky Way and beyond. In 2015, Sasselov is involved in the US$100 million-funded 'Breakthrough Life' initiative, to search for intelligent life in the universe. Announced by Stephen Hawking and Yuri Milner in July 2015, it became 'the most powerful, comprehensive and intensive scientific search ever undertaken for signs of intelligent life beyond Earth' (Breakthrough Initiatives 2010).

Among Hunter Valley residents, popular media coverage of space explorations is food for thought, and perhaps hope, in quotidian worlds. When asked about her thoughts on the future, Carla, a volunteer in an organic food cooperative, told the researchers she felt quite optimistic about humanity's future, if not the planet's. She said:

> *I'm always sort of deeply touched by things like on television. The other week they were interviewing an astronaut from NASA who'd just retired. He said 'the biggest thing that I take away from like all those trips to space is how much the planet has changed from when I first went to space and my last trips'. He said that the changes have been astronomical in terms of the human footprint. His conclusion is that like if we keep going at this rate we're just going to kill it. He said that's why it's good we've got space travel because we'll have to go somewhere else.*
>
> (Carla interview 2013)

The self-styled culture heroes of space exploration frequently compare their endeavours to those of Christopher Columbus, bringing to mind Becker's inquiry into the social forms of heroic transcendence of mortality in each human epoch (1975: 154).

Another 'Life on Other Planets' panellist and financial data analyst, Brad Durham, extolled Sasselov's vision of capitalist immortality:

> Businessmen once thought Columbus was ridiculous, but he was the adventure capitalist who helped create globalization. [He continued:] People in my field pay serious attention to Sasselov's work because what's knowable in our business can be thrown out the window real fast. It's likely going to take many lifetimes before we can take advantage of outer space as an emerging market, but it's best not to be hobbled by the lack of imagination on Earth.
>
> (quoted in Copetas 2010)

Physicist David Livingston has developed a *Code of Ethics for Off-Earth Commerce* to guide humankind's conduct in their contacts with aliens. He says: 'We're committed to ensuring a free-market economy off-Earth ... Treat outer space with respect, concern and thoughtful deliberation, regardless of the presence or absence of life forms' (quoted in Copetas 2010).

These values inform scientists' comments on the recent research data from the NASA (National Aeronautics and Space Administration)-funded Kepler space telescope, whose mission is 'to find terrestrial planets (i.e., those one half to twice the size of the Earth), especially those in the habitable zone of their stars where liquid water and possibly life might exist' (NASA 2013).

The discovery of exoplanet Kepler 452b, 'like Earth's "older, bigger first cousin"' and 12 similar planets (Yuhas 2015) has boosted speculation of other life forms in the Milky Way. But Kepler 452b, 'another place that somebody might call home', is 1,400 light years away, and its hot rocky surface and high levels of solar radiation suggest it may already be in a 'runaway greenhouse phase of its climate history' (Yuhas 2015), a site of exodus for any life forms that might exist there and a gloomy portent of Earth's future.

There are many differences between Christian fundamentalists and market fundamentalists, but they are similar in their commitment to immortality ideologies that seek new worlds, beyond the present Earth, when Earth is used up either by the fires of the Apocalypse or by exploitation, resource depletion and global warming.

Salvation by science takes many forms, and the neoliberal values that inform space exploration can also be discerned in the promotion of geoengineering to combat climate change: 'solar radiation management', sometimes termed 'albedo management', and 'carbon dioxide removal' techniques. These initiatives can be understood in theoretical terms through the concept of the 'free market cultural complex', a collective pattern of theory, perception and behaviour in which personal liberty and industrial capitalist modes of production and energy are pre-eminently valued (Marshall 2016). Like Hoggett's concept of perverse cultures discussed above, the free market cultural complex is anchored in the immortality ideologies of fossil fuel-intensive capitalist societies, in which immense social forces resist the disruptive effects of reducing GHG emissions, even at the cost of the environmental chaos and destruction of life forms that will accompany uncontrollable climate change. Marshall (2016: 252) writes:

> The main arguments for geoengineering depend on perceptions of social failure to reduce carbon emissions, and an aversion to challenging the forms of social organisation responsible for emissions. An ontology is implied in which it is simpler and less costly to control the natural world than to change society ... Geoengineering is framed as inevitable, further increasing chances of implementation.

In the moral universe of the free market cultural complex, all assessments of utility are subjected to cost–benefit analyses: reducing GHGs may be too costly. In the mythical universe, capitalism and its culture of consumption and endless renewal is life-sustaining; geoengineering is merely a necessary stabiliser, both of individual egos and of systems of extraction and exploitation (Marshall 2016: 253). From Hoggett's perspective, parasitic forms of capital and the egoistic pleasures of entitlement and narcissistic consumption, oblivious to the fate of Others, exist in a dysfunctional mutuality in perverse cultures (2013a: 60–1). The myth of geoengineering represses intimations of death and disorder from climate change, but Marshall suggests that it does have the virtue of acknowledging a problem, even if not diagnosing it correctly. He (2016: 258) remarks:

> as an imagining, it is paradoxical and potentially constructive as well as obstructive. In depth psychology, disruption, and the repressed, if attended to in ways initially acceptable to the ego, rather than feared and re-suppressed, can allow insight and useful change.

Geoengineering is an elite immortality ideology, apparently not shared by the public. Most of the geoengineering and off-Earth visionaries are men, like the explorers of former eras, inviting a gender analysis of forms of heroic transcendence that may be disconnected from women, and most earth dwellers. Naomi Klein's study of the world of geoengineering scientists and their funders came to the conclusion that: '... the Geoclique is crammed with overconfident men prone to complimenting each other on their fearsome brainpower' (2014: 267). A recent survey of Australian and New Zealand residents found that 'the public has strong negative views towards climate engineering ... Interventions such as putting mirrors in space or fine particles into the atmosphere are not well received' (Wright *et al.* 2014 cited in Klein 2014: 290). Tampering with the outer layer of the atmosphere and space beyond was not well received by Hunter Valley respondents in our survey, who were prone to attribute the *causes* of climate change to human interventions in the outer layers of the atmosphere and beyond:

> *I think they should stop sending people to space as I think that has a lot to do with climate change.*
> (Upper Hunter resident 2011)

> *What about all the rockets that are going up into the sky? I have noticed every time this happens there is some natural disaster that happens somewhere in the world.*
> (Lake Macquarie resident 2011)

Disrupting the atmospherical security of the Earth's shield seems to some people like piercing the uterine wall: dangerous and ultimately life destroying. Jeremy Walker (2016) delves into the ontology of multiple scales of enfolding spheres in a critique of science entrepreneurship at the microscale of the bioeconomy that mirrors in some respects the macroscale myths of geoengineering. Champions of synthesised microorganisms acknowledge that there is a problem with the use of fossil fuels and their eventual depletion, which can be reversed by the single-celled organisms of the industrial bioeconomy. These science entrepreneurs reproduce immortality ideologies of planetary salvation and endless economic growth, through their vision of the potential of microbial life 'to be re-engineered and synthesised as replacements for the destructive pyrochemical processes at the heart of industrial production' (Walker 2016: 264).

Walker dissects the inherent ambiguity in the imagined world of the bioeconomy. The harnessing of microbial life by the industrial bioeconomy may perpetuate the 'necrocapitalism' of our era: 'Our industrial present is animated by digging up the numberless dead of the buried biospheres of the deep past, setting ex-life to work for us in our dominance of the living one' (Walker 2016: 275).

Entrepreneurs see the synthetic biology of engineered organisms ushering in a mass speciation of hyperefficient microorganic producers that keep pace with ever-accelerating accumulation in the twenty-first century capitalist economy. By contrast, Walker argues that the bioeconomy's harnessing of the 'vital materialism' of photosynthesis could be accomplished without the harms of corporate biotechnology, and could drive the reduction of non-biodegradable wastes and render the petrochemical industry obsolete. Microbial biofuel plants, like much renewable energy technology, can be decentralised in many locations. Walker suggests that the planet's ubiquitous microorganisms, the 'pioneering ecological engineers of every corner of the planet' (2016: 264) may be harnessed in ways that create more democratic biotechnical commons and preserve the wild biosphere. Freed from capitalist accumulation, science may realise its transformative potential.

Generations

The citizens of the present era are sometimes characterised as the last generation to save the world from runaway climate change. In a recent article, the secretary-general of the United Nations, Ban Ki-Moon, said:

> We must aim high: for the adoption of an ambitious and universal agreement in Paris in December to keep the rise in global temperatures below the dangerous threshold of 2°C. Ours is the first generation that can end poverty, and the last that can take steps to avoid the worst impacts of climate change.
> (Ki-Moon 2015)

The 'we' is not specified except as a generation; it presumably means a 'generation in actuality' in Karl Mannheim's terms – in which 'similarly "located" contemporaries participate in a common destiny and in the ideas and concepts which are in some way bound up with its unfolding' (Mannheim 1923: 186). The contemporaries in the case of the 2015 UN Climate Change Conference in Paris are presumably empowered adults who are united by the historical experience of climate change threat. Ki-Moon implies that this is the generation with the responsibility and resources to act on climate change.

In the Hunter Valley research, those respondents who expressed worry about the future often talked about their children and grandchildren. There is a pervasive sense, from farmers, coal miners, council planners, suburban residents and climate activists among others, that their descendants may live diminished and even dangerous lives because of the environmental degradation of the planet, an unenviable 'common destiny'. This anticipatory mourning, in Freud's terms discussed above, seems to be a pervasive melancholia of adult generations. Even where climate change itself is not perceived as a threat, the evidence of environmental damage is everywhere. Older people we spoke to frequently compared the cleaner air, purer water and natural surrounds of their youth with the conditions they perceive today, which for some are tinged with the threat of climate change. While talk in quotidian worlds is mostly about the near future – what is happening next week, next month, next year – the prospect of planetary malaise propels future imaginings into a multigenerational time frame. Harry, the coal-miner, 'recyclist' and self-confessed climate sceptic, saw overpopulation and forms of environmental degradation like deforestation and pollution as a threat to his grandchildren's future well-being. He accepted the finitude of natural resources, but worried about the implications, commenting:

> As you get older you start thinking 'well my children have got another fifty years on this planet or more, my grandchildren have got another fifty-plus, eighty years on this planet'. What's this planet going to be like, in a hundred years? When my great grandchildren are around, what are they going to be like? Are we going to be fighting over oil, coal, natural resources? When does it run out? It's not an infinite product, any of them. And will products like solar be good enough? Or do we have to find some other way, or some other mineral, to survive on this planet?
>
> (Harry interview 2013)

Others put climate change front and centre of their concerns for the future of their children, as in these survey comments:

> We should have acted years ago about climate change. Our children will suffer greatly if we don't act now.
>
> (Lake Macquarie resident 2008)

> I believe what we do now affects the climate for our children and their children. Everyone should do something to help with climate change. Every little bit helps.
>
> (Upper Hunter resident 2011)

Maureen, a member of the Transition Newcastle group, and an active participant in environmental initiatives in her neighbourhood, admitted to feeling 'despondent' about the 'mounting evidence' of worsening climate change. She expressed particular concern about her son's future:

> I want to spend my life giving [my son] the best I can. Not in terms of material things, but in terms of care and education and opportunities for the future. I'm

worried if climate change becomes a reality and he's in a world that is so drastically changed and degraded and chaotic. And I don't think that's alarmist; I think that's a distinct possibility in his lifetime.

(Maureen interview 2013)

The immortality thinking in these parents' visions of the future is under challenge. Their melancholy is reality based, perhaps a recognition that the 'Faustian bargain' is collapsing, and the metabolic rift cannot be healed. Some 40 years ago, Ernest Becker (1975: 72) starkly identified the Faustian bargain modern humanity has struck with nature:

> the hope of Faustian man was that he would discover Truth, obtain the secret to the workings of nature, and so assure the complete triumph of man over nature, his apotheosis on earth. Not only has Faustian man failed to do this, but he is actually ruining the very theater of his own immortality with his own poisonous and madly driven works; once he had eclipsed the sacred dimension, he had only the earth left to testify to the value of his life. This is why, I think, even one-dimensional politicians and bureaucrats, in both capitalist and communist countries, are becoming anxious about environmental collapse; the earth is the only area of self-perpetuation in the new ideology of Faustian man.

Questioning of the sustainability of societies that are based on endless growth, consumption and profits, is now quite common. Writing in the 1960s and 1970s, when environmentalist thought and protective regulatory frameworks were on the ascendant, especially in the USA, Becker may have been correct in his attribution of growing concern to politicians and bureaucrats but naïve in his analytical neglect of the counterweight of fossil fuel-based political economies. He may also have been naïve about the chances of overcoming the seductive pleasures of consumerism. Nowadays, the 'green state', based on optimistic doctrines of ecological modernisation, holds out hope to consumers that they and their descendants will not have to relinquish the 'good life' built on commodity overabundance.

For most people, the problem of anthropogenic climate change is continuous with, or subsumed by, a host of other causes of environmental damage that they perceive: from coal mining to deforestation, industrial pollution to rocket launches, overpopulation to biodiversity loss, and so on. The environmental concerns of the broad spectrum of Hunter Valley residents that were part of this research suggest that people are most likely to engage in political struggles over local places they live in, care about and obtain livelihoods from.

People are motivated to protect valued places for future generations. Climate change has joined the list of activating issues for some, but exists in a space of cultural contradictions. A recent survey of Australian attitudes to climate and energy policy by the Climate Institute found that 63 per cent of respondents think that the current conservative government 'should take climate change more seriously, up six points from 2014' (Taylor 2015), and renewable energy policies, under attack by the government, are widely supported. However, the survey also found that the idea of a price on carbon (associated with the former Labor government) remains unpopular.

In Australia and elsewhere in the world, the real costs of consumption are obscured by the institutions of national and global political economies. This is not a generation that envisions itself propelled willy nilly into the hazardous uncertainties of the as yet officially unrecognised Anthropocene epoch, but rather a generation that anchors its consciousness and collective ontological security in the fleeting geological moment of the Holocene – an epoch whose relative climatic stability and bounteous planetary resources are taken as the foundational parameters of the future. The people whose experience of the Holocene is already unstable, such as the Circumpolar and South Pacific communities surveyed at the beginning of this book, have little influence in the geopolitics of climate change.

The fate of future generations of humans is often invoked in cautionary scenarios of planetary decline. Vast collectives of Others – life forms and their sustaining environments – form sacrifice zones, where extinctions proliferate, ultimately threatening the interdependent web of all life. The conditions for future planetary flourishing require ruptures and alternatives on a global scale in the imperative timeframe of the present. These include new myths to sustain different sorts of personhood and democratic leadership oriented to epochal timescales. The immense tasks of withdrawal from the capitalisation of nature and fossil fuel-based energy systems remain unfulfilled. Reworked social arrangements and value chains, transformative politics and reparative ecological practices are intrinsic to survival in this new epochal terrain. These changes have so far eluded the practical imagination of Anthropos but may find a purchase in the fragile human hopes for generational continuity, if the threat can be grasped as the urgent predicament of our present days.

Notes

1   Janis Dickinson (2009) has drawn on Becker's ideas to consider climate change responses, using the theory of 'terror management' that social psychologists have developed from Becker's work.
2   The religious adherents were mostly from Newcastle and Lake Macquarie, and included Anglicans and other Protestant denominations, Catholics, Quakers, Western Buddhists, Aboriginal and members of charismatic groups, recruited purposively through our network of research contacts.

References

Albrecht, G., Sartore, G., Connor, L., Higginbotham, N., Freeman, S., Kelly, B., Stain, H., Tonna, A. and Pollard, G. 2007. 'Solastalgia: The distress caused by environmental change'. *Australasian Psychiatry* 15 (Supplement): S95–98.
Baker, K. J. 2011. 'Getting Rapture Ready: The materiality of the Rapture in North America'. *Studies in World Christianity* 17 (2): 101–118.

Bauman, Z. 2005. *Work, Consumerism and the New Poor*. Berkshire: Open University Press.

Becker, E. 1973. *The Denial of Death*. New York: Simon & Schuster.

Becker, E. 1975. *Escape from Evil*. New York: The Free Press.

Breakthrough Initiatives 2010. 'Breakthrough Initiatives'. Available at www.breakthroughinitiatives.org/News/1 (accessed August 2015).

Brenman Pick, I. 2013. 'Discussion: The myth of apathy'. In: *Engaging with Climate Change: Psychoanalytic and interdisciplinary perspectives*. Weintrobe, S. (ed.). Hove, Sussex: Routledge.

Copetas, C. 2010. 'Harvard Star-Gazer Sasselov Maps Space Frontier From Davos. Bloomberg.com'. Available at www.bloomberg.com/apps/news?pid=newsarchive&sid=alLCE7adBQ_M archived by WebCite at www.webcitation.org/6b8N64oIF (accessed December 2010).

Curry, A. 2014. 'Germany Plans to Raze Towns for Brown Coal and Cheap Energy'. *National Geographic*. Available at http://news.nationalgeographic.com/news/energy/2014/02/140211-germany-plans-to-raze-towns-for-brown-coal/ archived by WebCite at www.webcitation.org/6b8KZateN (accessed June 2015).

Davidson, S. 2012. 'The Insuperable Imperative: A critique of the ecologically modernizing state'. *Capitalism Nature Socialism* 23 (2): 31–50.

Dickinson, J. 2009. 'The People Paradox: Self-esteem striving, immortality ideologies, and human response to climate change'. *Ecology and Society* 14: 34–53.

Foster, J. B. 1999. 'Marx's Theory of Metabolic Rift: Classical foundations for environmental sociology'. *American Journal of Sociology* 105 (2): 366–405.

Freud, S. 2005 [1916]. *On Transience*. Freud's Requiem. Riverhead Books.

German Federal Ministry of Economics and Technology 2012. 'Germany's New Energy Policy'. Available at www.bmwi.de/English/Redaktion/Pdf/germanys-new-energy-policy (accessed 20 August 2015).

Giles, D. B. 2016. 'The Work of Waste-making: Biopolitical labour and the myth of the global city'. In: *Environmental Change and the World's Futures: Ecologies, ontologies, mythologies*. Marshall, J. P. and Connor, L. H. (eds). London: Routledge.

Gillespie, S. 2016. 'Climate change imaginings and depth psychology: Reconciling present and future worlds'. In: *Environmental Change and the World's Futures: Ecologies, ontologies, mythologies*. Marshall, J. P. and Connor, L. H. (eds). London: Routledge.

Graham, M. 2016. 'Official optimism in the face of an uncertain future: Swedish reactions to climate change threats'. In: *Environmental Change and the World's Futures: Ecologies, ontologies, mythologies*. Marshall, J. P. and Connor, L. H. (eds). London: Routledge.

Hoggett, P. 2013a. 'Climate change in a perverse culture'. In: *Engaging with Climate Change: Psychoanalytic and interdisciplinary perspectives*. Weintrobe, S. (ed.). Hove, Sussex: Routledge.

Hoggett, P. 2013b. 'Reply: Climate change in a perverse culture'. In: *Engaging with Climate Change: Psychoanalytic and interdisciplinary perspectives*. Weintrobe, S. (ed.). Hove, Sussex: Routledge.

Hughes, P., Fraser, M. and Reid, S. 2012. *Australia's Religious Communities: Facts and figures from the 2011 Australian Census and other sources*. Victoria: Christian Research Association.

James, W. 1902. *The Varieties of Religious Experience*. London: Longmans, Green & Co.

Ki-Moon, B. 2015. 'We are the last generation that can fight climate change. We have a duty to act'. *The Guardian*. January 12. Available at www.theguardian.com/commentisfree/2015/jan/12/last-generation-tackle-climate-change-un-international-community archived by WebCite at www.webcitation.org/6b8ORmOAG (accessed July 2015).

Klein, N. 2014. *This Changes Everything: Capitalism vs the Climate*. London: Allen Lane.

Lertzman, A. 2013. 'The Myth of Apathy: Psychoanalytic explorations of environmental subjectivity'. In: *Engaging with Climate Change: Psychoanalytic and interdisciplinary perspectives*. Weintrobe, S. (ed.). Hove, Sussex: Routledge.

Mannheim, K. 1923. 'The Sociological Problem of Generations'. In: *Essays on the Sociology of Knowledge, Karl Mannheim [1998]*. UK: Taylor & Francis Books.

Mannheim, K. 1956. *Essays on the Sociology of Knowledge: Collected works of Karl Mannheim Volume 7, 2003*. USA and Canada: Routledge.

Marshall, J. P. 2016. 'Geoengineering, imagining and the problem cycle: a cultural complex in action'. In: *Environmental Change and the World's Futures: Ecologies, ontologies, mythologies*. Marshall, J. P. and Connor, L. H (eds). London: Routledge.

NASA (National Aeronautics and Space Administration) 2013. 'Kepler: A Search for Habitable Planets: About the Mission'. Available at http://kepler.nasa.gov/Mission/ QuickGuide/ archived by WebCite at www.webcitation.org/6b8NUqYId (accessed 2013).

National Space Society 2010. 'National Space Society'. Available at www.nss.org/ (accessed 28 June 2010).

New Oxford Annotated Bible 2007. Augmented Third Edition, New Revised Standard Version, Michael D. Coogan (ed.). New Testament Introduction to Revelation of John, p. 420. Oxford: Oxford University Press.

OECD (Organization for Economic Co-operation and Development) 2014. *OECD Environmental Performance Review of Sweden: Assessment and recommendations*. Available at www.oecd.org/env/country-reviews/sweden2014.htm (accessed 2 July 2015).

Pahle, M. 2010. 'Germany's dash for coal: exploring drivers and factors'. *Energy Policy 38* (7): 3431–3442.

Pew Research Center 2011. 'Global Christianity – A Report on the Size and Distribution of the World's Christian Population'. Available at www.pewforum.org/2011/12/19/ global-christianity-exec/ (accessed 20 August 2015).

Poloma, M. M. 2000. 'The Spirit Bade Me go: Pentecostalism and Global Religion'. Association for the Sociology of Religion Annual Meetings. Washington DC.

Randall, R. 2013. 'Great Expectations: The psychodynamics of ecological debt'. In: *Engaging with Climate Change: Psychoanalytic and interdisciplinary perspectives*. Weintrobe, S. (ed.). Hove, Sussex: Routledge.

Rank, O. 1932. *Art and Artist: Creative Urge and Personality Development*. C. F. Atkinson. New York: Tudor Publishing Company.

Rank, O. 1998 [1930]. *Psychology and the Soul: A Study of the Origin, Conceptual Evolution and Nature of the Soul*. Trans. G. C. Richter and E. J. Lieberman. Baltimore and London: John Hopkins University Press.

Surefoot Effect 2015. *Carbon Conversations*. Available at www.carbonconversations.org/ archived by WebCite at www.webcitation.org/6ZgbMexZ7 (accessed 15 June 2015).

Taylor, L. 2015. 'Australians fear Coalition is not taking climate change seriously, poll shows'. *The Guardian*. August 10. Available at www.theguardian.com/ environment/2015/aug/09/australians-fear-coalition-is-not-taking-climate-change-seriously-poll-shows archived by WebCite at www.webcitation.org/6b8TokCVG (accessed August 2015).

Thorpe, C. 2013. 'Artificial Life on a Dead Planet'. In: *The International Encyclopedia of Media Studies, First Edition*. Valdivia, A. N. (ed.). Blackwell Publishing Ltd. VI.

Walker, J. 2016. 'The Creation to Come: Pre-empting the evolution of the bioeconomy'. In: *Environmental Change and the World's Futures: Ecologies, ontologies, mythologies*. Marshall, J. P. and Connor, L. H. (eds). London: Routledge.

Weber, M. 1930. *The Protestant Ethic and the Spirit of Capitalism*. London and Boston: Allen and Unwin.

World Economic Forum 2015. 'World Economic Forum'. Available at www.weforum.org/world-economic-forum (accessed 21 August 2015).

Yuhas, A. 2015. 'Scientists identify Earth's "closest twin"'. *The Guardian Weekly*. July 31, p. 9.

Index

For Product Safety Concerns and Information please contact our EU
representative GPSR@taylorandfrancis.com
Taylor & Francis Verlag GmbH, Kaufingerstraße 24, 80331 München, Germany

www.ingramcontent.com/pod-product-compliance
Ingram Content Group UK Ltd.
Pitfield, Milton Keynes, MK11 3LW, UK
UKHW021828240425
457818UK00006B/125